Who Killed
John Lennon?

Who Killed
John Lennon?

Fenton Bresler

St. Martin's Press
New York

For David Moya

WHO KILLED JOHN LENNON? Copyright © 1989 by Fenton Bresler. All rights reserved.
Printed in the United States of America. No part of this book may be used or
reproduced in any manner whatsoever without written permission except in the case
of brief quotations embodied in critical articles or reviews. For information, address
St. Martin's Press, 175 Fifth Avenue, New York, N.Y. 10010.

Library of Congress Cataloging-in-Publication Data

Bresler, Fenton S.
    Who killed John Lennon? / Fenton Bresler.
        p.   cm.
    ISBN 0-312-03452-0
    1. Lennon, John, 1940- —Assassination. 2. Rock musicians-
-Biography. 3. Chapman, Mark David. 4. Assassins—New York
(State)—Biography. I. Title.
ML420.L38B75 1989
364.1′523′097471—dc20   89-6382
                                                               CIP
                                                               MN

First published in Great Britain by Sidgwick & Jackson Limited.

First U.S. Edition

10 9 8 7 6 5 4 3 2 1

Contents

Acknowledgments

When you have researched a book virtually single-handed for nearly eight years, there are a lot of people you have to thank for their help.

So I start at the beginning: with Sally Riley to whom I first mentioned the possibility of this book and who, with her natural enthusiasm, immediately introduced me to Sidgwick & Jackson, my English publishers. To Susan Hill, my editor at Sidgwick's, and to Jim Fitzgerald, her counterpart at St Martin's Press, my US publishers, who have proved both friends and a valiant support. And to Stephen Evers, my clerk, who has learned to accept my frequent 'sabbaticals' from the Bar to work on this book with good-natured humour.

Then, as to the actual research, I have to thank in:

New York: Allen Sullivan and Kim Hogrefe who prosecuted Mark David Chapman, Jonathan Marks who defended him and Justice Dennis Edwards who tried him, together with ex-Lieutenant of Detectives Arthur O'Connor and present or retired police officers Steve Spiro, James Moran and Tony De Palma. Also Judge Herbert Adlerberg, special assistant to the District Attorney Gerald McKelvey, ex-Attica Prison Superintendent Harold J. Smith, current Attica Superintendent Walter R. Kelly and Deputy Superintendent William R. McAnulty, Harry Brunger and Bonnie Mairs of the YMCA. Alice Urwand, wife of the owner of Lennon's favourite coffee shop, Philip Finn of the *Daily Express*, an old friend, and Thea Zavin of the Broadcast Music, Inc. (BMI), a new friend.

Atlanta: Harold and June Blankinship, the Rev. Newton Hendrix, Georgia Bureau of Investigation special agent Wesley Nunn and Diane Hunter, librarian of the *Atlanta Constitution & Journal*.

Hawaii: Walter Wright and Beverley Creamer of the *Honolulu Star-Bulletin* and John E. Simonds, the newspaper's executive editor. Janice Wolfe, Brook Hart, Jean Kapotani, 'Anne Jones', Ruth Brilhante and, above all, Captain Louis L. Souza of the Criminal Investigation Division of the Honolulu police.

Chicago: David C. Moore, Robert Morgan of United Airlines, Tony Ripley of the YMCA and Andrea Hinding, YMCA archivist at the University of Minnesota.

Carmel: The late Mrs Mae Brussel.

Washington: Daniel P. Sheehan.

Los Angeles: Professor Jon Wiener, Terry Nation, Tamar Cooper, Paul Baden, Paul Krassner, Art Seidenbaum of the *Los Angeles Times* for kindly arranging my use of the newspaper's excellent library and Douglas Conner, reference librarian, for his considerable help while I was there, Kevin Scott, David Goodwin and Ralph Martinez of Local 630 of the Teamsters Union.

I also have to thank Tony Adams of the YMCA and the Rev. Charles McGowan for two long telephone interviews, Barbara Walters, Alistair Cooke and Tim Rice for their personal thoughts on Lennon's death, Kevin Sim for his generous sharing with me of the fruits of his research and, above all, Yoko Ono, who was gracious and helpful when she called me on the telephone and who did me the inestimable service of putting me in touch with Jon Wiener.

Grateful acknowledgment is made to the authors, publishers and other copyright holders for permission to reprint previously published materials from:

Todd Rundgren song:
'AN ELPEE'S WORTH OF TOONS' from TODD (1974) © Fiction Music/Todd Rundgren/Screen Gems Music.

Books and magazines:
COME TOGETHER: JOHN LENNON IN HIS TIME by Jon Wiener. (1984) Random House, Inc., New York.
JOHN LENNON by Ray Coleman. (1984) Sidgwick & Jackson, London.
THE PLAYBOY INTERVIEWS WITH JOHN LENNON AND YOKO ONO by David Sheff. Excerpted from PLAYBOY INTERVIEW: JOHN LENNON AND YOKO ONO, PLAYBOY Magazine, (January 1981); Copyright © 1980 by PLAYBOY. All rights reserved.
THE LIVES OF JOHN LENNON by Albert Goldman, published by Bantam Press 1988. © 1988 Albert Goldman.
STRAWBERRY FIELDS FOREVER: JOHN LENNON REMEMBERED by Vic Garbarini and Brian Cullman, Barbara Graustark. Copyright © 1980 by Vic Garbarini, Brian Cullman, Barbara Graustark. Reprinted by permission of Bantam Books, a division of Bantam, Doubleday, Dell Publishing Group Inc.
RKO INTERVIEW WITH JOHN LENNON AND YOKO ONO. (1980) © RKO Radio Network Inc.
THE LAST LENNON TAPES by John Lennon, Yoko Ono and

Andy Peebles (BBC Radio One). (1983) Dell Publishing Co., Inc., New York.

SECRECY AND DEMOCRACY by Stansfield Turner. (1986) Perennial Library (Harper & Row, Publishers) New York.

OPERATION MIND CONTROL by Walter Bowart. (1978) Fontana, William Collins & Co. Ltd., Glasgow.

THE SEARCH FOR THE 'MANCHURIAN CANDIDATE' by John Marks. (1980) McGraw-Hill Book Co., New York.

PEOPLE for Jim Gaines' four articles in June 1981 and February/ March 1987.

NEW YORK for Craig Unger's article in June 1981.

ABOUT NEW YORK: MOURNERS COME AND GO TO SAD TONES OF BEATLES' MUSIC by William E. Farrell. Copyright © 1980 by the New York Times Company. Reprinted by permission.

8 December

The gun is sleek, snub-nosed and compact. Its two-inch barrel makes it ideal for both undercover detectives and murderers because it is so easy to conceal until needed.

In fact, its manufacturers – the Charter Arms Corporation of Bridgeport, Connecticut – call it proudly their 'Undercover .38 Special'. They once got an apology from the CBS Television Network for having called it 'a cheap handgun'. 'We are too dedicated to high quality in American-made handguns, and have poured too much into our products to have one of them even casually referred to as a "cheap handgun",' said an editorial in their company magazine.

It never misfires, there is no jamming, no bullet flying off line – and no gun exploding in your hands. When would-be assassin Arthur Bremer shot and paralyzed for life Alabama Governor George C. Wallace in May 1972, the bullet that tore into the politician's spine came from a Charter Undercover .38 Special.

It is a gun for people that mean business. And now, gripped by a podgy, blue-eyed young man, dropped into combat stance as if he knows what he is doing, with the gun held firmly in both hands, four bullets belch from the barrel in swift succession. They smash into the back and left shoulder of a dark-haired man in blue jeans, leather jacket and white shirt.

They are not ordinary bullets that merely tear through the flesh but hollow-points that fragment on impact, doing incalculable damage. The marksmanship is so good and they land so close together that people at the morgue the next day will get mixed up poking in the entrance wounds.

'Good shot group.' That is the firing-range term used by experts to describe such skill.

The victim has not got a chance. Almost killed outright by the first explosion of steel particles shattering into his body, he

1

manages to stagger up the five steps to the entrance office of the apartment block where he lives – only to fall flat on his face, gurgling and bringing up blood.

The white-haired doorman standing by cannot believe his eyes. 'Do you know what you have just done?' he screams at the killer. 'Yes, I just shot John Lennon,' is the cool reply.

PART ONE

SETTING THE SCENE

1

The Scenario

How on earth can anyone write a book about the murder of John Lennon, let alone research it for as long as I have done – ever since February 1981, two months after Lennon was gunned down on 8 December 1980 outside The Dakota, the apartment block in New York where he lived? Surely almost every thinking adult in the Western world – and quite a few in the Eastern – knows that basic fact and that date, set like pre-cast concrete in the shared memory of grieving millions.

For them, that day stands beside the outbreak of the Second World War, the Communist Revolution in Russia and the assassination of President John Kennedy as one that will for ever be writ large in their lives. Indeed, it *was* an assassination and not a murder: the only time in history that an entertainer has been stalked and cut down by a total stranger as if he were a president, a prime minister or some other political leader.

It was a madman who did it, wasn't it? One more 'lone nut' who so conveniently seems to have cropped up in recent American history to blow away with a gun a figure of stature who has excited the world's interest and, in some cases, even its love. Chapman, wasn't that his name? Mark David Chapman, a twenty-five-year-old fan – or ex-fan – who had got it into his head that he had to shoot Lennon because he thought that he was himself Lennon and that, in some weird psychological game with himself, he was killing himself through killing Lennon; or who believed that Lennon was a 'phoney', a billionaire rock star who preached peace and denial while enjoying the fruits of his vast wealth like any other super-rich capitalist; or who was simply a pathetic clapped-out failure in his early manhood who, in killing Lennon, dreamed that he could make himself famous – or who had whatever other motivation you like. How can you fathom the mind of a madman?

And how can you write a book about it? What is there to say or research in depth: a magazine article, perhaps yes – but a whole book?

It is exactly this kind of thinking that has blinded the whole world into accepting unquestioningly that Lennon's death was simply a one-off personal aberration: the work of one man acting alone and without a rational (or any) motive. Perhaps that is all it was. Perhaps in the end Chapman was only a 'lone nut' – but as someone who has practised at the Bar in England for nearly forty years, as well as journalistically investigated murder on both sides of the Atlantic for well over twenty years, I have never easily accepted the simplistic explanation for any homicide.

And in Lennon's case I have always thought it unlikely. Other international rock stars and entertainers from Elvis Presley onwards have received anonymous death threats from strangers and 'cranks' – but it is only Lennon who (without any prior threat) was gunned down. Why?

Flying to New York in February 1981, as then legal correspondent of London's *Daily Mail*, to do preliminary research to cover a trial that eventually (because of Chapman's guilty plea) never took place, I early forged links with prosecution and defence attorneys and others that I have since maintained and used as the basis for much further work both in the mainland United States and in Hawaii from where Chapman flew to commit the murder.

For there is another possible explanation for the tragedy: that Lennon, the politically most active rock star of his generation, and militantly left-wing politically active at that, was shot dead outside his own home by a killer who was merely a tool, a human gun used and controlled by others to destroy a uniquely powerful radical figure who was likely to prove a rallying point for mass opposition to the policies soon to be implemented, both at home and abroad, by the new United States government headed by Ronald Reagan. There is no evidence whatsoever that Mr Reagan knew of or had anything to do with such a deadly scheme; but it is an undoubted fact that, only one month earlier, the ex-actor had been elected for his first term as president and everyone knew he had the most determinedly reactionary programme of an American leader for many years.

For her part, Yoko Ono, Lennon's widow, would like to believe that Chapman is mad. Speaking from her New York apartment in

October 1985, she told me: 'He's a crazy man.' She did not want to talk about the past. 'I am more interested in the living John than the dead John,' she said.

But she sent me to see Jon Wiener, a professor of history at the University of California in Irvine whose study of Lennon's political and musical life, *Come Together*, she said was the best book yet written about her husband. 'He knows things I want him to tell you,' she said. Wiener, in turn, put me in touch with a radio journalist named Mae Brussell (sadly, dead prematurely of cancer in October 1988) out in Carmel, California, who first 'broke' the Watergate story back in 1972 two months before the Woodward-Bernstein exposé in the *Washington Post* made it national and international news. She was a controversial figure and not everyone agreed with her views but her verdict was sensational: 'It was a conspiracy. Reagan had just won the election. They knew what kind of president he was going to be. There was only one man who could bring out a million people on demonstration in protest at his policies – and that was Lennon.'

But who were 'they' and why get rid of Lennon in 1980 when the popular view – even discounting many of the so-called 'revelations' in Albert Goldman's sleazy biography *The Lives of John Lennon* – was that he had by then become mentally and spiritually 'fat', one more dollar-soaked billionaire playing at being a socialist?

The answer is that Reagan's rise to power coincided with Lennon's returning to his own former greatness. As record producer George Martin, 'the fifth Beatle' who helped mastermind their success, told the *Daily Express* in August 1988: 'The irony of John's death is that he had gone through a lot of rubbish with Yoko and going to America and the drugs scene and so on.

'But the year before he died he actually had got straight again. He had come through all that and found out the value of everything – the value of his relationship with his first son Julian, the joy of having his young second son Sean.

'He was coming round to becoming a happy middle-aged man. He was finding out what life was about. And then he was destroyed.'

Even Albert Goldman's negative biography quotes Jack Douglas, Lennon's last producer and close friend, as saying that as 1980 neared its end: 'John was totally satisfied with himself mentally and physically. He was starting to make a break. It had to do with

7

his fortieth birthday (on 9 October). He told me: "I'm happy to be forty years old. I'm in the best shape I've ever been in my life and I feel the best I ever felt."'

But this new joy in living was not only personal and professional. His five years of being a house-husband were over. He had just cut with Yoko *Double Fantasy*, his first album in five years. At forty, he had – like so many other men at that age – suddenly realized that life was passing and so much yet remained to be done. That was all true.

Yet there was something more. Says Jon Wiener: 'Not many people realize it but the very week that he was shot, he was due to fly to San Francisco with his wife and Sean to march in a rally in support of Japanese-American workers on strike on the West Coast. He had already bought the tickets. He was returning to the streets.'

So the argument goes that Lennon was once again becoming a political animal – and, as such, he could not be allowed to survive. He had to be cut down before the reasons for his death became obvious: before Reagan took the oath of office on 20 January 1981, before the world realized that Lennon was coming back to being the old Lennon, the man who sang 'Give Peace A Chance'.

Now, does that view stand up? Is it possible or even probable? Was Lennon's murder a political act? I have no personal axe to grind either way: my only concern is to get as near as I can to the truth. I have used no team of professional researchers. Unlike Albert Goldman, I have conducted all my own interviews and asked all my own questions. Nor have I paid for any information. The information you pay for is generally not worth having: the informant tends to say what he thinks you want to hear – not what necessarily happened. One retired New York detective would only talk to me if I paid him $2000 and let him set up further interviews that were unnecessary at that time – so I declined the offer. I did pay another ex-New York policeman $600 for the right to use certain documents in his possession.

Furthermore, I have in my possession the largest number of documents ever released by the FBI from their file on John Lennon under a Freedom of Information Act (FOIA) application: 217 pages as against the 89 pages they handed over to Jon Wiener back in 1981. I also have copies of the pitifully few documents that the CIA has released from its Lennon file. It is only a narrow chink

8

in the US government's armoury of secrecy but it does throw a penetrating new light on events.

For a start, let us get rid of the 'one more lone nut' theory. The widely accepted view of American political assassinations is undoubtedly that they have been the work of mad people. As Professor James W. Clarke of Arizona University has written in his study *American Assassins: the Darker Side of Politics*, 'Assassins are acutely disturbed persons who suffer from such a diminished sense of self that their lives become increasingly isolated, bitter and unbearable. Accordingly, this profound sense of failure translates into a generalized distrust of others to the extent that compensatory delusions of persecution and grandeur begin to dominate the subject's life.

'This distortion of reality is ultimately expressed in the irrational act of assassination. Some observers draw heavily on psychoanalytic concepts to explain this condition but the conclusions are essentially the same: the act is irrational and the assassin is, therefore, "delusional", "deranged" or "schizophrenic".'

The record simply does not bear this out. The plain, unadorned fact is that the majority of American political assassins have not been 'lone nuts'. I am not saying for one moment that they have all been 'Manchurian Candidates' triggered to commit their crimes or that behind most assassinations there has been a hidden conspiracy. That would be nonsense. But, if you look dispassionately at the history of political murder in the United States, you will see that most of the killers have been sane, normally law-abiding individuals who have for some reason that seemed best justified to themselves used assassination as the ultimate method of political protest.

From January 1835 when housepainter Richard Lawrence stepped from the crowd outside the Capitol in Washington DC and fired twice but unavailingly at the aged President Andrew Jackson, until March 1981 when rich man's son John Hinckley gunned down President Reagan outside a hotel in the same city, fifteen men and two women have attacked nationally prominent political leaders in sixteen separate incidents. Of those seventeen killers or would-be killers, only three have been ruled to be insane in law. Lawrence and Hinckley were both found mad by the verdict of a jury and, when John Schrank tried to

9

assassinate ex-President Theodore Roosevelt in October 1912, a panel of psychiatrists ('alienists' as they were called then) decided that he too was insane and was therefore exempt from criminal process.

Of the remaining fourteen assailants, three – Abraham Lincoln's killer John Wilkes Booth, Louisiana Governor Huey Long's assassin Carl Weiss and President Kennedy's murderer Lee Harvey Oswald – were shot down before they could stand trial; but all the other eleven were adjudged sane in court and treated by the country's legal, penal and medical authorities as fully responsible for their actions.

The 'lone nut' theory simply does not stand up as an all-embracing explanation covering all – or even most – instances of American political assassination. No one is saying that these men and women have all been completely 'normal' with absolutely nothing wrong with them in the mind or in the soul: indeed, there is a school of thought that all murderers must to some extent be unbalanced. How else could they kill without justification, and sometimes in cold blood, another human being? Indeed, Allen Sullivan, the New York County assistant district attorney who prosecuted Chapman, says: 'Nobody's suggesting the guy was normal, that he wasn't sick. The defence psychologists all agreed that he was a paranoid schizophrenic, though our medical people did not agree. But so what? We have convicted paranoid schizophrenics of murder before.'

Apart from John Hinckley, none of the living so-called 'lone nuts' – James Earl Ray who killed Martin Luther King Jr., Sirhan Sirhan who murdered Robert Kennedy, Governor George Wallace's assailant Arthur Bremer and Lynette Alice Fromme and Sara Jane Moore, who both tried to take pot-shots at President Gerald Ford – is detained in a mental institution. They are all in ordinary prisons for 'ordinary' criminals.

The United States is a vast melting-pot hybrid of a nation with a deep-rooted 'culture of violence'. 'The right of the people to keep and bear arms' is written into the Second Amendment to the Constitution. American private citizens own more than 55 million handguns. Lennon was the 701st person to be shot down in New York that year. About 25,000 Americans die every year from bullets fired accidentally or otherwise by their own country-men. About 62,000 gunshot injuries are sustained every year at a total cost to the nation in Medicare and state medical assistance programmes of almost a billion dollars annually, according to a report published in November 1988 by a group of researchers from the University of California. Carrying and using a gun – for sport or whatever purpose – is part of 'the American way of life'. An American does not have to be insane or a 'lone nut' to think that he can solve his own or his country's problems with a gun in his hand. On the day after Martin Luther King Jr. was assassinated, Robert Kennedy (several weeks before he too was murdered by gunfire) said: 'The victims of the violence are black and white, rich and poor, young and old, famous and unknown. . . . No one . . . can be certain who next will suffer from some senseless act of bloodshed. And yet it goes on and on in this country of ours. Why?'

Even with the horror of Lennon's murder less than twenty-four hours old, President-elect Ronald Reagan refused to be stampeded into a call for stronger gun control. 'I believe in the kind of handgun legislation we had in California,' he told a reporter. 'If somebody commits a crime and carries a gun when he's doing it, add five to fifteen years to the sentence.' But he refused even to contemplate making the nation's weak gun control laws stronger or more effective; and his wife Nancy told a Washington DC reporter that she kept for protection in a drawer near her bed a small gun that her husband had taught her how to use. 'Ronnie was away a lot, you know,' she said, 'during the time before he became a candidate. He was out speaking a lot and I was alone in that house in California.'

In the 1988 US presidential campaign, when Democratic candidate Michael Dukakis said he might favour legislation making it an offence for anyone other than the police or the military to own a handgun, his soon-to-be-successful Republican opponent George Bush retorted to ringing cheers at a Texas rally: 'That is not the American way! That is not the Texas way!' And this was in the very same state where another so-called 'lone nut' had asserted his constitutional right to carry a gun – with which he killed John Kennedy.

But, to be fair, the authorities have never said that Mark David Chapman is insane. Far from it. Their case has always been that, although allegedly acting alone, he was at all times sane and fully responsible legally for his actions. BS10, the blue-painted ten feet by seven feet isolation cell in which today he lives is not in some mental hospital (like John Hinckley) but at Attica State Prison in upstate New York. 'He is just another man in for murder as far as we are concerned,' said Harold J. Smith, Attica's superintendent, on the first anniversary of his crime. 'The status of Mr Chapman has remained constant during the past few years,' Walter R. Kelly, his successor as superintendent, wrote to me in May 1988.

This opens up a whole can of worms. For, if Mark was not a 'lone nut' and as sane a murderer as any other, why on earth did he kill John Lennon? Why did the God-fearing son of a law-abiding credit manager and ex-nurse from the Deep South, whom everybody believed until four years earlier would have had a full-time permanent career in the YMCA, drop into combat stance and destroy a fellow human being who had brought such happiness to the world?

Let us lead into it from a lawyer's angle. The prosecution had one theory as to the motivation for the murder, the defence had two of its own – both of which were self-contradictory. All three, on any objective assessment, are not supported by the facts. Therefore, one has to look elsewhere for the truth. It really is as simple as that.

The New York County district attorney's office took the view from the start, both in court and out of court, that Mark killed Lennon to become famous. On the first afternoon after the murder, Kim Hogrefe, Allen Sullivan's principal assistant, told Judge Martin Rettinger in Manhattan Criminal Court: 'The suspect has been cool, calm and rational. This was a deliberate, premeditated execution of Mr John Lennon.' Notice that vital word: 'rational'.

Four years later, when Mark was already at Attica, Sullivan himself told me, sitting back laconic and cool in his seventh-floor office adjoining the courtroom building: 'He wanted to be noticed. He hadn't done too well in his life and he just felt that he was deserving of great notoriety, great attention. He wanted attention. He really did, like a kid doing something naughty on the streets, want to be noticed.'

Mark wrote me in May 1988, 'If you wish, kindly write me from time to time and keep me abreast. I know you've worked hard and long on this' – but he would not see me. With only four exceptions, he has given no interviews to the media – although, unlike in most British gaols, prisoners serving their time in US prisons are perfectly at liberty to do so. He has talked at length to one American journalist, James R. Gaines, now managing editor of *People* magazine, who built up over the years a sympathetic, long-standing relationship with him which resulted in a major article in *People* in June 1981 and three later ones in February/March 1987. In 1983, Mark spent eight hours at Attica with Craig Unger, a New York journalist who had written about him two years before and was then planning a film about him, but the project apparently came to nothing. In February 1984, as we shall see later, he invited a reporter from the local *Buffalo Evening News* to interview him so that he could reply to a specific article in *Playboy* magazine that had annoyed him. And in 1987 he spent many hours with Kevin Sim, a British television documentary producer, although finally he would not let him use on camera any of the material: when the film *The Man Who Shot John Lennon* screened in Britain and the United States in early 1988, Sim had to be content merely with Mark's voice on the sound track talking to police and psychiatrists on old recordings made while he was awaiting trial. In fact, in a letter to David C. Moore, a long-standing YMCA friend, in April 1988 Mark wrote that the only thing he did not like about the television documentary was its final interview with a woman in which she said he was a seeker after publicity: 'That is nonsense. I turn away thirty to forty invitations from the media a year. I have never given an interview. I am not a seeker after publicity.'

Furthermore, if he killed Lennon to become famous, why did he ever plead guilty and so lose his supreme moment in the spotlight with reporters from all over the world describing his every gesture and hanging on his words as he told his story on the witness stand? His trial, if fought, would have been the 'Trial of the Decade'.

Confirmation of the basic implausibility of the district attorney's theory comes from, of all people, the lieutenant who was commanding officer of the detectives at the twentieth precinct of the New York police that dealt with his case. Arthur O'Connor, now retired after thirty years' service, has never before been interviewed on the murder. I traced him through the police pension fund – a standard method of getting hold of retired police officers throughout the world (which for some reason seemed to impress him). He says: 'It is definitely illogical to say Mark committed the murder to make himself famous. He didn't want to talk to the press from the very start. When I spoke to him about his wife on the night of the killing he was apprehensive about her finding out what he had done via the media. He didn't want the press. He didn't encourage it. He did not want the notoriety. He did not want the "glory" of a trial either.'

The defence's two theories stand up no better to the calm appraisal of logic, although both were – but of course! – supported by the opinion of psychiatrists. (In all my years in the law, I have never found a theory, however way out, put before a court that an honest psychiatrist, in perfect good faith, has not been able to support. It is not an exact science.) One theory was that Mark killed Lennon because he believed that he was himself Lennon and that only through killing this other part of his split personality could he be free. The other was that he killed Lennon because he hated him so much: he believed that he was a true-life 'Holden Caulfield,' like the sixteen-year-old hero of J. D. Salinger's novel *The Catcher in the Rye*, charged with the self-imposed task of ridding the world of 'phonies' of which Lennon was, to his mind, a paid up, eighteen-carat example.

But both theories cannot possibly be right. Mark cannot have killed Lennon because he identified himself so much with Lennon that he thought he was Lennon *and* because he thought he was Holden Caulfield ridding the world of Lennon the 'phoney'. It does not make sense and, if the case had gone for trial, the odds are, in my view, that a realistic New York jury would have thrown it out the window and refused to find him mad, so that he could go to a nice 'caring' mental hospital instead of a tough state prison.

So where are we? If both prosecution and defence theories do not stand up, we have to look elsewhere for the explanation for the murder. And the amazing thing is that the New York police did not do so. There was no proper investigation of complicity in this crime: that may be hard to believe but it is true. Albert Goldman quotes ex-New York detective Ron Hoffman: 'We knew that when this case went to trial, no matter what happened, we were gonna be criticized for years, for generations to come. We did our best. There was nothing too insignificant to go into. Nothing!'

This is difficult to accept. Says his ex-boss, retired lieutenant of detectives Arthur O'Connor: 'This case was a grounder. In any kind of criminal investigation, primarily a homicide investigation, a case in police vernacular in New York City is considered grounded when a case is solved. This case was solved with the arrest of Mark Chapman. He remained on the scene voluntarily. He was not physically restrained. Seventy-five feet away was an entrance to the subway. If he wanted to, he could have gotten clean away. He had a 75 per cent chance, in my book, of never being apprehended. But he wanted to get caught. Now, if he had got away, then there would have been one hell of an investigation!

'As it was, there was no extensive investigation: there did not have to be. We had our man! As for Sullivan, the assistant district attorney, he did not have too much homework to do either, though I grant you he is a very thorough man: it didn't matter, he was primarily concerned with Mark's mental condition. He knew that would be the essential issue at the trial. Mark was going to plead insanity – and that is what occupied Sullivan's mind.

'Investigate a possible conspiracy? Whatever for? Nobody cared to pursue that line. When a case is grounded, it's grounded – and this one was from the start. Mark acknowledged his guilt that first night at the precinct. What more was there to do? You don't go looking for a conspiracy. I had no information about one – and I did not look for it.

'Look! I only had twenty detectives in my precinct for a whole area in which a million people lived. We had just finished a massive investigation – and that really was one! – into the Metropolitan Opera House murder in July when a young stagehand, who worked there, a guy called Craig Crimmins, killed a girl who was a violinist in a visiting orchestra from Berlin. That case really had vibes! The pressure was on from all sides to get it solved. But even after the arrest at the end of August, it dragged on for months. Crimmins finally got bail at the beginning of December and then – bang! – John Lennon is killed. We needed that like a hole in the head – but fortunately it was grounded!'

This view of the investigation – or lack of it – is confirmed by Wesley Nunn, a special agent with the Georgia Bureau of Investigation (GBI instead of FBI), who did follow-up research for the New York police in the Atlanta area. He says: 'Apart from wanting me to go check on where Mark got his bullets from, the primary thrust of my enquiries was into his background. What sort of a guy he was, that kind of thing. I got the impression the

DA in New York was more concerned with fighting a defence of insanity at the trial than anything else.

'Conspiracy? I know nothing about that. No one mentioned anything to me about the possibility and I certainly didn't get into that area.'

Similarly, in Honolulu, another local detective – Louis L. Souza, now a captain in the criminal investigation division – made local enquiries for the New York police; but he primarily limited himself to background information on the arrested man. When Gloria Chapman, Mark's wife, refused to see him because she said she was too upset, he did not insist on an interview; 'I checked with the New York authorities and they did not want to press the issue so I didn't pursue it.' Frankly, to my mind, this seems amazing; she could have given vital first-hand information not only as to Mark's state of mind in the days and weeks before the killing but also as to his associates and the actual mechanics of his getting to the mainland – and the finance for it. The Castle Memorial Hospital where she worked, and from whose credit union it is believed she borrowed $2500 to finance the second of his two trips to New York, refused to disclose to Souza their accounts on the basis of confidentiality: 'Maybe we could have gone to court to get that information,' he told me; 'but at the time I guess they didn't feel in New York that it was important where he got the money from to make the trips. The fact is that he did take the trips.' Souza did not, on his own admission, even try and interview Mark's mother who was by then living on the island. My only comment is that it is impossible to imagine anything more half-baked by way of investigating a major crime. I do not criticize Souza: he was merely following the line dictated by New York.

As we shall see later, there is a vitally important question as to the exact date when Mark left Honolulu on his final mission to kill Lennon and even whether he flew direct to New York (as all published accounts have it) or had a three-day stop-over at Chicago on the way – as I believe to be the case. Souza traced the United Airline ticket agent who sold him his ticket – 'But I don't have his address nor did I interview him because my only concern at the time was to establish that Chapman acquired an air fare out of the state and the ultimate location.'

I know that real-life detectives and police officers, whether in

Britain or the United States, do not always carry out their duties with the smooth, calculating efficiency so often seen on television, with no legitimate channel of enquiry unexplored; but the police work on the John Lennon murder really does strike an all-time low.

And what makes it all the more lamentable is that, in June 1988, Arthur O'Connor admitted to me: 'It's possible Mark could have been used by somebody. I saw him the night of the murder. I studied him intensely. He looked as if he could have been programmed – and I know what use you are going to make of that word!' He was speaking with the advantage of hindsight. At the time, the thought just genuinely did not seem to have occurred to him.

So let us do our own investigation, such as we can, with no rights of arrest nor recourse to the courts for writs of subpoena or legally enforceable demands for the production of documents. Speaking to the media on the day following the murder, Mark's long-standing YMCA friend David C. Moore said in Chicago: 'I don't think it was Mark who pulled the trigger – maybe his body but not his mind. To say that Mark, the bright, sensitive young man I knew, did this thing makes me wonder if I could have done it, if anyone could have done it, given similar circumstances. And that is horribly frightening.'

The 'frightening' story now begins.

2

The CIA, YMCA and Others

In May 1960, Lennon was twenty years old and had the previous month formed the Beatles in their native Liverpool: they were total unknowns. Mark was only five and living with his parents, David and Diane Chapman, in a small town in Indiana, while his father, recently having left the US air force, was taking his first steps on the corporate ladder as a junior credit official with the giant American Oil Corporation.

In this same month, in the luxurious setting of the thick-carpeted Fontainebleau Hotel overlooking the Atlantic at Miami, Florida, a secret meeting took place between three men that, if a movie camera had been present, would have looked like a scene from an old-style Hollywood thriller – only this one was for real. Robert Maheu, ex-FBI man, freelance CIA agent and right-hand man to reclusive billionaire Howard Hughes, had come to talk to two leading Mafia mobsters about murder. Johnny Roselli from Los Angeles and Sam Giancana from Chicago, both later murdered and both with roots going back to Al Capone, were experts in that field. But they, like Maheu himself (who was on direct orders from CIA director Allen Dulles), were only middle-men. They were there on behalf of 'Don' Santos Trafficante, who had been the undisputed boss of the Mafia in Cuba until January 1959 when, on the downfall of the corrupt, US-supported dictator Fulgencio Batista, he had been booted out by Fidel Castro.

The proposition that Maheu put to Roselli and Giancana was one that he knew in advance would appeal to them: pooling CIA and Mafia resources to set up 'political assassination units' to get rid of Castro and so get them back their fat profits. But it was not only Castro himself who was to be killed but also his brother

18

Raul, the charismatic young fighter Che Guevara and five other Cuban revolutionary leaders.

If this was not so well documented, the whole story would seem ludicrous – and unbelievably evil. For the CIA to plot with the Mafia to kill the prime minister of a neighbouring country (Castro did not become president until 1976): how far-fetched can you get? But it did happen. It was true – and it was not even the first high-powered US government project against the new rulers of Cuba: in late 1959 the US National Security Council had set in train a secret CIA operation, code-named 'Operation 40', to use expatriate right-wing Cubans who had fled to the States to undermine, weaken and eventually overthrow the new revolutionary government. The joint CIA/Mafia 'shooter teams' now agreed to be set up, with assassins trained at a secret 'triangular-fire training base' at Oaxaca, Mexico – like something out of a James Bond film – were only a more deadly extension of Nixon's original brain-child, 'Operation 40'.

Did the President himself, then ex-World War Two military supremo Dwight D. Eisenhower, know of the 'shooter teams'? In December 1986 in the US District Court in Florida, Daniel Sheehan, a Washington-based attorney and leading civil rights activist, filed an affidavit in a lawsuit brought for $17 million damages by two American journalists injured in a bomb blast in Nicaragua in 1984, alleged to be the work of direct descendants of the original 'shooter teams'.[1] Sheehan stated that the May 1960 meeting took place with Eisenhower's full knowledge and

[1]The lawsuit was filed in May 1986 on behalf of Tony Avirgan and Martha Honey by the Christic Institute, a fact-finding Washington-based public-interest law firm co-founded by Sheehan and his wife and drawing its name from a Jesuit philosopher. It charged that the bombing was the work of an alleged 'secret team' of ex-CIA operatives, right-wing activists, arms merchants, drug smugglers and mercenaries stemming right back to the original 'shooter teams'. The twenty-nine defendants included such names as retired Army General John Singlaub, retired Air Force General Richard Secord, ex-CIA senior official Theodore Schackley, Contra leader Adolfo Calero, Colombian cocaine kingpin Jorge Ochoa and John Hull, an American rancher in Costa Rica.

With its allegations of three decades of illegal covert operations, drug smuggling, gun running, terrorist acts, political assassinations and undercover wars around the world, the suit sounded preposterous to most of the American public until many of the same names began cropping up in the high-profile congressional hearings into the Iran-Contra affair in the summer of 1987.

approval. It was Eisenhower who, three months later, on 18 August 1960, at a meeting of the National Security Council, was to call angrily for straightforward action to 'dispose of' the erratic and pro-Soviet Congolese prime minister Patrice Lumumba. Even though he was forced to resign three weeks later, Lumumba remained a considerable power in his strategically important Central African country and was perceived to be a continuing major threat to American interests. In January 1961, he was murdered and fifteen years later a Senate Select Committee, chaired by Senator Frank Church, found:[1] 'The chain of events revealed in the documents and testimony is strong enough to permit a reasonable inference that the plot to assassinate Lumumba was authorized by President Eisenhower.' The old soldier would probably not have found it too difficult to contemplate Castro's murder either.

The 'shooter teams' were neither the first nor the only time that the US government linked hands, in covert operation, with the Mafia. During the Second World War, General William J. Donovan, chief of Office of Strategic Services, the undercover intelligence organization out of which the CIA grew, had enlisted the help of the leading New York mobster, 'Lucky' Luciano, in

---

1

But, on 23 June 1988, just three days before the suit was to be heard in Miami, twenty-eight years and one month after the original CIA/Mafia meeting in the Fontainebleau Hotel, US District Judge James Lawrence King, appointed to office by Richard Nixon, when Republican president, dismissed the case on a summary judgement ruling based on insufficient evidence – an extraordinarily late time to do so.

Daniel Sheehan promptly said that the desire to protect then Vice-President George Bush, ex-CIA director and Republican candidate for the presidency in the upcoming elections in November 1988, from the taint of the trial was the real reason for the summary judgement. He pointed out that Robert Owen, one of the defendants, had worked for Senator Dan Quayle, Bush's right-wing running mate for vice-president, and claimed that 'politics' was the basis of the case's dismissal.

An appeal against Judge King's ruling was immediately lodged, and the Institute boasts that it will succeed and one day their evidence will be heard. But when? Recalling their most famous victory to date, the Karen Silkwood case, which established the right of citizens to seek remedies for nuclear hazards under state laws, Sally Schwartz, a spokesperson for the Institute, told the *Los Angeles Times* in September 1988: 'We're trying to remind people that the Silkwood case took for ever. It took ten years.'

protecting the Mafia-controlled docks on America's East Coast from attempts at Nazi sabotage – in return for which at war's end Luciano's long prison sentence was commuted and he was deported to his native Italy.

Over thirty years later, in March 1975, Seymour Hersh, a leading investigative journalist, reported in the *New York Times*, after having talked extensively to a senior CIA undercover agent 'whose knowledge of the CIA seemed extensive', that 'the Mafia was relied upon' to 'assault targets selected by the CIA'.

A common purpose can make strange bed-fellows.

Yet, for all the sinister undertones of the Castro assassination project, in practice the combined efforts of the CIA and the Mafia over the next five years, under the code-name 'Operation Mongoose', until President Lyndon B. Johnson called the whole thing off, would make a superb comic thriller movie. They tried to kill or humiliate the Cuban leader with bombs, telescopic rifles, a poisoned pen, poisoned pills and darts, an exploding seashell to be placed near his favourite bathing spot as well as poisoned cigars, a contaminated scuba diving suit and even a coating of thallium salts in his shoes so that, when he bent down to tie up his laces, the fumes would make his beard fall out so he would look ridiculous when broadcasting to his people on television.

It all sounds nonsense but Lyndon B. Johnson was convinced that Castro took it all so seriously that he was behind the assassination of President Kennedy. So much for *that* particular 'lone nut' murder.

It is, indeed, established fact that the CIA has been involved in assassinations and assassination attempts around the world. A Senate Committee of Inquiry chaired by Senator Frank Church in the mid-1970s reported that, on the evidence disclosed to them, no foreign leader had ever been directly assassinated by the CIA but that 'American officials encouraged or were privy to plots which resulted in the deaths of Rafael Trujillo (in the Dominican Republic), Ngo Dinh Diem (in Vietnam) and General Rene Schneider (in Chile).'

What is not generally known, however, is that there are good grounds for believing that the hit-teams that were set up by the Maheu-Roselli/Giancana meeting in May 1960 did not cease to exist when the Castro project came to an end. Interviewed in

June 1988 in his office in Washington DC, Daniel Sheehan, the civil rights attorney who filed the affidavit dealing with Nixon and the 'shooter teams' eighteen months earlier, said: 'I am confident that it was a generic programme and that there was a lot more in their sights than just Castro, Che Guevara and those five guys. There had been all that earlier talk about killing Patrice Lumumba in the Congo and there'd been discussions about how, to set up such an operation, you had to get hold of someone from organized crime who could possibly know how to do that kind of stuff. It was clear that there was a generic kind of conversation going on. To have that type of general capacity to carry out that kind of direct action or "executive action", as the CIA calls it, was in fact what they were talking about.

'The objective was to have a generic programme available to take out individuals whom they felt they were at war with. That still continues to this day.'

Successive CIA directors have always claimed that, until President Gerald R. Ford specifically outlawed assassination as a legitimate working tool, it only took place outside the USA. No one was ever 'disposed of' by the CIA or their associates inside the United States, they have always said. But how can one be sure? How can one ever believe what the CIA says? The agency was, for instance, happy for the world to know that both Ford's successors, President Carter and President Reagan, had also signed Executive Orders prohibiting CIA involvement in all assassination either direct or indirect. Yet in October 1984 an Associated Press wire report disclosed that, despite those three presidential decrees, a CIA guerrilla-warfare training manual, written by the later so-called 'All-American Hero', Colonel Oliver North of Iran-Contra fame, advocated the 'neutralization' of Nicaraguan judges and police. The news exploded like a bomb in Washington DC. The United States was going to the polls next month to elect a new president, and Reagan, the incumbent, was the front runner against ex-Democratic Vice-President Walter Mondale. Reagan was supposed to have curbed the CIA: how could this new development possibly be true – or be allowed to be perceived as true?

CIA director William J. Casey had publicly, and much to his personal distaste, to eat humble pie and the White House rushed out a statement: 'The administration has not advocated or condoned political assassination or any other attacks on civilians, nor will we.'

What else could they say?

Old habits die hard, if ever. Executive Order 12333, signed by President Reagan in 1981, bars the CIA from activities 'intended to influence United States political processes, public opinion . . . or media'.

Yet in September 1988, the highly respected and politically independent newspaper, the *Los Angeles Times*, revealed that, according to documents unearthed by the congressional Iran-Contra Committee in the previous year, a covert White House propaganda campaign had been mounted with CIA backing, 'to manipulate the American public, Congress and the news media in support of Contra military aid in Nicaragua'. The documents disclosed that this domestic operation, directed out of the National Security Council, had been crafted by a senior CIA propaganda veteran and staffed, in part, by US army psychological warfare specialists.

As the Iran-Contra Committee had been writing its report in the autumn of 1987, House investigators had drafted a chapter on this illegal activity. It said that the campaign had used 'one of the CIA's most senior specialists sent to the NSC by director Casey, to create and coordinate an inter-agency public diplomacy mechanism. [This network] did what a covert CIA operation in a foreign country might do – attempted to manipulate the media, the Congress and public opinion to support Reagan administration policies. The problem with all this is: they tried to do it in America, to their own people, to their own Congress, to their own free press.'

What happened to that chapter? It did not appear in the Iran-Contra Committee's report. And why not? The *Los Angeles Times* gave this typically tawdry political explanation: 'Inside the committee, the chapter's dramatic conclusion was hotly opposed by Republicans (Reagan's own party), who argued it was outside the panel's investigative mandate, and by some Democrats, who feared it would jeopardize support for the report's chief findings from moderate Senate Republicans. In the rush to complete its work, the committee dropped the draft chapter.' As so often has happened, expediency was all.

'A rogue elephant out of control,' Senator Frank Church has called the CIA. That was over ten years ago – but nothing changes.

Against this background, there are many, therefore, who believe that CIA involvement in political assassination is not a thing of the past, that it was not so in December 1980 – and furthermore that it has never been a product reserved for export only. The official CIA line has always been quite the contrary. Until Executive Orders by President Ford in 1976, President Carter in 1978 and President Reagan in 1981 gave the agency a certain limited authority to act internally, the agency has always maintained that it has not operated at home anyway, in whatever kind of activity. Undoubtedly, it was never supposed to.

The agency was created by the National Security Act of July 1947, taking over from the transitional Central Intelligence Group (CIG) which had been established two years earlier when President Truman had discontinued the old wartime derring-do undercover organization, the Office of Strategic Services (OSS), a few weeks after the Japanese surrender in 1945. It was to perform a role in the Cold War of the late 1940s and beyond similar to that which the OSS had played in the Second World War: fight, on the intelligence front, the new enemy of Soviet Communism as against the old foes of Nazi Germany and Imperial Japan.

From the very beginning, the agency was 'sold' to the American people as restricted solely to activity outside the USA: in fact, Congress wrote into its charter that it was prohibited from exercising 'police, subpoena or law-enforcement powers or internal security functions'. Congressional debate made it clear that the nation's legislators anticipated that it would simply not operate at home: any domestic work that needed to be done would be handled by the FBI.

But from very early on, in one covert operation after another, the new organization cocked a snook at Congress – and the law. As Admiral Stansfield Turner, appointed by President Carter as CIA director in the hope of cleaning up the organization during the four years of his administration (1977 to 1981), has written in his memoirs: 'Some 300,000 Americans considered to be potentially "dangerous" to our national security were indexed in a CIA computer, and separate files were created on approximately 7,200' (including, as we shall see, John Lennon). 'Millions of private telegrams were obtained between 1974 and 1975. Countless "dangerous" citizens were placed under surveillance,' (again, as we shall see, including John Lennon) 'with bugs on their telephones, microphones in their bedrooms or warrantless break-ins of their homes. There was extensive use of fellow citizens as informants. Tax returns were obtained from the IRS and scanned for information about citizens. Army intelligence infiltrated domestic dissident groups, collected information on prominent citizens sympathetic with such groups, and created an estimated 100,000 files on Americans.'

It was all illegal. All totally contrary to the agency's own charter. But what did that have to do with anything? Such considerations have seldom got in the way of a zealous CIA official pursuing what he considers his duty. This agency has its own concept of honour in the service of its country.

That is why President Bush was such a popular CIA director in the twelve months he held office from January 1976 until January 1977 when Jimmy Carter became president and shortly afterwards appointed Admiral Turner to the post. 'The reason they had a great love for George Bush [at the CIA] was that he let them do whatever they wanted,' Turner has said. 'He came in and said, "What do you want to do?" And then he said, "OK, go ahead and do it".'

For the first time in its history, the United States now has a leader who is a former head of the CIA. As vice-president, he was the keynote speaker at a testimonial dinner for ex-CIA director Richard M. Helms who, as it happened, had six years earlier pleaded 'no contest' to two charges of failing to testify 'fully, completely and accurately' to Congress about the agency's covert operations in Chile. That little detail did not prevent Mr Bush declaring his 'respect and admiration' for Helms' work in building an intelligence agency 'second to none'. At the same time he praised the CIA for being 'fastidious in respecting the law of the land'.

Such talk is for fairy tales. The true picture has been more accurately painted by Victor Marchetti and John D. Marks in their book *The CIA and the Cult of Intelligence*: '[The agency] penetrates and manipulates private institutions, and creates its own organizations (called "proprietaries") when necessary. It recruits agents and mercenaries; it bribes and blackmails foreign officials to carry out its most unsavoury tasks. It does whatever is required to achieve its goals, without any consideration of the ethics involved or the moral consequences of its actions.'

'I wear my directorship of that organization as a badge of honour,' President Bush has said. The justification for its activities has always been the same: to keep America 'strong' and to combat the world menace of Soviet Communism. With that aim, anything and everything goes. As the *Los Angeles Times* quoted an unnamed CIA source as saying in November 1988, 'Covert action is something George Bush feels comfortable with. He is a supporter of having that instrument of power available. . . . He will use it as it should be used – as a surgical instrument.'

Such thinking has always been behind the agency's exercise of power. It has been the justification for its widespread, and sometimes illegal, intrusion into so many aspects of American life, internal as well as external.

It has set up its own airlines and business firms to infiltrate ordinary commercial activities. It has formed dummy foundations to funnel secret money into domestic cultural groups, educational publications and labour unions. The more respectable the cover, the more desirable it has been.

The agency's corrupting touch has reached out even to the young. In February 1967, the editors of *Ramparts Magazine* took full-page advertisements in the *New York Times* and the *Washington Post* to announce that their forthcoming March issue would lift the lid on a fifteen-year scandal: 'The CIA has infiltrated and subverted the country's student leadership. It has used students to spy. It has used students to pressure international student organizations into Cold War positions, and it has interfered in a shocking manner in the internal workings of the nation's oldest and largest student organization.'

The March issue and subsequent disclosures revealed this was no overstatement. The National Students Association, with chapters on 340 campuses, had to concede that it had received more than $3 million from the CIA from 1952 to 1966, and for most of that time only the association's two top officers had known the source of the money.

Even the nation's Christian missionaries did not prove immune. After reports had appeared in the press in the late 1960s of 'systematic use of American missionaries by the CIA', the magazine *Christian Century* protested: 'Since the CIA specializes in keeping everyone in the dark – friend and foe alike – there is no way to know how widespread the practice has been.'

26

In February 1973, James Schlesinger was appointed CIA director by President Nixon to take over from the long-serving (1966–1973) and case-hardened Richard M. Helms. As a newcomer, Schlesinger was shocked by the agency's increasingly tarnished reputation and decided to uncover all the skeletons in the CIA's closet for himself before the newsmen did. He asked every CIA employee to inform him of any instance of improper activity they knew about. The list ran to a staggering 683 pages and was called sarcastically 'The Family Jewels'.

But Schlesinger served only five months (before leaving to become defence secretary) and it fell to his successor, William Egan Colby, the first – and only – CIA director to be appointed from within the agency, to decide what to do about it. He took what Admiral Turner, in his memoirs, calls 'a considerable number of corrective actions'; but the floodgate of disclosures in those post-Watergate years could not be dammed. On 22 December 1974, the balloon really went up with the publication of a sensational but deeply researched article by Seymour Hersh in the *New York Times*. Under the headline, 'Huge CIA Operation Reported in US Against Anti-War Forces, Other Dissidents in Nixon Years', Hersh charged: 'The Central Intelligence Agency, directly violating its charter, conducted a massive illegal domestic intelligence operation during the Nixon administration against the anti-war movement and other dissident groups in the United States, according to well-placed government sources.'

In Admiral Turner's phrase, 'The fat was in the fire. In-house corrections would no longer satisfy critics. Demands mounted for a full-scale investigation.'

In January 1975, President Ford appointed his vice-president, Nelson D. Rockefeller, to head a blue-ribbon commission – with ex-Californian Governor Ronald Reagan as one of its members – to investigate Seymour Hersh's allegations. Like so many official inquiries on both sides of the Atlantic, its efforts ended five months later in a soothing whitewash: 'A detailed analysis of the facts has convinced the commission that the great majority of the CIA's domestic activities comply with its statutory authority. Nevertheless, over the twenty-eight years of its history, the CIA has engaged in some activities that should be criticized and not permitted to happen again.'

But the setting up of this expectedly pliant commission had

not calmed public disquiet. Later in January 1975, the Senate appointed a Select Committee on Intelligence to inquire into the CIA under the chairmanship of Senator Frank Church and the following month the House of Representatives followed suit with its own Select Committee under the eventual chairmanship of Representative Otis Pike. Although in the end, all that either body gave the agency in their reports was a slight slap on the wrist – both were over-awed by claims that the organization had throughout acted only in what it considered 'the national interest' – for the next two years a surprising spate of revelations spewed out.

Specifically on the aspect of the CIA's involvement with the churches and Christian organizations, agency witnesses claimed to Senator Church's committee that over the years the CIA had made 'direct operational use' of only twenty-one individual missionaries – but how can one ever tell if this figure is accurate? Or when – or if – such activity has ceased? And one is left wondering how men and women of God can ever bring themselves to accept that it is morally right to lie or spy, even for one's own country.

Which brings one to the American Young's Men's Christian Association.

In all the literature on the CIA, there is scarcely any reference to any possible link between the agency and the YMCA. But, if one thinks about it, the value of such an association would be tremendous: with YMCA offices in ninety countries around the world, all linked to the American 'Y' in the World Alliance of Young Men's Christian Associations, there could be no better cover for an international intelligence network – however unofficial. This is an objective fact; although I make no suggestion whatsoever that such a link was known to, or participated in, by the YMCA management, whether national or international.

This laudable and esteemed organization, whose 'mission' in the American 'Y's' fact sheet is given as 'To put Christian principles into practice through programmes that build healthy body, mind and spirit for all,' was founded in England as long ago as June 1844. A twenty-three-year-old drapery clerk in London named George Williams suggested to his eleven fellow young live-in clerks above the Hitchcock and Rodgers shop facing St Paul's Cathedral that they should call their prayer and Bible study group for evangelicals the Young Men's Christian Association. His goal was to save his fellow-workers, who like him had been drawn to the capital by the need for work, from the wicked life on the streets of the big city.

By the time he died in November 1905, knighted by Queen Victoria and with a last resting place in the very cathedral opposite which he used to work, his brain-child had already spread across the Atlantic to the United States and Canada and become a world-wide institution. The World Alliance of YMCAs had been formed in 1855, and the avowed aim of this new international organization had been proclaimed as: 'To unite young men' – women were added later – 'who have accepted Jesus Christ as God and Saviour and who wish to be His disciples in faith and life and extend His Kingdom amongst young men.'

The YMCA has branches in no Communist or Iron Curtain country. To be devoutly Christian is not necessarily to be aggressively anti-Communist but, although the organization has always maintained that it is non-political, the odds must surely be that the sort of person who opts for a working life within the 'Y' is likely to feel more deeply anti-Communist and emotionally more opposed to the anti-Christ than the average person who matter-of-factly calls himself a Christian.

Officially, the CIA, for its part, has no religion but the very inscription on the marble wall of the main lobby at its headquarters at Langley, Virginia, outside Washington DC is a quotation from the New Testament: 'And Ye shall know the truth and the truth shall make you free' (John, VIII:32). There has never been a non-Christian – or even Jewish – CIA director; and one somehow feels that there are very few open atheists or even agnostics on its permanent staff. In all but name, it is a Christian-oriented organization and, to boot, has always and everywhere been militantly anti-Communist. If, as we have seen, it has reached out successfully to Christian missionaries to enlist them in its work, it is almost inconceivable that it would not, at least, have tried to do the same to the God-fearing men and women and young people who make up the YMCA. Why should they be such 'untouchables'?

In 1979, when I was researching a book on *The Chinese Mafia* with top-level cooperation from the US Drug Enforcement Agency, a DEA agent who was also an ex-CIA case officer boasted to me, over a steak dinner in The Hague, Holland, about the agency's use of the YMCA as a superb front for their activities. He was not specific, and I did not press him: at that time, it was no part of my concern. We had other, more immediate things to discuss and this was just a pleasant social occasion at the end of a long, grim working day – but I have always remembered what he said.

Philip Agee, the first-known defector from the CIA, names in his classic 1974 book *Inside the Company: CIA Diary* the YMCA in a list of organizations used by the agency and, as an ex-Latin American operator, specifies the 'Y's' office in Quito, the capital of Ecuador, as being a contact base for agents and potential agents. Two Quito CIA station officers were actually on its board of directors.

Nor was this any quiet, uneventful posting. In 1961 and again in 1963, while Agee was serving in Quito, the CIA was instrumental in successfully toppling two successive anti-US governments. Those two 'YMCA directors' did their job well.

Agee's disclosures on the most intimate workings of the CIA are not to be dismissed as just one more sensationalist, allegedly 'tell-all' kind of book. In its 600 pages, the first ever of its kind, he named several hundred CIA officers and informants besides identifying scores of cover organizations and laying bare the agency's relationships with governments and companies. The authorities took his revelations very seriously indeed. 'The book will affect the CIA as a severe body blow does any living organism,' said one review written by an ex-CIA official. 'Some parts obviously will be affected more than others, but the health of the whole is bound to suffer. A considerable number of CIA personnel must be diverted from their normal duties to undertake the meticulous and time-consuming task of repairing the damage done to its Latin American programme, and to see what can be done to help those injured by the author's revelations.' In January 1981, the US Supreme Court ruled that, by his efforts, Agee had forfeited the right to hold a US passport: those efforts included blowing the cover on the CIA/YMCA link.

As we shall see later, Mark David Chapman had an undoubted and continual involvement with the YMCA throughout most of his life until he assassinated Lennon. He went, as a young man of twenty, to Beirut for them in 1975. He toured the world, staying in YMCA hostels around the globe in 1978. He actually worked for them for five months in 1975 at a camp for Vietnamese refugees in Arkansas and at six summer camps at his home 'Y' in Georgia from 1969 to 1976, first as full-time camp counsellor and then as assistant camp director.

Andrea Hinding, a helpful and dedicated archivist with the YMCA central archives at the University of Michigan, says that she would have expected to find some record of all his time on the pay-roll in her archives but, despite the most diligent searches, she has drawn a blank. Admittedly, the records are not 100 per cent complete but other people, with similar service, *are* in the records. Why should that particular file, with all Mark's personal details, be missing?

The fact remains that, if he was, indeed, a CIA-trained killer 'on hold', there could have been no better cover than the YMCA for his activities – and no better reason for his dossier to be missing from the organization's central archives.

3

Mind Control I

The term 'Manchurian Candidate' came into the language in 1959, when Richard Condon made it the title of a best-selling novel that later became a classic movie starring Laurence Harvey and Frank Sinatra. It told the story of a US army officer captured by the Communists during the Korean War and brainwashed at a secret location in Manchuria into a remote-controlled assassin programmed to kill the American president. The subject was so hot that, when the movie was made in 1962, Sinatra had to ask President Kennedy personally to intercede with the president of United Artists to ensure the backing for the film. After Kennedy's assassination the following year, a deeply shaken Sinatra, who owned the copyright, withdrew the film from circulation only allowing it to be re-issued twenty-five years later in 1988.

Why Manchuria? Condon consulted with a wide variety of experts while researching his book; and John Marks, a former Senate aide and State Department official, whose own factual book *The Search for the 'Manchurian Candidate'* caused a minor sensation when it appeared in 1979, has speculated that some inside sources may well have filled him in on the gist of a discussion that took place at a meeting in 1953 at CIA headquarters on behaviour control. Marks quotes one participant: 'Individuals who had come out of North Korea across the Soviet Union to freedom recently apparently had a blank period of disorientation while passing through a special zone in Manchuria.' Marks tried to follow up this oblique reference but could come up with no further information.

The fact remains that, ever since Condon's brilliantly conceived novel first hit the bookshops, people have been asking: 'Do real-life "Manchurian Candidates" exist?'

32

The answer has to be: almost certainly, yes – but we are unlikely ever to know for sure.

The notion of a 'Manchurian Candidate' programmed to kill seems chillingly modern but to trace its development you have to go back to the mid-eighteenth century and to an Austrian physician named Anton Mesmer. He was the father of modern mind control for it was he who invented hypnotism or – as it was called for over half a century – mesmerism. Introduced to metal magnets by an astronomer at the court of the great Empress Maria Theresa in Vienna, Mesmer found that he could relieve pain by applying magnets to the bodies of his patients. In some way it drained off their hurt and their discomfort. But then he found that it was not the magnets that were responsible but himself: his own eyes and hands, the almost unreal quality of his touch, the impact of his charismatic personality. Recognizing that the vital factor was himself rather than the metal magnets, he evolved the theory of 'animal magnetism' – hence, the term that many people still use today without realizing its origin.

Shunned by his colleagues, Mesmer moved to Paris where he quickly became a great success. Long before the days of modern drugs and anaesthetics, Mesmer could rid his patients of pain and make them disregard their symptoms merely by throwing them into a hypnotic trance. When they came round, it was as if they were cured. Their mind, controlled by Mesmer, had taken over their body and freed them from torment.

In 1784, the French Academy of Science appointed a committee of the most eminent scientists in the country to explore just what 'mesmerism' was all about. They could come to no firm conclusion, except that the Austrian doctor's amazing results came from a combination of the suggestibility of his patients and the powerful impact of his own personality and touch.

But the phenomenon outlived its founder. After Mesmer's death, the medical profession gradually adopted some of his techniques – especially in the use of an induced trance as an early form of anaesthesia for medical operations. In fact, it was a Scottish surgeon named James Baird who coined the term 'hypnotism' in 1843. From then, it has had a strange history: at times, in great vogue and at other times scorned and dismissed as the play-thing of quacks. For a while, Sigmund Freud himself used hypnosis to plumb his patients' subconscious but then he too turned away

33

from it to develop the notion of 'free association' with the patient encouraged to talk at will with no restrictions imposed upon him.

Over two hundred years after the French Academy of Sciences first reported on the phenomenon, we still know little about its nature. As Paul H. Wedner and Donald F. Klein write in their book *Mind, Mood and Medicine*: 'Hypnosis has never been satisfactorily explained. It is not related to the power of a hypnotist over a subject, since all of its effects can be generated through auto-hypnosis. What is known is that it is not sleep – and may not represent any special state of consciousness at all. . . . Induction of hypnosis with suggestions of sleep, of heaviness, of entering a trance, may not be necessary.'

It was not until the Second World War that anyone thought of using hypnosis as a means of killing someone. A sort of murder by remote control. But a Bostonian industrialist named Stanley Lovell, who was head of research and development at the CIA's wartime precursor, the Office of Strategic Services (OSS), had the neat idea of hypnotizing a high-ranking German prisoner of war into hating the Gestapo and the Nazi regime and then arranging for him to 'escape' back to Germany with the hypnotically induced mission to assassinate Adolf Hitler. He 'would be under a compulsion that might not be denied,' Lovell wrote.

But when he checked it out with two leading New York psychiatrists, they reported that the weight of evidence showed that hypnotism could not make people do what they did not want to do. Unless the guinea pig, high-ranking German prisoner of war happened to start off not liking Hitler anyway, he could not be hypnotized into wanting to kill him. The idea was shelved.

In fact, at that time the majority of psychiatrists and psychologists in the United States accepted this presumed limitation on the effectiveness of hypnosis as, I rather think, many laymen still do today in the world at large. But Professor George 'Esty' Estabrooks, head of the Psychology Department at Colgate University, took a different view. Although he accepted that hypnosis did not work on everyone and that only one person in five made a good enough subject to be placed in a deep trance, he was sure that, once you had such a person, you could make him do whatever you wanted him to do – regardless of his pre-hypnotic disposition. He had watched prim and proper people make fools of themselves at the hands of stage hypnotists and he had made his own students reveal their deepest fraternity secrets and even the details of their love affairs. So he suggested to the OSS that they conduct an experiment to see if a perfectly 'normal' person could be hypnotized into killing someone. 'Any "accidents" that might occur during the experiments will simply be charged to wastage in human life which is part and parcel of war.'

But General William J. Donovan, head of the OSS and an old-style military hero (he had been the United States' most highly decorated officer in the First World War for his bravery in the trenches), was not prepared to go along with such a disgraceful suggestion.

It was left to the more steely, less honourable men of the post-war CIA – and the emergence of drugs as a sophisticated new aid to hypnosis – for investigation to be made into carrying Lovell's and Estabrooks' theories into practical effect.

From 1950, within three years of the CIA's coming into existence, the agency was experimenting with a whole range of on-going investigations into the possibility of inducing what it called 'behavioural modification' in individuals.

For over twenty years this research was classified information and hardly any news of it leaked out; but now we do have some scattered notion of the agency's grim dedicated involvement in the seemingly science-fiction world of mind control. Our knowledge comes, in great part, from the pioneering inquiry, however restricted, of Senator Frank Church's Intelligence Committee in the mid-1970s and three subsequent major books by authors availing themselves of the right to demand information from the US authorities under the Freedom of Information Act, of which sadly there is still no equivalent in Britain. The three books are *Operation Mind Control* by Walter Bowart, John Marks' *The Search for the 'Manchurian Candidate'* and John Ranelagh's *The Agency: The Rise and Decline of the CIA*, and I freely acknowledge my debt of gratitude to them.

The story begins in February 1949 when Cardinal Mindszenty, head of the Roman Catholic Church in Hungary, pleaded guilty before a state court in Budapest to treason. Arrested two months before, he was clearly a broken man. With a glazed look in his

35

eyes, he 'confessed' in public to crimes which it is impossible to believe he had committed. Sentenced to life imprisonment, his performance recalled the Moscow purge trials of 1937 and 1938 when tough Communist Party senior officials had likewise, and with equally zombie-like faces, admitted to a long series of improbable offences. These and a string of post-war trials in other Eastern European countries seemed staged, eerie and unreal. How had the Russians and their puppets done it? What was their secret to assert so masterly a control on stalwart men? The CIA determined to find out.

In the summer of 1949, a senior CIA official visited Western Europe 'to apply special methods of interrogation for the purpose of evaluation of Russian practices': i.e., he experimented with drugs and hypnosis on refugees and prisoners returned from behind the Iron Curtain. Back in the United States, he recommended setting up a team skilled in the 'special' interrogation methods he had just tried out.

And so was born, in April 1950, PROJECT BLUEBIRD, the CIA's first mind control 'baby' with teams consisting of a psychiatrist, a lie detector expert trained in hypnosis and a technician checking out agents and defectors for the agency. Within two years this had progressed into the substantially enlarged PROJECT ARTICHOKE. According to a later CIA internal memorandum, PROJECT ARTICHOKE was intended to 'exploit operational lines, scientific methods and knowledge that can be utilized in altering the attitudes, beliefs, thought processes and behaviour patterns of agent personnel. This will include the application of tested psychiatric and psychological techniques including the use of hypnosis in conjunction with drugs.' In turn, only one year later, in April 1953, PROJECT ARTICHOKE became MKULTRA, the generic name for a series of on-going investigations by the agency's Technical Services Staff (TSS) under a charismatic scientist who lived in a former slave cabin on a fifteen-acre farm outside Washington DC. Over the next twenty years, there were to be at least 149 MKULTRA sub-projects and 33 allied sub-projects, often pursued in conjunction with US Armed Forces' Intelligence and Chemical Research Units.

That all sounds very clinical and scientific. The reality was obscene and evil: man playing at God and treating the human mind as if it were just a piece of vegetable. Human dignity meant nothing. The sanctity of life itself was meaningless. One CIA report boasted of the agency's work 'in effecting psychological entry and control of the individual'.

As early as 14 July 1952 a CIA memo to the Director of Central Intelligence cited a successful application of narco-hypnotic interrogation undertaken by the agency. It related how drugs had been used to enhance the effect of hypnosis on two Russian suspected double agents:

> In each case, a psychiatric-medical cover (i.e., the two men were in hospital) was used to bring the ARTICHOKE techniques into action.
>
> In the first case, light dosages of drugs coupled with hypnosis were used to induce a completely hypnotic trance. The trance was held for approximately one hour and forty minutes of interrogation with a subsequent total amnesia produced by post-hypnotic suggestion.
>
> In the second case (an individual of much higher intelligence than the first), a deep hypnotic trance was reached after light medication. This was followed by an interrogation lasting for well over an hour. However, a partial amnesia only was obtained at this time, although a total amnesia was obtained for a major part of the test. Since further interrogation was desired, a second test was made on this individual in which the ARTICHOKE technique of using a straight medication was employed. On this test, highly successful results were obtained in that a full interrogation lasting two hours and fifteen minutes was produced, part of which included a remarkable regression. During this regression, the subject actually 'relived' certain past activities of his life, some dating back fifteen years, while, in addition, the subject totally accepted Mr (deleted) [the case officer and interpreter at this time] as an old, trusted and beloved personal friend whom the subject had known in years past in Georgia, USSR. Total amnesia was apparently achieved for the second entire test on this case.

The memo revealed that sodium pentathol and the stimulant desoxyn were the drugs used to aid these two hypnotically induced trances. It continued:

> For a matter of record, the case officers involved in both cases expressed themselves to the effect that the ARTICHOKE operations

were entirely successful and team members felt that the tests demonstrated conclusively the effectiveness of the combined chemical-hypnotic technique in such cases. In both cases, the subjects talked clearly and at great length and furnished information which the case officers considered extremely valuable.

But it did not just rest with exploring new interrogative techniques with which to prise information from uncooperative subjects. The whole realm of drugs and their effect on human behaviour was examined – using unwilling and unknowing guinea pigs as human putty in the hands of agency personnel. Just consider the reality behind these soothing, almost white-washing words in the memoirs of Admiral Stansfield Turner, a subsequent CIA director: 'Although the purpose was reasonable, many of the CIA's methods for learning about the effects of drugs were deplorable. Some of the experimentation took place in CIA-owned houses in New York and San Francisco where there were elaborate decorations and two-way mirrors. Some of the testing was done by inducing an individual to leave a bar and come to one of the houses. The drugs were then administered without the individual's knowledge and his or her reactions observed, sometimes through the two-way mirrors.'

But this ennobling work went beyond paying prostitutes to take back unsuspecting clients to rooms where they were given mind-blowing drugs and CIA men watched their subsequent antics – with, of course, no element of personal sexual enjoyment. In at least two accredited instances, mind control experiments by the CIA and related government agencies actually killed two totally innocent American citizens.

Both deaths occurred in the very early days: in 1953. The first concerned an army civilian scientist named Frank Olson. He was one of a group of ten scientists working on MKULTRA and Army Chemical Corps projects who, in November of that year, gathered in a log cabin by a lake in the Appalachians for a twice-yearly informal two-day conference to discuss their work. The atmosphere was professional but relaxed. Appropriately, on the last evening, after dinner, the scientist handed around a bottle of Cointreau – but only he knew it had been laced with a very small dose of LSD. Two of the men present did not drink any, one had a heart condition and the other was a reformed alcoholic; but Olson was among the eight that did. The other seven all had only temporary effects from the drug; a 'trip' usually lasts only about eight hours. But with Olson it was different: in the weeks following this bizarre experiment, he seemed increasingly depressed and, according to his family, his whole personality changed. Realizing that something was seriously wrong, the scientist sent him for psychiatric treatment and a doctor decided to place him in a sanatorium.

One month after drinking the laced Cointreau, at 3.20 in the morning that he and a CIA companion were due to leave for the sanatorium, Olson crashed through the closed window in his New York hotel room, splattering himself onto the pavement ten floors below.

What to do? The agency knew it had 'triggered' Olson's suicide; so cover-up and whitewash were the order of the day. His widow Alice was told first that he had died of a 'classified illness', then that he had jumped or fallen out of the window. She was given a full pension.

For over two decades no one told Mrs Olson the truth. Then, in June 1975, the Rockefeller Commission, although still masking a great deal of the CIA's illegal domestic activities, reported that a man fitting Olson's description had leaped from a New York hotel window after the CIA had given him LSD without his knowledge. The Olson family read about the incident in the *Washington Post* and pressed for more details. On television, Mrs Olson and each of her three children took turns reading from a prepared family statement: 'We feel our family has been violated by the CIA in two ways. First, Frank Olson was experimented upon illegally and negligently. Second, the true nature of his death was concealed for twenty-two years.'

Congress passed a bill the following year to pay $750,000 in compensation to the Olson family and President Ford personally apologized to them; but a man was dead – cynically and unnecessarily.

The truth about the other innocent American citizen killed by the US government in a mind control experiment that went wrong – or, at least, the only other one we know about – came to light solely because of the publicity caused by the revelations in the Olson's case. In the wake of the scandal, the US Army Chemical Corps relaxed its own cover-up about the death of a forty-two-year-old tennis professional from New York named Harold Blauer twenty-two years earlier. But his surviving family – two daughters – had to wait a further twelve years before the US government paid them compensation, and then only by order of a court.

When Blauer voluntarily entered a psychiatric hospital in Manhattan on 5 December 1952 he was suffering from depression after his divorce. He did not know that the hospital had a secret contract with the US army to study the effect of injections of army-supplied mescaline derivatives on patients in a chemical warfare experiment to see if soldiers and civilian populations could be temporarily immobilized – literally 'spaced out' for a while.

The derivatives were a hybrid of mescaline and amphetamine, varying in strength and proportions. Mescaline itself is a notoriously powerful hallucinogenic drug similar to LSD. It seems incredible but a doctor at the hospital admitted injecting these substances five times into Blauer without knowing or checking whether they had ever been tested on humans.

The first four injections seemed to do Blauer some good. There was talk of his soon being able to leave hospital on a few days' leave to visit his thirteen-year-old daughter, Elizabeth. But the fifth injection – which was the same as the first but sixteen times stronger – delivered at 9.53 in the morning of 8 January 1953 killed him: he began sweating profusely and threshing his arms about wildly, then his body stiffened and he frothed at the mouth. He lapsed into a coma and was dead in just over two hours.

The hospital did not disclose to New York's Chief Medical Examiner (the equivalent of an English coroner) the nature of the drug or the army's involvement. It merely told Mrs Blauer that her ex-husband had died of 'an overdose of a drug' and, when she sued the hospital's owners two years later for damages for negligence, they settled her claim for a paltry $18,000. The US government secretly contributed half that amount on condition that its role in the death was kept secret. Mrs Blauer died in 1974, a year before the truth came out.

When the truth did emerge, the US government still refused to pay Blauer's daughter, Elizabeth Barrett (as she had then become) and her younger sister any further damages. The government's lawyers, trying every trick in the book, claimed she was barred by the earlier settlement for $18,000 that her mother had accepted. Only in May 1987 did Judge Constance Baker Motley finally order the US government in the Manhattan Federal District Court to pay the two women $700,000 damages. 'This court is faced with assessing a sad episode in the conduct of the government and a personal tragedy for an unsuspecting victim and his family,' she said. In a judgement that ran to 109 pages, she castigated the US government for having 'covered up its involvement in the affair' and dubbed the truth about Blauer's death a 'shocking revelation'.

But how many people at that time even knew about the case or about Judge Motley's precedent-making decision? I know I did not. I only heard about it a year later from Daniel Sheehan: his friend, Eugene Scheiman, happened to be Elizabeth Barrett's lawyer.

MKULTRA formally came to an end in 1973 – but only after most of the records had been destroyed in accordance with what was considered to be its duty.

Precious little detail, therefore, survives – despite the work of the Church Committee and the three subsequent leading authors – and we have to be content with occasional chinks in the armour of secrecy. One such insight derives from an amazing indiscretion perpetrated by one Lt Commander Thomas Narut, a US naval psychologist assigned to the US Regional Medical Centre at Naples in July 1975. At a NATO conference in Oslo on 'Dimensions of Stress and Anxiety', he startled the assembled 120 psychologists by boasting, in the course of a talk with the horrendous title of 'The Use of a Symbolic Model and Verbal Intervention in Inducing and Reducing Stress', about his work in teaching 'combat readiness units' to cope with the stress of killing. He then followed this up, during private questioning with a small group of listeners (including Peter Watson, then of the London *Sunday Times*), with the most amazing disclosures about these 'units' which comprised men programmed to kill. They were, he said, 'hit men and assassins' (his own words) made ready to kill in selected countries should the need arise. He told Watson and the others that US naval Intelligence had taken convicted murderers from military prisons, conditioned them as political assassins and placed them in American embassies around the world – notably in Athens.

He claimed that he was personally involved with such programmes in both Naples itself and San Diego, back home in America – but, when the story ran in the London *Sunday Times*, the US navy published an official denial and Narut explained that he had been talking 'in theoretical and not practical terms'.

In the literature on the subject, we do know positively of one hypno-programmed CIA agent – but she was a courier, not a killer. In his book *The Control of Candy Jones*, published in 1976, Donald Bain has told the story of Candy, a Second World War pin-up who on a USO tour in the Pacific in 1945 fell ill with various tropical diseases that landed her in a military hospital in Manila, where she met a young medical officer. Years later in civilian life, when she was running a modelling school in New York, he was to hypnotize her into doubling up as a courier for the CIA. For twelve years, she had a double life: Candy Jones and the hypno-programmed courier, Arlene Grant. It only came to an end when she married an old friend whom she had unexpectedly met again – and gradually the truth about her strange life-style came out.

The name of this pivotal ex-military physician who hypnotized Candy and made her for so many years an unknowing worker for the agency has never been disclosed, not even in Donald Bain's book written with her cooperation and that of her husband. But Walter Bowart, in his *Operation Mind Control*, writes that it may have been a Dr William Jennings Bryan who died, in March 1977, aged fifty, 'allegedly of a heart attack'. Fifteen years earlier, Dr Bryan had been the technical consultant for the film *The Manchurian Candidate*.

4

Mind Control II

It is one thing to programme convicted murderers into killing again and to hypnotize innocent people into performing non-illegal acts, such as being a courier, in the name of their country. Your true 'Manchurian Candidate' is someone who is not, by natural disposition, a killer but is yet programmed into being an assassin and in such a way that he cannot tell the truth afterwards about what has happened to him. Indeed, he does not really 'remember' it or know it himself.

Now, is *that* possible? Has *that* actually happened?

In 1977, when – in answer to a Freedom of Information Act request made by John Marks for his book *The Search for the Manchurian Candidate* – documents overlooked for destruction by former CIA director Richard Helms and Dr Sidney Gottlieb came to light, Admiral Stansfield Turner, the 'new broom' director appointed by President Carter to clean up the agency, released them to Marks and also immediately informed the Senate Intelligence Committee, now under the chairmanship of Senator Dan Inouye. Admiral Turner gave evidence to the committee and once again repeated the official agency line that the CIA had stopped all drug testing. As Walter Bowart has commented, 'He was not asked nor did he volunteer information about *new* technologies of mind control. He did not say the mind control operations had stopped, only that the experiments had stopped.'

John Marks' conclusion is an open one: 'I have tried to weave together a representative sample of what went on, but having dealt with a group of people who regularly incorporate lying into their daily work, I cannot be sure. I cannot be positive that they never found a technique to control people, despite my definite bias in favour of the idea that the human spirit defeated the manipulators.'

Yet there is evidence to indicate that this is merely a forlorn hope. Marks himself quotes Milton Kline, a New York psychologist and former president of the American Society for Clinical and Experimental Hypnosis who has served as unpaid consultant on CIA hypnosis research, as saying that the idea of creating a real-life Manchurian Candidate is not impossible. 'It cannot be done by everyone,' says Kline. 'It cannot be done consistently, but it can be done.' (Kline, incidentally, later served for a while as an expert witness for the defence in the case of Mark David Chapman.)

There seems little doubt that sophisticated techniques have now reached the stage where, if murder is desired, a killer, once programmed and 'on hold', can be triggered into action by a phone call or by use of a particular book (such as perhaps happened to Mark Chapman with *The Catcher in the Rye*) or by a hypnotic session (as did happen to Candy Jones for twelve years whenever she was needed as a courier) – if necessary, with built-in memory loss for after the event. If this seems far-fetched, I can only counter that way back in the early days of MKULTRA, in the late 1950s and early 1960s, hypnotically induced amnesia had already been brought to such a point that one senior CIA official is alleged to have wanted to advance it to the stage of seeing whether it would stand up to torture. Fellow CIA official John Gittinger told John Marks that, so far as he knew, this devilish experiment – torturing your own human guinea pig – was not carried out. 'I still like to think we were human beings enough that this was not something we played with,' he said.

But Marks comments that such an experiment could have been performed, as was apparently suggested, by friendly and none too fastidious police in a 'sympathetic' Third World country like Taiwan or Paraguay. Marks states positively: 'CIA men did at least discuss joint work in hypnosis with a foreign secret service in 1962,' but his efforts to follow this up with a request under the Freedom of Information Act were stymied by a specific CIA denial of access to any document concerning the testing of hypnosis and psychedelic drugs in cooperation with foreign intelligence agencies. They said that releasing such documents would reveal intelligence sources and methods, which were exempted by law.

Daniel Sheehan, whose Christic Institute has carried on into the late 1980s the investigative work in this field pioneered by Bowart and Marks, does not rule out this possibility. Speaking in his office in Washington DC in June 1988, his measured words bring a new dimension of authority to the subject:

'We have discovered in doing the kind of investigations that we've done, with regard to the Karen Silkwood killing, the killing of the people in Greensboro and other places, that we've come to the point of not speculating on things like that. We know we can find out but you cannot find out really responsibly without looking very specifically at each particular case and analysing it.

'Now we have made no enquiries into the John Lennon killing – but I would definitely assume, as a generality, from what we know about the MKULTRA programme and other things that the CIA was definitely into trying to create a hypno–programmed Manchurian Candidate.

'As for the specifics, I don't know one way or the other about Mark Chapman whom you say may have been programmed to kill and then kept "on hold" with built-in memory loss, but we have uncovered a sort of halfway spot to that situation. We have talked to half-a-dozen individuals who have told a startlingly similar story about how, at a very young age, usually between twenty and twenty-five, they were contacted, usually within the context of military training, and told: "Look, we've got a special deal for you. You're going to come into the service under the normal designation of being an infantryman but you're going to leave the service after a while and you're going to have special training, and you're going to be brought into a special programme."

'They're sent to special places where they are trained by mercenaries and then they're told: "You're going to be called upon from time to time to do some things for us."'

The Christic Institute's researches brought up one such young man who was approached at an army recruiting centre and, in due course, handed over to an official of the Bureau of Alcohol, Tobacco and Firearms Division of the US Treasury. He was given a special mission to infiltrate the Hell's Angels motorcycle gangs. He had to dress up as a member of an opposing gang and then assassinate the leader of a rival gang – so that the two gangs would fight and partly destroy each other. 'A bizarre law-enforcement kind of thing,' Sheehan calls it.

This same individual was also sent to 'a place where they were training people to carry out an assassination in Central America'. That place: Hawaii – the group of islands with a strong US naval and military presence where Mark Chapman lived for three years before killing Lennon. He also was sent into Thailand to try and find 'MIAs', US soldiers 'missing in action' in neighbouring Vietnam during the 1965–1973 Vietnam War.

Sheehan says that, in this 'halfway spot' of programmed undercover operators, his institute had also come across 'a very weird group of people who it's very hard to get a handle on how they got into this kind of thing, but it also happened when they were very young – like, between twenty and twenty-five – and they ran into someone who was like this mentor type of guy in the context of some sort of authoritative structure.' (The YMCA, linked to the CIA, comes immediately to mind as a possibility.) 'And again they get some kind of special training' (as Mark Chapman may have done in war-torn Beirut topped up by seemingly innocent instruction as an armed security guard), 'and then they go and do this sort of stuff – kill someone on orders.

'But the only thing is they don't just allow these guys to walk up and shoot somebody and get caught – like Mark did. It would be too dangerous. They would start talking and tell people about their exploits. These guys have a great tendency to do that – that is how we've gotten them to talk to us!'

But what about if Mark had been programmed not to do that with drugs such as sodium pentathol or desoxyn (or more advanced variations thereof) used as well as basic hypnosis to ensure built-in memory loss? After all, we know that the New York police did not test him for drugs upon his arrest: it was 'not normal procedure', according to ex-lieutenant of detectives Arthur O'Connor. Everyone can make their own assessment of Sheehan's answer: 'We haven't run into that yet. There is no direct evidence of it having actually happened – but it is a plausible kind of situation. It is clear that the MKULTRA programme was where they were experimenting to see if they could get people to behave in that way – and I cannot say it has not happened.'

Allegations have persisted over the years that the three great political assassinations of the 1960s, President John Kennedy, his brother Senator Robert Kennedy and Dr Martin Luther King Jr. were all the work of programmed real life 'Manchurian Candidates' – or that, at the very least, all were the result of conspiracies. The men who pulled the trigger in each case – Lee Harvey Oswald, Sirhan Sirhan and James Earl Ray – may all have been somewhat unstable characters but that only made it easier to label them 'lone nuts'. In fact, so run the theories, none of them acted alone.

Seeing conspiracies where none may exist is a boom industry in the United States. There is even an 'Assassination Archives and Research Center' in a five-room suite in the heart of downtown Washington DC established in 1984 as 'a long needed, centrally located and permanent centre for the study of assassinations'. Investigative journalists and commentators like the late Mae Brussell in Carmel, California, thrive on stories of 'conspiracy' in which they passionately believe. Whole shelves of books exist which seek to establish – or state as a positive fact – that the Kennedy brothers and Martin Luther King did not die at the hands of lone killers.

Walter Bowart has succinctly stated the case for a possible conspiracy angle behind these three major assassinations: 'Those who support the "lone nut" theory point to the fact that no clear political motive could be attributed to any of the three assassins. Yet even to a casual student of history each of the three murders was of obvious political benefit to the extreme right: John and Robert Kennedy and Martin Luther King were all independent thinkers who could not be bought off. They worked for expanded civil rights in a manner the right wing interpreted as Communist. . . .

'The Kennedys were not only on the wrong side of Hoover's FBI, they were on the wrong side of the CIA as well. JFK fired several top intelligence officers (he asked for Allen Dulles' resignation) and at the time of his death he was privately talking about reorganizing the entire US Intelligence Service. Robert Kennedy, as Attorney General, was waging a tireless campaign against organized crime. His campaign cut across the alliance the CIA had formed with gangsters who had lost their gambling and drug concessions in Cuba.

'Robert Kennedy was a close friend of Dr King, and one rumour persists that the assassins had issued a dire warning that RFK not run for president, and that King was sacrificed to show that the group meant business.'

Yet, despite all the talk and all the print, no one has yet conclusively proved anything either way – and it is difficult to see how they ever will. As Daniel Sheehan puts it, 'The problem is that you get one strike, one hit, out of ten guesses in that kind of stuff – and then you're probably doing well.'

Yet these three murders all have a striking parallel with the killing of John Lennon: none of them was followed by a trial bringing all the facts into the glare of courtroom examination. Lee Harvey Oswald who – in a 1976 Harris Poll, 80 per cent of Americans said they believed did not act alone – was conveniently gunned down in the basement of Dallas police headquarters by Jack Ruby who, with almost equal convenience, already had within him the seeds of the cancer that was also to kill him. James Earl Ray saved himself from an almost certain death sentence by pleading guilty and getting ninety-nine years in prison – only for the House Assassinations Committee to conclude nine years later: 'There is a likelihood that he assassinated Dr Martin Luther King as a result of a conspiracy.' Sirhan Sirhan in the end pleaded not guilty to Robert Kennedy's murder – but the only real courtroom battle was, as with Mark Chapman, over his state of mind and not the facts of the murder. I can reveal that, in fact, he wanted to plead guilty – so that in his case as well, there would have been no kind of trial at all.

Interviewed in Los Angeles in May 1988, Sirhan's junior trial lawyer, Luke McKissack, told me twenty years after the event that both senior prosecution and defence attorneys had agreed upon a plea bargain. Sirhan would plead guilty to murder in return for the prosecution not asking for the death penalty (as was their right under Californian state law) – and, surprisingly, the Kennedy family would have gone along with this. The only problem was that Judge Herbert Walker would not accept it, and insisted on a trial. As McKissack commented bitterly, 'This seventy-seven-year-old jurist wanted his judicial swan song to be a warble and not a mere chirp. And so we had to go ahead although nobody had really adequately investigated the many, many issues of the case.' It was assumed throughout Sirhan Sirhan's trial by both prosecution and defence counsel that the defendant had shot Robert Kennedy and that he had done so alone. The only question was: 'Was he insane?'

The jury said 'No,' and he was sentenced to death – only to

be saved from the gas chamber by a US Supreme Court decision that the death penalty was unconstitutional. The court later took a different view, but not with retrospective effect.

This does not alter the fact that, if Sirhan Sirhan had had his way, he would have saved himself from execution by pleading guilty – and, as with Mark Chapman, there would have been no trial.

But there is an even stronger individual link between the Kennedy and Lennon assassinations. There is evidence to suggest that both could have been the work of programmed killers.

When the public defender asked Sirhan about Kennedy's shooting, he replied: 'I don't remember much about the shooting, sir, did I do it? Well, yes, I am told I did it. I remember being at the Ambassador (the hotel where Kennedy was shot). I am drinking Tom Collinses. I got dizzy. I went back to my car so I could go home. But I was too drunk to drive. I thought I'd better find some coffee. The next thing I remember I was being choked and a guy was twisting my knee.'

An eye-witness to the murder described Sirhan as being 'enormously composed'. 'Right in the midst of this hurricane of sound and feeling, he seemed to be almost the eye of the hurricane. He seemed purged. . . .'

When a local attorney for the American Civil Liberties Union interviewed him in prison, Sirhan looked at him through tear-filled eyes and said: 'I'm a failure. I believe in love and instead of showing love . . .' Then the attorney remembered him muttering 'something about having betrayed his own primary beliefs'.

When you come to read in detail about how Mark Chapman behaved after Lennon's murder, you will find a striking parallel between the 'dazed', as if in a trance-like, condition of the two men. Mark remembered more of the actual killing but otherwise their reactions were almost identical. And remember what ex-lieutenant of detectives Arthur O'Connor has said: 'I saw him the night of the murder. I studied him intensely. He looked as if he could have been programmed – and I know what use you are going to make of that word!'

When, seven years after Sirhan's crime, abortive efforts were made on his behalf to re-open the case, recorded interviews with his psychiatrists in prison were analysed by a newly developed 'truth detector' called Psychological Stress Evaluator (PSE).

Unlike the old-fashioned 'lie detector' or polygraph, it does not have to be connected to the body to measure stress. Instead it measures micro-tremors in the human voice inaudible to the human ear but which form a distinct pattern when transferred to a chart. Charles McQuiston, described by author Walter Bowart as a 'former high-ranking US Intelligence Officer', one of the originators of the PSE, reported: 'I'm convinced that Sirhan wasn't aware of what he was doing. He was in a hypnotic trance when he pulled the trigger and killed Senator Kennedy. . . . Everything in the PSE charts tells me that someone else was involved in the assassination – and that Sirhan was programmed through hypnosis to kill RFK. What we have here is a real live "Manchurian Candidate".'

When Dr John W. Heisse, Jr, president of the International Society of Stress Analysis, examined Sirhan's PSE charts, he agreed with McQuiston. 'Sirhan kept repeating certain phrases,' he said. 'This clearly revealed he had been programmed to put himself into a trance. This is something he couldn't have learned by himself. Someone had to show him and teach him how.

'I believe Sirhan was brainwashed under hypnosis by the constant repetition of words like "You are nobody. You're nothing. The American dream is gone" until he actually believed them. At that stage someone implanted an idea, "Kill RFK," and under hypnosis the brainwashed Sirhan accepted it.'

Another expert, Dr Herbert Spiegel, a leading medical hypnotist, said of Sirhan: 'It's very possible to distort and change somebody's mind through a number of hypnotic sessions. It can be described as brainwashing because the mind is cleared of its old emotions and values which are replaced by implanting other suggestions. . . . This technique was probably used with Sirhan. From my own research, I think Sirhan was subjected to hypnotic treatment.'

This is all very impressive stuff – or pure nonsense according to your individual reaction; but I cannot quote what any psychiatrist or psychologist has said about the possibility of Mark Chapman having been narco-hypnotically programmed to commit his crime because no psychiatrist or psychologist, whether for the prosecution or the defence, ever appears to have been asked to consider that situation – either in the run-up to his trial or at any time since. Furthermore, there has been no PSE evaluation of his many hours of taped interviews with prosecution and defence psychiatrists and psychologists.

There is an odd footnote to all this: the principal medical defence witness for Sirhan was Dr Bernard Diamond of the University of California, one of America's leading psychiatrists who used hypnosis in his work. Thirteen years later he was to be one of the defence psychiatrists in Mark's case. His diagnosis for the two men was the same: paranoid schizophrenia. Yet he seems not to have used hypnosis in either of his two interviews with Mark, although he hypnotized Sirhan on six of his eight visits to great effect. For instance, when Dr Diamond asked Sirhan where he had concealed his gun while waiting for Kennedy, Sirhan, in his trance, went for the inside of his belt on the left side – and the police at last knew where he had carried the weapon.

Early in his sessions, Dr Diamond found that Sirhan was happier answering questions in writing, when interviewed under hypnosis, than in speaking. 'It is called automatic writing,' Diamond later explained, 'and the term aptly describes the way Sirhan would write like a robot and keep on repeating a word or phrase until I stopped him.'

A crucial piece of evidence against Sirhan, to prove premeditation, was a page from various notebooks found in his bedroom in which he had written these jumbled words:

May 18, 9:45 a.m. – 68. My determination to eliminate RFK is becoming more the more of an unshakable obsession . . . RFK must die – RFK must be killed Robert F. Kennedy must be assassinated RFK must be assassinated RFK must be assassinated . . . Robert F. Kennedy must be assassinated before 5 June 68 Robert F. Kennedy must be assassinated I have never heard please pay to the order of of of of of of of of this or that please pay to the order of . . .

In fact, his notebooks were full of strange writings, often with words repeated three times or more. Sirhan said that he did not remember writing in the notebooks but he agreed that he must have done. So at one point Dr Diamond showed him a photocopy of one of the bizarre entries and questioned him about it, while he was still in a hypnotic trance.

'Is this crazy writing?' Diamond asked.

'YES YES YES,' Sirhan wrote.

'Are you crazy?'

'NO NO.'

'Well, why are you writing crazy?'

'PRACTISE PRACTISE PRACTISE.'

'Practise for what?'

'MIND CONTROL MIND CONTROL MIND CONTROL,' was the written reply.

So How is it Done?

How do you convert a law-abiding, God-fearing (as in Mark Chapman's case) individual into a murderer?

It is really quite simple:

You catch him young or at his most vulnerable – the two often go together. You work your way into his confidence, perhaps under the guise of some benevolent paternalistic organization to which you both belong. You flatter him. You make him feel important, set aside for a special mission that only he can accomplish.

You subject him to hypnosis, with or without the help of drugs (which, with many youngsters these days, will not be all that difficult to tempt him to try).

Then you keep him under surveillance, watched by close friends whose 'advice' or helpful suggestions he readily accepts. If necessary, for a while you take him off to a totally alien setting (say, Lebanon in the middle of a civil war) where he is both disoriented for the first time in his life and also 'blooded' by close contact with the stench of human destruction.

You do not rush at it. You keep him 'on hold' for months, even years. But he is always there: ready to be triggered for action.

And, once alerted, you never let him relax. You maintain the pressure. You do not let him off the hook of his own inner torment.

The telephone rings. He picks it up. A familiar voice says: 'Do it, do it, do it!' – and rings off.

The phone rings again: 'You are Holden Caulfield. You are Holden Caulfield. You are Holden Caulfield,' says the same voice in dry monotone.

He returns home to find a note waiting for him pinned to the front door: 'Lennon is a phoney. Lennon is a phoney. Lennon is a phoney.'

The telephone rings in the middle of the night. He wakes up, reaches for the receiver and hears: 'Catcher, Catcher, Catcher! You are "The Catcher in the Rye" of this generation!'

He dials an outside call and the same voice butts in: 'Kill the phoney. Kill the phoney. Kill the phoney!'

He never knows when he is next going to hear that voice on the telephone which soon becomes almost indistinguishable from that other voice which is now inside his head repeating relentlessly the same patterned phrases.

And when it is over and the man he has shot is lying dead at his feet, he is at peace. He has achieved his destiny. Some may even claim that he has only done it to make himself famous.

PART TWO

BUILD-UP TO MURDER
(December 1971 to November 1980)

5

Enter Lennon

As the moon's rays fought their way through the darkened clouds above, a slender dark-haired man wearing glasses stepped forward, with his wife, to the greatest roar of welcome of the night. He struggled to be heard. The noise, the shouting, the cries were too great. Finally, he said with the soft intonation of his native Liverpool: 'We came here tonight to say that apathy isn't it. And that we can all do something. So Flower Power didn't work. So what? We start again!'

It was a strange setting for an English rock star in December 1971. To be sure, there was an audience of 15,000 cheering, jubilant, semi-hysterical young fans – many of them high on marijuana – but they were not the usual crowd of happy-go-lucky youngsters out for a good time. They were all seriously motivated campus kids: university undergraduates and their friends.

It was 3.00 on the morning of 11 December. The Chrysler Arena at Ann Arbor, the relaxed, laid-back small town forty miles west of Detroit that is still home to the University of Michigan, had rocked for seven hours to explosions of light and sound as leading performers of the time such as Phil Ochs, Bob Seager, Archie Shepp, country rock artist Commander Cody and Stevie Wonder had played.

But the air had also been full of passionate, angry speeches about the Vietnam War, then raging in all its senseless horror; pleas were made for liberty, human rights – and the need for revolution. Four defendants from the recent Chicago Seven Conspiracy Trial were on the platform, convicted (though later successful on appeal) of trying to disrupt by violence the 1968 US Democratic Presidential Convention; and they were not silent.

'The only solution to pollution is a humane revolution!' shouted Chicago defendant Bobby Seale. 'This is the first event of the Rock Liberation Front. What we are doing here is uniting music and revolutionary politics to build a revolution around the country!' yelled fellow defendant Jerry Rubin. He called for 'a million of you to turn up at the Republican National Convention in August to humiliate and defeat Richard Nixon' in his bid to seek nomination for re-election as president. There were immense cheers.

Even in the middle and late 1980s, when the old dividing line between active involvement in politics and pop music has been shattered, when Bob Geldof can with one brilliant single, Band Aid's 'Do They Know It's Christmas?', shame the entire world into effective action to feed the starving millions of African famine, when Bob Dylan can sing songs of freedom in Moscow and Bruce Springsteen, Sting and Peter Gabriel can head a six-weeks' 'Human Rights Now!' 35,000-mile world tour for Amnesty International, such open and unambiguous calls to violent political change are still not heard amid the sounds of music. In the early 1970s, it was like declaring war on the US government.

As the kids quietened and the lights dimmed, John Lennon took a guitar and sang a song he had specially written for the occasion: 'John Sinclair'.

It was most certainly not the best song he had ever written, but the recording made by his sound unit that night earned it a track on his next album: *Some Time in New York City*.

But that was not the only recording made that night. Unknown to Lennon and his companions on the platform, the spools of secret tape recorders were quietly whirring hidden in the clothing of undercover FBI agents sprinkled around the arena. This was his first concert appearance in the United States since the Beatles waved goodbye at San Francisco's Candlestick Park five years earlier – and now he was under top-secret surveillance. Sixteen days later, attached to a report that I have obtained under the Freedom of Information Act, the Special Agent in Charge (SAC) of the FBI's Detroit field office sent his boss, J. Edgar Hoover, the bureau's veteran director, verbatim copies of all the speeches – and of that one song.

For this was no ordinary rock concert. It was a 'Freedom Rally', sponsored by the left-wing 'Committee to Free John Sinclair'. Nowadays few people remember who he was, but in the early

1970s he was a hero for the New Left and a bogey-man for the Far Right. A commune leader and wild-rock musician, he founded in 1967 a magazine calling for guerrillas who 'should understand they will be engaged in combat'. In 1968, he formed the White Panther Party, a white-skinned version of the terrorist Black Panthers, with a crazy, 1960s-style hippy policy of 'rock 'n' roll and dope and fucking in the streets'. In 1969, he proclaimed proudly: 'With our music and our economic genius we plunder the unsuspecting straight world for money and the means to revolutionize its children at the same time. . . . We will use guns if we have to. We have no illusions.'

The Detroit police determined to get him, and they did. It proved not too difficult: in July 1969, he was gaoled for ten years for selling two joints to an undercover woman police officer. A bit extreme, even if it was his third conviction. One can understand why Lennon sang: 'They gave him ten for two.'

The rally did the trick. Next day, the *Michigan Daily* wrote: 'One couldn't distinguish where the songs left off and the politics began' – but it had been timed virtually for the eve of Sinclair's appeal court hearing, and within fifty-five hours of Lennon and Yoko leaving the stage, Sinclair was set free. Jerry Rubin hailed it as 'an incredible tribute to the power of the people'.

So it was – but I believe that it could have started John Lennon on the path that nine years later, almost to the day, would bring him face to face with Mark Chapman and the assassin's hollow-point bullets searing into his flesh. On a 'secret' memorandum dated 12 January 1972 sent to the Special Agent in Charge of the FBI's New York office by another SAC, whose precise field office is blacked out in Lennon's file, are the words, 'ALL EXTREMISTS SHOULD BE CONSIDERED DANGEROUS', hand-written in capital letters and underlined.

They look grimly menacing scrawled across the bottom of the page.

Lennon had always been 'the thinking man's Beatle'. It was he who, at the age of nineteen, had founded the group in early 1960. He was the first one to be married – to fellow ex-Liverpool Art College student Cynthia Powell – in August 1962. He was also the most restless, outspoken and creative of the group.

In later years, he styled himself 'a working-class hero', the title of his brilliant song recorded in October 1970; and this was factually true. His roots were solidly embedded in the vast amorphous British working class. His father Fred was a ship's steward, his mother Julia a cinema usherette.

But early in his life came contradiction and turmoil. Fred deserted Julia when she was pregnant; she found another man and Lennon was brought up by his adoring but stern aunt, Mimi Smith, and her husband George. She had, in British class terms that almost everyone else in the world finds difficult to understand, 'improved herself' by her marriage.

George Smith had a small dairy business. The young John Lennon was thus brought up in a comfortable lower-middle-class home in the suburbs, with flowers in the back-garden. He went to grammar school and not elementary school: he was almost accepted – but not quite. 'You want to belong, but you *don't* want to belong because you *can't* belong,' he said later.

In his inner life as well, there were different swirling currents from an early age. Integrated into his aunt's home, spoiled by his uncle, who taught him to read and bought him his first mouth organ (then died when the boy was only fourteen), his mother reappeared on the scene in his early teens and for a while they found each other again – only for her then to disappear for ever. She was run over and killed by a car driven by an off-duty policeman. The driver stood trial but he was acquitted. 'Murderer!' cried Mimi Smith in court, as she lunged at the man with her stick.

Lennon was seventeen. He never got over it. Twelve years later, he ended *John Lennon/Plastic Ono Band*, his first studio album recorded after the break-up of the Beatles, with the song 'My Mummy's Dead'.

Tony Palmer, writing in *London Magazine* in September 1967, complained: 'What we have . . . singularly failed to realize is that the Beatles are not one person but four, and not four equal persons, but one giant, his side-kick and two midgets.' That is grossly unfair to the major talent of Paul McCartney and the necessary balance supplied by George Harrison and Ringo Starr (born Richard Starkey); but the dominating force of the group, in purely musical terms, was always Lennon. As early as *Rubber Soul*, his songs have a dark power of their own, 'as if he were impacted with anger and depression', in Lloyd Rose's telling phrase.

Her perceptive article in the *Boston Phoenix* in December 1985 hits the nail exactly on the head: 'It had always been obvious that mixed in with the anger and the pain were not only wit, brains and talent but a peculiar innocence, egotistical yet genuine. . . . It was the unique fusion of innocence and viciousness that kept him from being just another superstar jerk.'

The Beatles' legacy to the world of music can never be repaid. Since the 1960s, they have put their indelible stamp on generations of the world's young people – some of whom are now not quite so young. They were a unique phenomenon. The sadness, the joy, the lustrous melancholy tinged with hope of many of their ballads struck something deep in the consciousness of millions that no other pop group has achieved.

Lennon was still repeating the same message ten years later, in September 1980, shortly before he was killed, in an interview with *Playboy*: 'You make your own dream. That's the Beatles story, isn't it? That's the Yoko Story. That's what I'm saying now. Produce your own dream. If you want to save Peru, go save Peru. It's quite possible to do anything, but not if you put it on the leaders and the parking meters. Don't expect Carter or Reagan or John Lennon or Yoko Ono or Bob Dylan or Jesus Christ to come and do it for you. You have to do it yourself.' No Victorian moralist or Margaret Thatcher could have put it better.

Of the four Beatles, only Lennon could have been so honest and forthright – and so indiscreet – as to give to Maureen Cleave of the London *Evening Standard* that famous interview in March 1966, when he said: 'Christianity will go. It will vanish and shrink. I needn't argue about it; I'm right and I will be proved right. We're more popular than Jesus now; I don't know which will go first – rock'n'roll or Christianity. Jesus was all right but his disciples were thick and ordinary. It's them twisting it that ruins it for me.'

I have printed the vital paragraph in full, to put it in its context in the newspaper as it first appeared. Expressed with the callousness of a twenty-six-year-old, it yet is more of an attack on Jesus's 'thick' disciples than on the man himself. It is an expression of atheism, if not agnosticism, that is, in essence, unexceptionable to thinking adults. Voltaire two centuries earlier had said much the same thing but with far more elegant grace: 'Oh Lord, if there is one, save my soul – if I have one!'

In Britain, the remark passed unchallenged – indeed, unnoticed. But four months later, when reprinted in the July issue of the American teenage magazine, *Datebook*, on the eve of the Beatles' fourth US tour in two years, it caused almost a nation-wide outburst of anger – especially in the South. The message went out – wrongly – that he had claimed that the Beatles were 'bigger than Jesus Christ'.

Young and old Christian America united in outraged condemnation. In the name of God, the US Constitution and the Ku Klux Klan, bonfires of Beatles albums flared throughout Alabama, Texas and Georgia (where an eleven-year-old boy called Mark David Chapman was growing up). One outraged community provided rubbish bins labelled 'Place Beatle Trash Here'; another hired a tree-crushing machine to pulp the music of the anti-Christ; Pastor Thurmond Babbs of Cleveland, Ohio, threatened to excommunicate any of his flock who dared to attend a Beatles concert. Their records were banned by thirty-five radio stations from Ogdenburg, New York, to Salt Lake City, Utah.

Despite their manager Brian Epstein's frantic efforts to calm things down and Lennon's own perplexed apology at a press conference in Chicago: 'I wasn't saying whatever they're saying I was saying. . . . I'm sorry I said it, really. I never meant it to be a lousy anti-religious thing. . . . I apologize, if that will make you happy. I still don't know quite what I've done,' the tour was a disaster. Hatred was in the air. They beat out their music to rows of empty seats. They never returned to the United States to sing.

Yet, under Lennon's leadership, a new political edge had already crept into their public image. That summer had seen an escalation of the Johnson administration's war in Vietnam. In June, the United States had bombed Hanoi for the first time and announced a policy of systematic bombing in North Vietnam. The voice of anti-war protests had grown louder.

When they arrived in New York in the last week of their tour, a newsman asked them at the standard press conference if they had any comment on the Vietnam conflict. Brian Epstein had warned them about this: 'Cool it, lads,' he had said, 'we've got enough problems already.' But 'We don't like war, war is wrong,' they answered the reporter's question in unison. And Lennon gave his own solo endorsement: 'We think of it every day. We don't like it. We don't agree with it. We think it's wrong.'

As Jon Wiener comments in his biography *Come Together*: 'It was a bold and risky move. . . . It was unprecedented (at that time) for a leading rock group to take a political stand of any kind. That was only for Bob Dylan and Phil Ochs.'

But the political evolution of John Lennon had only just begun. On 9 November of that year, he walked into the Indica Gallery in London and there among ladders, spyglasses, nail boards and other props of her art, was Yoko Ono.

Seven years his senior, Yoko was to prove the mother/lover/creative partner for whom he had been searching all of his adult life.

Not that she seemed the most likely consort for a working-class Liverpool lad. The daughter of a well-to-do Japanese banker, she had been born in Tokyo but moved with her family to New York when she was nineteen. There she had soon thrust herself into the avant-garde art world.

Her first husband was a Japanese musician. Her second an American film producer named Tony Cox, by whom she had a daughter Kyoko – whom she once brought on stage at a concert as 'an uncontrollable instrument'. In September 1966, the family moved to London to further Yoko's career and in November she took her exhibition of 'Unfinished Paintings and Objects' to the Indica Gallery in London.

Lennon would probably have broken up with the Beatles anyway and moved forward into his own more radical concept of music and art, and of the world beyond both. But there is no doubt that Yoko accelerated the process. She gave him the impetus and the support for what would, in any event, have eventually occurred.

It did not happen overnight. It was seventeen months before, in early May 1968, they spent their first night together: thereafter, Lennon's marriage and the Beatles' future as a group were equally doomed. A unique new working and emotional partnership had been formed.

On 30 May 1968 the Beatles recorded Lennon's 'Revolution' – their first attempt at a political song – and it was light years away from the earlier soothing balm of 'All You Need Is Love'. This new single, released in the United States in August of that year, began: 'You say you want a revolution . . .' It was, as yet, uncertain in its tone. It suggested that Lennon, who took the solo lead, although prepared to go along with the idea of revolution, would not support one in fact until he could see 'the plan'. His straight critics thought he was entering an area where a pop music writer had no business to go, his radical critics objected to his ambivalence; but Jon Wiener astutely observes, 'The song marked John's decision that he had political responsibilities, and that he ought to fulfil them in his music. That was a momentous decision' – and it was one that Yoko helped him to make.

She was also involved, in October 1968, in an event that was to have a catastrophic effect upon their lives, and serve to fire Lennon's burgeoning anger against what he saw as the ever-present forces of government repression. On 18 October, the two were arrested on a drugs bust in Ringo's London apartment in Montagu Square, where they were staying. They were charged with possession of one and a half ounces of marijuana. 'The thing was a set-up,' Lennon later declared. He had been warned two weeks before by a friendly journalist that the police were out to get him because he was a 'loudmouth': 'So believe me,' he said, 'I'd cleaned the house out.' The same 'head-hunting cop', Detective-Sergeant Norman Pilcher, later gaoled for two years for planting evidence in other cases, 'went around and busted every pop star he could get his hands on', including Mick Jagger and Keith Richards. Wiener quotes Lennon as saying: 'Some of the pop stars had dope in their houses, and some didn't. It didn't matter to him. He planted it. That's what he did to me. He said, "If you cop a plea, I won't get you for obstruction, and I'll let your missus go."'

And so it worked out: at Marylebone Magistrates' Court on 28 November 1968 the police withdrew charges against Yoko Ono, Lennon was fined £150 with £21 costs – and 'an offence of moral turpitude' went on his record rendering it very difficult for him ever again to be granted a visa to enter the United States, or to work or live there.

But that was not all. Yoko was pregnant at the time of her arrest. She almost suffered a miscarriage that day and, although immediately hospitalized, she lost the baby a month later. On being told the end of their child's unborn life was near, Lennon had a tape recorder brought into the hospital room and, with a stethoscope microphone, he recorded his second son's failing heartbeats before he died.

But, at first, it took a form that many people thought somewhat ridiculous. His and Yoko's two 'bed-ins for peace' struck even some of his most loyal fans as preposterous. The first was in the presidential suite at the Amsterdam Hilton in March 1969 for a week during their honeymoon (they had been married in Gibraltar on 20 March), and the second was in May–June 1969 at the Queen Elizabeth Hotel in Montreal (which was the nearest they could get to New York, because he was refused a US visa on account of his drugs conviction). 'Make love not war' was a good slogan but the sight of these two long-haired people, one of them long-bearded, sitting up in bed in white pyjamas holding court and talking about peace did not seem the most effective way of getting their message respected and understood.

But perhaps even in those early days there was a premonition of danger. 'Laurel and Hardy, that's John and Yoko,' he said. 'And we stand a better chance under that guise because all the serious people like Martin Luther King and Kennedy and Gandhi got shot.'

Even amid nonsense, his talent – and now dedicated sense of protest – shone through: on 1 June, the last night of the Montreal 'bed-in', Lennon gave everyone in the room the words of his new song, and recorded on an eight-track portable tape recorder his first single since the break-up of the Beatles, 'Give Peace A Chance'. In September 1988, as I type these words in my rented apartment in Venice, California, where I have come to write this book, an activist promoting the cause of Democratic presidential candidate Michael Dukakis on the sea-front just round the corner from where I sit, has that emotive phrase displayed large on a banner. Released in the United States in July 1969, the song reached number 14 on the American charts in September and number 2 in Britain. It received 'Top Forty' radio play for nine weeks in the States, and sold over a million records world-wide.

Its success was not only commercial. On 15 November, Vietnam Moratorium Day was declared in Washington DC and nearly half a million massed demonstrators sang the song at the Washington Monument. Said *Newsweek*: 'The peace movement has found an anthem,' and so it has remained to this day.

Whatever may have been the circumstances of his private life, however many drugs he or Yoko may have sent crashing into their systems, he was entering a new dimension of political awareness – and effectiveness. He was no longer just a singer, however gifted. He had become a prophet for his time.

It was not without personal loss: the man was being torn apart by his internal dilemmas, the pressures of his two emergent contrasting life-styles as 'entertainer' and left-wing activist – and by the drugs that were at that time taking ever greater toll upon his mind and body. On 23 April 1970, with a visa granted by the US authorities on medical grounds, he and Yoko boarded TWA Flight 761 to fly to Los Angeles for four months of intensive therapy with local psychologist, Arthur Janov. Janov's theory, as explained in his book, *The Primal Scream*, was that 'the suppression of feeling' was the basic cause of emotional deprivation: a child's 'terrible hopelessness of never being loved' had to be brought out in the open, faced up to – and conquered. 'That's for me!' had said Lennon, when Janov's publisher had sent him the book unsolicited in the mail for a possible review.

Even Albert Goldman, who seldom has the grace to write anything generous or kind about Lennon in the 699 pages of his biography, has to admit: 'Though John Lennon spent only four months in therapy, a very short time as such treatments are usually measured, he profited enormously from the experience. He recovered from a serious nervous breakdown, learned lessons about himself that he never forgot, and found the material for his most important album.'

That was *John Lennon/Plastic Ono Band*, recorded in October 1970, at Tittenhurst Park, Lennon's huge white Georgian mansion in Ascot, Surrey. An eight-track studio in a two-centuries-old house with seven bedrooms, three bathrooms and three reception rooms standing in seventy acres of rolling parkland, was an extremely unlikely place in which to record songs with titles like 'Mother', 'Hold on (John)', 'God', 'My Mummy's Dead' – and 'Working Class Hero' – but that was Lennon's style by now.

This last track was the most powerful and politically militant song that Lennon had created to date: nearly twenty years later, the words still scream at you in rage.

Lennon knew exactly what he was doing. In a 30,000-word interview that December with Jann Wenner, the editor of *Rolling Stone*, who ran it in two parts and later published it as the book *Lennon Remembers*, Lennon called it 'a song for the revolution. . . . It's for the people like me who are working class . . . who are supposed to be processed into the middle class. . . . It's my experience, and I hope it's a warning to people.'

He told Wenner that the workers were still 'fucking peasants', despite all the appearance of change in the 1960s (when British Prime Minister Harold Macmillan had coined the condescending phrase: 'You've never had it so good') because 'the people who are in control and in power, and the class system and the whole bullshit bourgeois scene is exactly the same except that there are a lot of middle-class kids with long hair walking around in trendy clothes. . . . The same bastards are in control, the same people are runnin' everything. . . . They're doing exactly the same things, selling arms to South Africa, killing blacks on the street, people are living in fucking poverty with rats crawling all over them. It's the same. It just makes you puke. And I woke up to that too. The dream is over.'

With Lennon, rock had become revolutionary – and for real. He and Yoko took part in demonstrations, they campaigned for a public inquiry into the case of James Hanratty, convicted of murder and hanged in the early 1960s; they protested against a prosecution of the underground magazine *OZ* for obscenity; they marched for the IRA and they called for help for striking shipbuilders. All from the large Georgian house in Ascot.

In March 1971, an interview appeared in the underground magazine *Red Mole*, which began uncompromisingly: 'I've always been politically minded and against the status quo,' and continued from there. 'It's pretty basic when you're brought up, like I was,' he told Marxist activist Tariq Ali, then the scourge of middle-class Britain, 'to hate and fear the police as a natural enemy and despise the army as something that takes everybody away and leaves them dead somewhere. . . . I'd like to incite people to break the framework, to be disobedient in school, to insult authority.' When *Ramparts*, the same US magazine that had four years earlier exposed the

CIA's clandestine funding of the National Student Association, reprinted the *Red Mole* interview in its June 1971 issue, it did so under the banner headline: 'The Working Class Hero Turns Red.'

As if this was not enough, on the day after his *Red Mole* interview, Lennon picked up the telephone to Tariq Ali. 'Look,' he said, 'I was so excited by the things we talked about that I've written this song for the movement, so you can sing it when you march.' The song was 'Power to the People', released in March 1971. It hit the charts in both Britain and the United States – and became a marching song for tens of thousands of political demonstrators. The caution of 'Revolution' only three years before had now gone.

The out-pouring did not stop. In September 1971 in the United States, and in the following month in Britain, appeared the album *Imagine* with Lennon's hauntingly beautiful song of the same name on the first track.

In New York's Central Park, not far from where just over nine years later he was shot, that one word 'Imagine' has been set into the ground in the middle of a mosaic circle; and people come to stand and ponder.

By the time the album had appeared in the record shops, Lennon and Yoko were no longer living in Britain. 'Due to unexplained intervention by the State Department with the Immigration and Naturalization Service,' as a FBI secret memo was later tartly to comment, Lennon's embargo on US entry because of his drugs conviction was lifted by a special waiver. On 13 August 1971 the two left Tittenhurst Park for the last time and came to the Big Apple to live with the aim of spending the rest of their lives there together.

Why New York? Because 'it's a fantastic place', Lennon later enthused. 'There's an unbelievably creative atmosphere on this little island of Manhattan. Like they say, there just isn't anything you can't get in New York. . . . I love all the gear here, whether it's cheeseburgers or more TV channels. There's definitely more energy in America, and I don't think it's the size of the country or the amount of people here. It's just that Americans have more energy. America is more my speed.'

And, as he also later said, 'I landed in New York and the first people who got in touch with me were Jerry Rubin and Abbie

Hoffman' – two Chicago Seven Conspiracy Trial defendants. Those two somewhat battered relics of the 1960s, then still trailing some shades of glory, had set their sights on Lennon. He was the man they had been waiting for. It was inevitable that less than four months later, under their influence, Lennon and Yoko would step out on to the platform at Ann Arbor's Chrysler Arena to an audience of predominantly young people – and undercover FBI agents.

6

Followed by the FBI
and the CIA

It will amaze most people, but the FBI had developed an interest in Lennon long before the 'Free Sinclair Rally' – it was from way back, long before he was even living in the United States.

On 11 January 1969 the Special Agent in Charge (SAC) of the bureau's office in New Haven, Connecticut, reported to J. Edgar Hoover on a campus demonstration at the University of Hartford. Two days earlier 200 students and five faculty members had held a 'standing room rally' to protest the dean's suspension of the campus newspaper for having reprinted 'nude photographs, front and back, of Beatle JOHN LENNON holding hands with his girlfriend YOKO ONO'. It somehow did not seem to matter to the worthy dean nor to the diligent SAC that the same photographs were readily available in almost every record shop in the country: they were on the cover sleeve of Lennon and Yoko's recently released album, *Two Virgins* (better known in the United States as the *White Album*).

Indeed, the SAC thought it all so important that he sent copies of his report to the US army, to military intelligence and to the secret service. It is difficult to believe that he would have done this, seemingly as a matter of routine, if there had not already been in existence a substantial file on this troublesome English singer – which (for whatever strange reason) also involved the armed forces and the secret service.

In fact, no outsider can say when the FBI opened its file on Lennon. The New Haven memorandum is the earliest in point of time in a two-inches' swadge of documents released to me by the bureau in September 1987, in answer to my application under the

Freedom of Information Act (FOIA) for their file on Lennon. But that means nothing. The swadge is out of order, uncorrelated and obviously woefully incomplete: many documents refer to others that simply are not there. There is no way of knowing whether there are any more documents in the file before 11 January 1969, the date of the Hartford University memorandum, or after 13 August 1976, the date of the last document in the swadge when FBI director Clarence Kelley sent this written order to his New York SAC:

> No investigation should be conducted concerning subject but your sources should be alerted to the subject's presence in the area covered by your office. Any information developed indicating activity outside the scope of the intended purpose while in the United States should be promptly furnished to the bureau.

That does not read like the end of the story to me. Seventeen days earlier, on 27 July 1976, Immigration Judge Ira Fieldsteel had finally allowed Lennon to remain as a permanent resident in the United States, and he had been handed his long-sought green card, number A17-597-321. He said after the hearing that, 'the same as everyone else', he planned to devote himself to his 'wife, kids and a job'.

It would be fascinating to know why, after all Lennon's long battle in the courts, the New York FBI chief should still have to 'be alerted to [his] presence in the area' – and for how long.

In answer to an FOIA application by Jon Wiener in 1981, the Bureau released only 89 pages, although Wiener claimed that 'the main Lennon file' amounted to 288 pages. In 1983, he got another eight pages. Backed by the American Civil Liberties Union, he is still fighting the issue in the courts. There are 217 pages in my swadge but nowhere does the FBI tell me how many pages there are in the whole file. Even on the released documents, substantial sections and sometimes even whole pages have been blacked out 'in the interests of national defense or foreign policy'.

So who knows when the file really began – or when it really ended? Under the 1976–80 Carter administration, documents could be withheld or passages obliterated only if disclosure would cause 'identifiable damage to national security'. An executive order by President Reagan in 1981 removed the word 'identifiable'. The FBI now does not even have to identify the so-called 'damage to national security' that releasing Lennon's file to me nearly seven years after his death would cause.

Sadly one cannot trust the American authorities to reveal all that, under their own law, they should reveal. In Britain, until finally they reform the Official Secrets Act, at least you know where you are: you are entitled to nothing from official government and law-enforcement agencies' records. And so you have semi-frightening nonsense, such as the 'Spycatcher' fiasco that dragged on in the British courts over the two years 1987 and 1988, when the Thatcher government tried relentlessly – and in the end unsuccessfully – to prevent the publication of ex-MI5 official Peter Wright's memoirs.

But, in the United States, government agencies are supposed to tell you what they have done in your name, except in very tightly restricted circumstances.

That still does not mean you will get anything like the whole – or even partial – truth out of the CIA. Three documents in the FBI's swadge actually state: 'Original and Copy to CIA'. Yet, when Professor Wiener, in June 1984, obtained from the CIA (for use in a possible second edition of his biography) the agency's file on Lennon, all that came in – via the FBI, as it happened – were four measly documents. He has passed them on to me, and they do not even include the three documents of which my FBI swadge says they were sent copies; Wiener's four CIA documents cannot possibly be the total file. I say that, not only because they all relate to the month of February 1972 and do *not* include two of my FBI documents marked as having copies sent to the CIA which are dated that same month, but my third FBI report copied to the agency is dated over four years later: 27 July 1976. Where are the documents in the CIA file from February 1972 to July 1976 – and did the reporting continue even after that time?

Despite the missing pages and the blacked out sections, the information released by the two agencies contains startling revelations of clandestine activity. The implications are awesome for a free society – and deeply disturbing when you consider what role the CIA may have played in Lennon's eventual assassination.

For a start, the undercover FBI agents in the audience at the 'Free

Sinclair Rally' were not the first to keep their tabs on Lennon. In the previous chapter, you will have read how, on 23 April 1970, Lennon and Yoko flew to Los Angeles on TWA's Flight 761 to start four months of primal therapy with Arthur Janov. In fact, they were accompanied by fellow Beatle, George Harrison, and his then wife, Patti Boyd.

But none of them knew as they settled into their comfortable first-class seats – and this is the first time it is revealed – that a few hours earlier J. Edgar Hoover had sent this secret memorandum to his Los Angeles and New York offices:

JOHN LENNON
GEORGE HARRISON
PATRICIA HARRISON
INFORMATION CONCERNING
On 4/22/70 [the American version of the British 22/4/70] a representative of the Department of State advised that the American Embassy in London had submitted information showing the captioned individuals planned to depart from London, England on 4/23/70 via TWA Flight 761 which will arrive in Los Angeles at 7:15 local time. These individuals are affiliated with the Beatles musical group and Lennon will be travelling under the name Chambers and the Harrisons are using the name Masters.

While Lennon and the Harrisons have shown no propensity to become involved in violent antiwar demonstrations, each recipient remain alert for any information of such activity on their part or for information indicating they are using narcotics. Submit any pertinent information obtained in form suitable for dissemination.

Needless to say, my swadge of documents is silent on whatever 'pertinent information' was obtained.

The paranoia shown in the FBI and CIA files gives an insight into the way in which these people's minds worked, alone in their secret world. As someone who has been in the law for nearly forty years, I know that the police mentality is a different one from that of ordinary folk: everything and everyone is suspect. The only people you think you can trust are your own kind. London's policemen call the Metropolitan Police 'The Firm', CIA agents call their agency 'The Company': the way of thinking, the sense of being cut off from the life of everyone else outside is identical.

The very language employed in the FBI reports reveals the blinkered thinking of the men behind them.

• Attached to the transcript of the speeches and Lennon's song about John Sinclair that the Detroit SAC sent his pug-faced director after the Ann Arbor rally, is a memorandum naming the 'sources', i.e., the undercover FBI men in the audience, and saying that the information was classified confidential (and, therefore, blacked out in the released document) 'to protect the identity of sources whose identities, if disclosed, could be detrimental to the national defense interests of this nation'. 'Defense interests' in a rally to free a drug-saturated hippy?

• Whoever dictated the typed notes accompanying the transcripts felt the need to explain that Lennon, then one of the most famous rock stars alive in the world, was 'formerly with group known as the Beatles'.

• The writer of a later report (on 27 July 1972) was similarly constrained by his institutionalized way of thinking to describe Lennon, in stereotyped police pattern, as if he were a petty criminal with a past conviction for shoplifting:

Name:	John Winston Lennon
Race:	White
Date of Birth:	October 9, 1940
Place of Birth:	Liverpool, England
Hair:	Brown to Blond
Weight:	160 pounds
Height:	Approximately six feet
Build:	Slender
Nationality:	English
US Residence:	105 Bank Street, New York City
Arrest Record:	1968 Narcotics Arrest, in England for Possession of Dangerous Drugs (Cannabis) Pled Guilty

• On 10 April 1972, Hoover directed his New York SAC to 'promptly initiate discreet efforts to locate subject and remain aware of his activities and movements. Handle inquiries only through established sources and discreet pretext inquiries. Careful attention should be given to reports that subject is heavy narcotics user and any information developed in this regard should be furnished to narcotics authorities and immediately furnished to bureau in form suitable for dissemination'. One can almost picture Gene Hackman in the role of Hoover dictating the memorandum to an actress playing his secretary in a Hollywood movie.

• In San Diego, a man was arrested by FBI agents 'for Conspiracy to Injure Government Property and Trespassing for the Purpose of Injuring Government Property' during anti-Vietnam War demonstrations, and an address book with 395 names and addresses was found in his possession. One set of names was 'John and Yoko Lennon'. The San Diego SAC promptly, on 18 May 1972, sent his New York counterpart a copy of the address even though it was only a post office box: 'Old Chelsea Station, PO Box 654, New York, NY 10011'.

• Two reports, 23 May and 24 May 1972, referred to Lennon's subject-matter in the file as: 'Revolutionary Activities', as if they believed the singer was truly engaged in a conspiracy violently to overthrow the established government of the United States.

These are just psychological give-aways of the mental process of the individuals who wrote, and acted upon, these reports; but in one of the few post-1972 documents, dated 18 September 1973, there is something more concrete. It is so important an indiscretion that one wonders how on earth the censor wielding the bureau's thick black crayon managed to overlook it. It is a memorandum to recently appointed FBI director Clarence M. Kelley from Henry E. Petersen, Assistant Attorney General at the Criminal Division of the Justice Department, Washington DC. It asks the new director to furnish one Robert P. Weidner in the Government Regulations Section of the Criminal Division with:

Any memoranda, including reports to the Department of Justice, which expand or summarize the portions of . . . logs [of Lennon's telephone conversations obtained by any lawful electronic surveillance] or which demonstrate pertinent leads which may have come from the illegal electronic surveillance.

Notice that absolutely vital 'the' in the last line. The request predicated that there was illegal electronic surveillance. The Justice Department was saying that they knew positively in September

1973 that Lennon's telephone had been illegally bugged – but they were not expressing shock or disapproval. They merely wanted to know what he had said.

Indeed, Lennon knew from early in 1972 that he was under constant surveillance, being followed in the streets and with his telephone tapped. 'I'd open the door, there'd be guys on the other side of the street,' he told Capital Radio in London in 1975. 'I'd get in the car, and they'd be following me in a car. Not hiding. They wanted me to see I was being followed.'

In December 1975, he told *Hit Parader* magazine: 'We knew we were being wire-tapped on Bank Street (an early New York address), there was a helluva lot of guys coming in to fix the phones.'

More ominously, in late 1972, he told Paul Krassner, a left-wing friend of Yoko's in San Francisco from the early 1960s: 'Listen, if anything happens to Yoko and me, it was not an accident.' In the light of what happened to him eight years later, those words, repeated to me in October 1988 by Krassner, take on a possible significance that is chilling.

What really got the FBI and CIA so geared up about Lennon was not merely his attendance at the Sinclair Rally or even the wild words shouted by others from the platform. It was the spin-off idea, fuelled by the rally's success in achieving Sinclair's freedom, for a 'revolutionary road show', starring Lennon and Yoko. This combination of rock music and radical politics was to barnstorm its way across America in the early summer and end up in a giant protest rally outside the Republican National Convention at San Diego, where President Nixon was almost certain to be nominated for re-election at the presidential elections that November. The aim was a huge 'political Woodstock' that would successfully accomplish at San Diego in 1972 what Jerry Rubin and his colleagues had failed to achieve at Chicago in 1968: the disruption of a major party's national convention. An organization originally named the Allamuchy Tribe, and then the Election Year Strategy Information Committee, was set up with headquarters in the basement of Lennon and Yoko's apartment in Greenwich Village.

What federal law was being broken in all this? Absolutely none, but it concerned a president of the United States, and a Republican president at that – and that was enough to get the FBI and CIA crucially involved. On 21 January 1972, the New York SAC sent Director Hoover a coded message that his office was 'opening a separate case captioned "Allamuchy Tribe" [with a] copy provided San Diego due to interest in forthcoming National Convention.' On 2 February 1972, he told both Hoover and the Washington SAC:

John Winston Lennon re-entered the United States holding a temporary visa which expires end of February instant. Lennon has applied for (varied) status leading up to becoming a United States citizen. He is presently married to Yoko Ono Lennon . . . Washington Field Office immediately review INS (Immigration and Naturalization Service) file regarding Lennon and forward background including photo of subject to New York Office.

Does this mean they not only had Lennon under illegal surveillance but had also secret photographs of him? The New York office was surely not short of ordinary photographs of the famous rock star.

Hoover's answering memorandum on 3 February is so blacked out as to be almost unreadable, as is the New York SAC's immediate communication in reply. On the very next day, Strom Thurmond, the veteran (born 5 December 1902) Republican diehard who still sits as Senator from Southern Carolina, kept up the pressure with a superb idea designed to do away with all their troubles.

On 4 February, in his capacity as member of a Senate Internal Security Sub-Committee, he sent the late John Mitchell, Richard Nixon's personal friend and Attorney General (who was later to go to prison for his involvement in Watergate), a secret memorandum drafted by the staff of his subcommittee and headed: 'John Lennon.' After noting that Lennon had appeared at the Sinclair Rally with members of the Chicago Seven, it continued:

This group has been strong advocates of the programme to 'dump Nixon'. They have devised a plan to hold rock concerts in various primary states for the following purposes: to obtain access to college campuses; to press for legislation legalizing marijuana; to recruit persons to come to San Diego . . . in

August. They . . . intend to use John Lennon as a drawing card to promote their success. . . . This can only lead to a clash between a controlled mob organized by this group and law enforcement officials . . . *If Lennon's visa is terminated, it would be a strategic counter-measure* (my italics).

In case the point was lost on the none too astute Mitchell, who had a notorious drinking problem, Senator Thurmond added a personal endorsement: 'This appears to me to be an important matter, and I think it would be well for it to be considered at the highest level as I can see many headaches might be avoided if appropriate action is taken.' As if this was not enough, knowing with whom he was dealing, he handwrote at the bottom: 'I also sent Bill Timmons [a White House aide] a copy of the memorandum.' Thurmond did, indeed, want his suggestion taken to 'the highest level'.

There can be little doubt that it was. On 14 February, Mitchell's deputy, Richard Kleindienst, sent a note to INS Commissioner Raymond Farrell: 'Ray, please call me about the attached. When is he coming? Do we – if we so elect – have any basis to deny his admittance?' He seems not to have been all that much better informed than Mitchell, but no matter. Even without White House intervention, the FBI and the CIA already had the matter well in hand, off their own bat. An FBI report dated 7 February (one of the two in my swadge specifically marked 'Original and Copy to CIA'), under the heading Election Year Strategy Information Center, refers again to Lennon's application to become a US citizen and, although almost all the two-paged report is blacked out, reveals enough to indicate that the bureau was already thinking it would be a good idea if Lennon was simply booted out of the country. Towards the end, it specifically notes: 'CIA has requested that all (relevant) information be classified "Secret – No Foreign Dissemination/No Dissemination Abroad". CIA has requested details of information we furnished in daily summary teletype.'

The second FBI secret memorandum that specifically mentions the CIA is even more explicit, though equally prodigiously blacked out. On 15 February, Hoover told his New York, Los Angeles, San Diego and Washington DC offices: 'Recipients are reminded that investigative instructions relating to possible disruption during Republican National Convention must be handled on expedite basis and by mature, experienced agents. Recipients carefully note dissemination instructions.'

Nor did the CIA drag its feet – even before the cumbersome machinery of the INS had motivated itself to act on the White House-backed suggestion. On 23 February 1972, some unknown CIA agent reported in the only one of the four agency documents released to Jon Wiener that contains anything of real significance:

> Some American participants at the Soviet-controlled World Assembly for Peace and Independence of the Peoples of Indochina, held 11–13 February 1972 in Paris/Versailles, attempted unsuccessfully to include a call for international demonstrations to take place at the time of the Republican National Convention. . . .
>
> John LENNON, a British subject, has provided financial support to Project 'YES' [one of Yoko's radical brain-child organizations], which in turn paid the travel expenses to the World Assembly of a representative of leading anti-war activist (and Chicago Seven defendant) Rennie DAVIS. . . . In Paris this representative in the World Assembly met at least once with officials of the Provisional Revolutionary Government of South Vietnam; it is not known if the Republican National Convention was discussed.

This is the first secret CIA document naming Lennon to be publicly quoted. To many, it will read like something from a novel by John le Carré or a James Bond film-script.

So far, this had all been shadow-boxing: with surveillance and phone-tapping and secret reports while Lennon went about his normal life. But that soon was to end: as an undated INS document, included in my FBI swadge, says in the cold language of bureaucracy the whole world over:

> On March 1, 1972 the District Director in New York City notified Lennon in writing that his stay had expired on February 29, 1972 and gave him until March 15, 1972 within which to depart voluntarily without the institution of deportation proceedings. Upon learning that he did not plan to depart, the District Director notified Lennon on March 6, 1972 that this privilege of voluntary departure was revoked. Thereafter

an order to show cause was issued on March 7, 1972 with hearing scheduled for March 16, 1972.

Lennon fought the deportation proceedings with a passion that was deep and committed. He adored living in the United States and he wanted to stay there. At the first full hearing of the INS court case against him on 18 April 1972, he told reporters defiantly that the Nixon administration was only trying to get him and Yoko out of the country 'because we're peaceniks'. This was duly translated for J. Edgar Hoover's benefit later that day, in an 'urgent' secret report, as: 'Lennon was observed by a representative of the FBI to make a press release in which he inferred INS was attempting to deport him due to his political ideas and present policy of the US government.'

On their way to court, they had spoken at a midtown Manhattan anti-Vietnam War rally and six days later Lennon's first overtly feminist single, 'Woman is the Nigger of the World', backed by Yoko's equally militant 'Sisters, O Sisters', was released.

But the pace was already heating up. Three days earlier, on 21 April, E. L. Shackleford, a supervisor in the FBI's New York office, had sent E. S. Miller, one of his men, and later one of the only two FBI agents ever to be convicted of crimes committed in the execution of his duty (he was pardoned by President Reagan in 1981), a memorandum which, amid all the blacked-out sections, speaks of Lennon as being a 'currently reported heavy user of narcotics' and states:

> In view of successful delaying tactics to date, there exists real possibility that subject will not be deported from US in near future and possibly not prior to Republican National Convention. Subject's activities being closely followed and any information developed indicating violation of Federal laws will be immediately furnished to pertinent agencies in effort to neutralize any disruptive activities of subject.

Even on the basis of the limited information contained in my FBI swadge of documents, there can be no doubt that President Nixon himself was now, if not before, officially in the picture. The same memorandum attached 'for approval' a letter to 'Honorable H. R. Haldeman at the White House', Nixon's closest aide and later to go to prison for him because of his involvement with Watergate. In the light of all the controversy in the newspapers about the administration's efforts to cast Lennon out of the country, it is inconceivable that the president himself did not know – and fully approve of – what was going on. Leon Wildes, Lennon's immigration lawyer, told Jon Wiener in 1983: 'Nixon took such an intimate interest in the smallest of details. Remember that was the first year they gave eighteen-year-olds the right to vote in a presidential election. Lennon was the guy who could have influenced the eighteen-year-old vote the most. In my mind there is a moral certainty that Mr Nixon had discussions about Mr Lennon.'

Four days after the Haldeman memorandum, on 25 April, the Acting Attorney General sent J. Edgar Hoover a memorandum, substantially blacked out, concerning Lennon, which stated:

> This information is also being furnished to the Honorable H. R. Haldeman, Assistant to the President, at the White House. Pertinent information concerning Lennon is being furnished to the Department of State and INS on a regular basis.

Somehow the message got back to Lennon that, if he wanted to stay in the United States (which was his first personal priority, not only because of his own personal preference but because Yoko was still desperately trying to obtain custody of her daughter Kyoko, who was living in the States with her father, Tony Cox), he had to pull in his horns. Revolutionary activity and asking the courts to let you stay in the country did not easily go hand in hand.

He began declaring in private and in public that he had cancelled the 'revolutionary road show'. In May 1972, he went on Dick Cavett's TV talk show and said: 'They think we're going to San Diego, or Miami or wherever it is [by now, the Republican National Convention had been re-located to Miami]. We've never said we're going.'

It was a major climb-down in sheer self-defence, forced upon him by Leon Wildes' shrewd advice; but he felt sick at heart. His supporters understood. Even John Sinclair told Jon Wiener eleven years later, 'Cancelling the tour plan was wise. I know how much it meant for them to stay here – partially because of the thing with the kid. I understood perfectly.'

It was sheer political opportunism by the Nixon administration. They knew that in Lennon's 1968 marijuana conviction they had a trump card in trying to get him out of the country. The INS all along maintained that it was merely complying with US Federal law and that their opposition to Lennon's continued sojourn in the country was purely routine. They were undeterred by leading journalist Jack Anderson's revelation in his nationally syndicated column that over 100 aliens with drug records had, unlike Lennon, been granted 'non-priority decisions' permitting them to stay in the United States indefinitely.

In May 1972, President Nixon ordered Haiphong Harbour to be mined and massive new bombing raids to take place. Anti-war feeling reached new heights of intensity throughout the country. Lennon and Yoko took part in a 'candlelight vigil and procession for peace' on 20 May in Washington DC marching side by side with many other similarly minded celebrities, including the Hollywood actor Robert Ryan; but there was a limit to what they could safely do. It went against all their principles; but they had to remain comparatively silent throughout the rest of that year while their deportation battle, destined to endure for four more years, dragged on.

On 7 November 1972, Nixon was triumphantly confirmed in power. On 8 December 1972, the New York SAC notified Hoover's temporary successor, L. Patrick Gray, Nixon's nominee as acting FBI director:

> In view of subject's inactivity in Revolutionary Activities and his seemingly rejection by NY Radicals, captioned case is being closed in the NY Division.
>
> In event other information comes to New York's attention indicating subject is active with Revolutionary groups, the case will be re-opened at that time and the Bureau advised accordingly.

In other words, the FBI's – and presumably the CIA's – surveillance on Lennon was put 'on hold'.

But Lennon was left physically and mentally exhausted. As he later explained to his British friend, Anthony Fawcett: 'In 1972, it was really gettin' to me. Not only was I physically having to appear in court cases, it just seemed like a toothache that wouldn't go away. There was a period where I just couldn't function, you know. I was so paranoid from them tappin' the phone and followin' me.' It did not get very much better. In March 1973, he was again ordered by the INS to leave the country, although they granted Yoko permanent residency. His reply was spirited but weary: 'Having just celebrated our fourth wedding anniversary, we are not prepared to sleep in separate beds. Peace and love, John and Yoko.' Fighting to stay in the country now became almost a full-time job. Everything else, even the occasional protest demonstration, had to take second place. As Jon Wiener has written, 'Along with the feelings of powerlessness and fear instilled by the government came a loss of artistic energy and confidence.'

Then, in June 1973, Lennon and Yoko rented the home of Robert Ryan, the actor who had marched with them in the Washington DC 'candlelight vigil and procession for peace' the previous year and who was now sadly dying of cancer. It was Apartment 72 in an enormous granite-fronted block built in 1884 by the Singer sewing machine millionaire Edward S. Clark. It was then located so far out of town it was given the ironic name of The Dakota, a remote mid-Western territory that had not yet even achieved its modern twin-statehood of North Dakota and South Dakota, but by the early 1970s it had become one of the most desirable blocks in the city.

Lennon, dispirited and at the lowest of his powers, moved in to what was to prove to be his last and happiest permanent home.

7

Enter Mark

A month before Lennon and Yoko moved into Robert Ryan's old apartment, an eighteen-year-old youth with brown wavy hair and blue eyes, wearing a rented tuxedo, adjusted his floppy bow-tie and smiled warily at the photographer of his high school's graduation yearbook. He looked like any other of the 300 young men and women of the 'Class of 73' of Columbia High School in the comfortable middle-class suburb of Decatur on the outskirts of Atlanta, capital city of the state of Georgia.

The faces in the 300 photographs are all very similar: clean, well scrubbed, well fed, white-skinned – and slightly nervous of what adulthood had in store for them.

Ten years later, in May 1983, most of these youngsters gathered together for their tenth anniversary reunion. A pamphlet containing alumni notes recounted their progress:

'I attended Georgia State University and am currently a computer programmer. . . . I enjoy cats, running, aerobics and reading. . . . My husband, Ed, and I have been married for eight years and have two daughters. . . . My hobbies are raquetball, scuba diving, piano and snow skiing. . . . I am employed as a CPA-tax manager for Price Waterhouse and Vickie takes care of Kurt . . .' And so on, and so on. Life styles of the successful and prosperous, or soon to be.

But there was no entry for Mark David Chapman, the young man with the floppy bow-tie. By then he was in Attica prison garb. And when his youthful face was seen on an old school slide, with a group of other youngsters, immediately after John Lennon's voice had been heard singing a song from the Beatles' *White Album*, 'Happiness is a Warm Gun', several people looked uncomfortable. 'It was tactless,' Tommy Morris, a friend of Mark both from school and the local South De Kalb YMCA's summer camp, told a reporter from the *Atlanta Journal*.

Like others who remembered Mark during his five years at school, from the eighth grade through to the twelfth grade and graduation, Morris was adamant that between May 1973 and the series of gunshots that felled Lennon in December 1980, something very strange must have happened. 'The Mark Chapman that I knew I just didn't picture as the Mark Chapman who killed John Lennon,' he said.

The Rev. Newton Hendrix, another school friend of Mark's of the same age, talking to me in May 1988 in his office as musical director at the Jefferson Avenue Baptist Church, is more reflective: 'Obviously, there's a lot of water under the bridge from '73 to '80 but still, looking back, you can see all these things and think: well, maybe that was part of it, you can maybe see some instability there. But, I mean, you can look back on me and see the same thing, you know.

'Alright, you've just read me a quotation from the *Atlanta Journal* where another classmate said he didn't think Mark was any more confused than the rest of the class of '73. I agree with that! But you've got to understand the context.

'We were all part of a generation called baby boomers. Our fathers were part of World War II. They all came home, they married, they had families – and that's us: their kids. Now we're like ages twenty-eight to forty-two but it was a time when people were moving to the suburbs and leaving the city. Momma stayed home, kept house, daddy drove to town to go to work, the kids all went to school in new neighbourhoods.

'There's a lot of characteristics of this time that sociologists are looking at now and we seem to be a confused generation, a lot of us. There were just a lot of people looking for answers. But a lot of them are stockbrokers now. They outgrew it. It had no lasting effect. Yet at that time, as teenagers, looking at what was going on with the college students who were just ahead of us, we were confused. Not all of us went out and did drugs, as Mark did, or free sex or anything else either – but it touched us all.

'Even so, there was nothing about Mark's behaviour, nothing he ever said to me, that would make me want to say: "John Lennon had better be careful because he's coming after him."

Nothing he ever did that made me think he would not end up just a normal person.'

Why then did he become the most famous murderer of his generation? There is an old Swedish proverb: 'Children are certain sorrow but only uncertain joy,' and Mark's parents David and Diane Chapman must surely agree with that. The only problem is that children can often say the same about their parents.

'My father was never very emotional; I don't think I ever hugged my father,' Mark told Dr Lee Salk, a psychiatrist who visited him in gaol while he was awaiting trial. 'He never told me he loved me, and he never said he was sorry. We just never ever really got along. He smashed my head down in a plate of spaghetti one time.

'He never showed any emotional love, just maybe if I needed money for school, he would give it. Mom always told me that my father couldn't show these kinds of things but he'd try in other ways. You know, he was always home and he never drank and things like that, but I needed more than just a father who was responsible, morally – not morally, but maybe ethically – for his family. I needed more than that.'

For her part, Diane Chapman told writer Jim Gaines in 1987: 'I pretty well know there was nothing that drastic in our lives that would cause anything like [our son killing John Lennon]. As far as I can see, we were pretty normal. It's true that Dave didn't show his emotions, but he would do anything for Mark. That's where it's so unfair. What more did you want from a person? Did you want total understanding? Who gets that? My father didn't even look up from the paper at me half the time. I didn't care.'

At a practical level, there can be no doubt that the Chapmans did their best for Mark and his younger sister, Susan.

David Chapman, credit manager at an Atlanta bank when his son shot Lennon, was a sergeant in the US air force and his wife a night nurse when Mark was born at Fort Worth, Texas, on 10 May 1955. A few months later the family moved to Indiana, where David received at Purdue University a bachelor's degree in electrical engineering. He went to work for the American Oil Company and in 1962, when Mark was seven and David had moved over to the credit side of the organization, they settled in a new three-bedroom house on a shady corner plot in Decatur. Even today, the house and the area are purest middle-America, southern-style, with broad roads lined with towering trees and large gardens, front and back. It looks like a clearing in a forest; and, indeed, the road is called Green Forest Drive. (The only difference since the Chapman family lived there is that then it was 100 per cent white. Now most of the prosperous residents with their two- or three-car families are black. Social change has come, even to this part of the Deep South.)

The family, as with so many in the South, where most of the towns have more churches than service-stations, were deeply religious Christians. David Chapman did his best to be a good father: he taught guitar at the local YMCA, and he showed Mark how to play.

The boy was musical and the Rev. Newton Hendrix remembers meeting him for the first time at choral practice at Columbia High, when they were both thirteen and had just come into the school in their eighth grade. 'Somehow he seemed so innocent looking. His hair cut was very short, very neat. He just had an innocent look on his face. A wet-behind-the-ears kid, coming into high school.'

The following year, aged fourteen and at his father's bidding, Mark, like most other local white youngsters at the time, joined his nearest YMCA, the South De Kalb branch. Tony Adams, then thirty-one, was executive director. He was to be Mark's supervisor, friend and confidant as the boy grew to young manhood. 'He trusted me and, even though he loved his father, he confided in me just as much,' he said after Lennon's murder. Mark was 'one of the three most top-notch young people I have met in sixteen years with the YMCA.'

Mr Adams told Jim Gaines in 1981: 'I'd say it was a very happy family and Mark was a happy, well-adjusted boy.' Which only goes to show how difficult it is sometimes for even the most astute outsider to know what is really going on inside the comfortably reassuring exterior of a suburban home – anywhere in the world.

In fact, almost from the time he joined Tony Adams' YMCA, Mark was rebelling at home. He smoked his first marijuana joint at fourteen, by fifteen he had taken his first hit of LSD and was well into a whole variety of drugs, including heroin. Sometimes he would 'trip' for five days in a row. Columbia High, at that time, had an unenviable fame as 'Number 1 for drugs in the State of Georgia', and Mark slipped so deeply into the subculture that he became known as a 'garbage-head', someone who would take anything.

'He had several bad LSD experiences,' Gary Limuti, his best friend at the time, later told a *Newsweek* reporter. 'He suffered a great deal of anxiety and he feared for his sanity.' His parents did their best but he could not easily be controlled: once after he had been locked in his room, he took the door off its hinges, left it downstairs and stormed out of the house. He twice ran away from home.

Then suddenly in the summer of 1971, when he was sixteen, God came into his life and rescued him – or, at least, that is how he always afterwards regarded it. In fact, a Californian evangelist named Arthur Blessed was in town. Mark went to one of his meetings, and had a genuinely moving religious experience. Mr Blessed certainly had a powerful style. Here is a sample from one of his sermons from that period:

Many of you just made a real commitment in your life to Jesus Christ, and in His place when someone turns on to Jesus we have them share their testimony and many are loaded on drugs or have drugs in their possession. So we go into the restroom and we have a toilet service and we read a passage of Scripture and we say a word of prayer and then we drop the drugs in the john and, just as we start to mash the Hell down, we sing a little song that says 'Down, down, down, down, all my dope is gone', and we flush it down.

Remember, Jesus Christ *is* life's greatest trip!

The change in Mark was overnight. He no longer looked 'like a hood' when the teenage Newton Hendrix came across him in the corridors, 'with long hair, old army jackets, baggy looking trousers, green draft coat and stuff like that'. Now he was 'a lot calmer, softer spoken, his hair was short. He was still wearing the large coat and some of that stuff – but now he always wore a large wooden cross round his neck.' In fact, never one to do anything by halves, Mark had gone right to the other extreme and become 'a Jesus freak', although, after Hendrix used that expression to a reporter, he 'got into a whole lot of flack'. This was after all Georgia where nobody could be called a freak for loving Jesus Christ, even to excess.

There are three major misconceptions about Mark that have appeared in most that has been written about him since he committed the murder. At this early stage in the narrative of his life, let us get rid of them once and for all.

First, he is nearly always depicted as a dedicated admirer of John Lennon. 'Lennon's alter ego', *Newsweek* called him on 22 December 1980. 'Fan of Lennon stalked him', said the *Los Angeles Times* on 10 December 1980. 'A devout Lennon fan', was the expression used in December 1980 by two newspapers so far apart as the *Honolulu Star-Bulletin* and the London *Daily Telegraph*. Nearly eight years later, in October 1988, Mike Wallace on the US top television documentary programme *60 Minutes*, in an item on the upcoming film, *Imagine: John Lennon*, was still calling him 'a deranged fan'.

Why should 'a devout fan' have killed his idol? The truth is that, at the time he shot Lennon, Mark was *not* a particular fan, 'devout' or otherwise, of the man he killed.

That tag has been applied to him almost from the very start almost entirely because of one impromptu remark made by his court-appointed counsel, a fifty-year-old New York attorney named Herbert Adlerberg, representing him on legal aid, after Mark's arraignment for Lennon's murder on the afternoon following the crime.

At the arraignment itself, he told Judge Martin Rettinger that his client had not been 'coherent' when he questioned him. 'His answers were not connected with the question in any way,' he said. And he continued: 'He admired the Beatles very much. He doesn't value himself too much.'

That was all he said in court: there was no particular reference to Lennon. But outside the courtroom, Adlerberg was set upon by a posse of reporters. The scene was bedlam. Blinding sets of hand-held television lights competed with each other, microphones on sticks thrust frenziedly into the air, radio-reporters' hand-cassettes jostled for place in front of his mouth. One answer that Adlerberg gave in this high-pressured jamboree has passed into the folk-lore of the murder. 'He told me he had admired Lennon very much since he was ten years old,' said the beleaguered attorney, adding: 'My impression was of a very confused character.'

'Confused' was the operative word for everything that was going on. At this initial court hearing, the prosecution got two

'Chapmans' mixed up and told Judge Rettinger that *this* Chapman had a serious criminal record although, in fact, it belonged to the other Chapman. Kim Hogrefe, District Attorney Allen Sullivan's assistant, told Judge Rettinger that Mark had 'convictions dating back to 1972 and an arrest this year for armed robbery and abduction for which there is a warrant outstanding'. The mistake was put right within an hour in a statement to the press by Sullivan explaining that law enforcement officials in Florida had given the New York police the wrong record. But the odd thing is that the Florida man's name was not even Mark David Chapman but William Alan Chapman. So how come the error was made? According to the *New York Times*, the Florida Chapman 'had the same birth date and the same general characteristics as New York's Chapman'.

Similar turmoil seemed to be reigning in the defence camp. Before going into Judge Rettinger's courtroom Adlerberg had (as we shall see later) no time for proper consultation. Interviewed two months later, in February 1981, he told me: 'I only got to defend Chapman in the first place that morning because my name was next on the Court's Homicide Panel. So I got nailed! I got called – and all for twenty-five bucks an hour!' He had only seen his client for twenty-five rushed minutes before going into court. 'My first impression was that this guy was a little crazy and I thought I had better have him committed for psychiatric evaluation and see where we go from there. That is more or less what I told the judge and he agreed. He ordered the guy to be confined for psychiatric examination at Bellevue Hospital to see if he was fit to stand trial pending a further hearing on 6 January. And that was it!

'But then when I came out of court I was bushwhacked by reporters from all over the place. That's when I felt my first pang of fear, it was a very peculiar feeling because, after twenty-one years, I knew that building like the back of my hand. They stuck microphones in my face, the cameras were shooting – and I wondered who else was in that crowd. I remembered watching on TV when Jack Ruby went to a police station and killed that poor bastard Harvey Oswald. I thought it might happen to me. So I said, "Let's get out of the hallway" and we went to the press room,' where he parried the newsmen's questions as best he could. He has admitted to me that, at that moment, he had only got the haziest picture of events from his client. 'I was going to go up to Bellevue the next day to get a more extensive interview with him.'

Adlerberg could not remember whether he had specifically asked Mark, in their short time together, whether he was a fan of Lennon's or whether Mark had volunteered the information. Or whether the word 'fan' was even mentioned. We do not know what questions the baffled and somewhat reluctant attorney asked of his client in his short time with him, in an effort to make sense of what must have seemed such a senseless crime. But, however 'incoherent' or 'confused' Mark may have been (or however efficiently programmed to give that particular piece of throwing-off-the-scent information), the amazing fact remains that it was later an essential part of the prosecution's case, although never revealed in open court, that, in the words of Allen Sullivan, Mark 'had no particular interest in John Lennon during the ten year period between age fourteen and twenty-four'. It was to be a vital weapon in their armoury that Mark was *not* any particular fan of Lennon's but had cold-bloodedly and calculatedly chosen to kill him as a guaranteed way of becoming famous. As we shall see, they would claim that any other celebrity of equal fame would have done as well.

Admittedly, in his early days at school, Mark had been a fan of the Beatles just like millions of other American youngsters – despite what Lennon had said about the Beatles being more popular than Jesus Christ. That did not come into it. After the dust from the first explosion of anger had settled, young Americans soon went back to being beguiled by the music of the 'Fab Four'. 'He liked Lennon's wit and cynicism. He was our favourite Beatle,' Gary Lumuti told *Newsweek*.

But Mark's attachment to the Beatles or Lennon was not exceptional for a kid growing up at that time. He was never, even when very young, a *devout* Lennon fan. Says the Rev. Newton Hendrix (and remember that music is one of the things they had in common, both being members of the school choir): 'He never expressed strong views on the Beatles or Lennon to me. He played the guitar and may even have written some songs, but it was not "Beatles type music". All of his feelings, very strong feelings, I might add, towards John Lennon and the Beatles were new to me when I heard of them in 1980. To me he never expressed a dislike or made any comment at all that I remember.'

Indeed, this seems to have continued into later life. Brook Hart, the astute Honolulu lawyer who represented Gloria Chapman, Mark's wife, in the difficult months following the murder, has told me: 'I have more Beatles records in my collection than Mark had.'

Then there was the mysterious affair of the 'cassette recorder with about fourteen hours of Beatles tapes' that, according to some newspaper reports at the time, Mark was supposed to have had on him when arrested and which, according to other reports, he was supposed to have listened to while waiting for Lennon and Yoko to return to The Dakota: does not that show he was an avid fan, at least of the Beatles, if not of Lennon? It might perhaps do so if the recorder and tapes existed. Steve Spiro, the New York policeman who arrested Mark, has given me a list of the objects that Mark had on him when he took him into police custody. It includes Mark's copy of *The Catcher in the Rye*, the key of his New York hotel room and his Bank of Hawaii Visa Card – but there is no cassette recorder listed and no tapes of any kind, not of the Beatles nor of anyone else. Thus is legend created from the mind of some imaginative reporter not bothered too much about truth getting in the way of a good story.

Captain Louis L. Souza of the Honolulu police, who spent over a month after Lennon's murder inquiring into Mark's background on the island, has also told me: 'I did not come to the opinion that he was a John Lennon nut. It appeared like he was just the opposite. He was not particularly in favour of that type of music. He was not a particular fan of John Lennon. He did not express any views on Lennon, he didn't talk about him.'

Newsweek, on 22 December 1980, stated that, when working at a local apartment block in the year before Lennon's murder, Mark stuck a strip of masking tape over the name tag on his chest and 'rebaptized himself' with the name John Lennon 'scrawled on the smudged tape'. It was a nice story, reported in good faith; but Captain Souza found no evidence to support it.

What about the famous remark supposed to have been made in Mark's prayer group at Columbia High in 1972 when *Imagine* was released? 'There were some kids in the group who had a joke about it,' one member telephoned the *Atlanta Journal* shortly after the murder. The so-called 'joke' was picked up by the rest of the world's press: 'They chanted, "Imagine, imagine if John Lennon was dead!"' Did that really happen? 'I don't know anything about it,' says Hendrix. 'I really don't know whether it was said or not or, if it was, if it was made in jest. You know how kids are! I cannot believe it was really meant – not at a prayer group, of all places!'

Two years after leaving school, Mark *did* say to a YMCA friend, David C. Moore: 'John Lennon shouldn't have said the Beatles are more important than Jesus Christ. . . . It sounds arrogant. It's only going to do the Beatles harm.' But Moore insists: 'I want to emphasize he said all this without anger. He didn't seem upset.' In other words, it was no big deal so far as Mark was concerned. It was certainly not of such continuing importance as to have been a factor in motivating him to kill Lennon five years later – as has sometimes been suggested.

In fact, by 1973, Mark's graduation year, his real rock idol, to whom he remained devoted right up to the murder and beyond, was Todd Rundgren, a musician at a totally different range of the spectrum from Lennon. Lennon even once called him 'Todd Runtgreen' after a short feud between them in the pages of the magazine *Melody Maker* when Rundgren attacked him in print: 'John Lennon isn't a revolutionary. Shouting about revolution and acting like a fool. It just makes people uncomfortable.'

For all of Rundgren's alleged use of bad language, it did not seem to put off the 'reborn Christian' Mark – nor did the fact that, as an unmarried father with two children, he did not exactly follow the church's guidelines for life-style.

His lyrics are on a totally different wave-length from Lennon's: no political attitudes for him. He adopted a diametrically opposed viewpoint. This is what he wrote in his song 'An Elpee's Worth of Toons', about 'a crazy man' who thought that he could bring about anything in the real world merely by a song:

> *A portrait of a crazy man trying to make a living out of an LP's*
> *worth of tunes.*
> *A picture of a soul in pain trying to change the world with an LP's*
> *worth of tunes.*
> *There's something at the heart of it that is simply awful.*
> *A man who makes a living off a plastic waffle.*
> *Sweat is forming on my brow.*
> *Not a thing can help me now.*

My life is on the line for an LP of tunes.
A man would simply have to be as mad as a hatter.
To try and change the world with a plastic platter.

Two years after his graduation, Mark was to tell an old schoolfriend, Miles McManus, in a recorded cassette he sent him, that this song had moved him to tears. Its message could not be more different from that of John Lennon, whose 'devout fan' Mark is supposed to have been.

The second popular misconception about Mark relates to J. D. Salinger's famous novel, *The Catcher in the Rye*. The theory is that he had always identified himself with Holden Caulfield, the book's phoney-hating sixteen-year-old hero, ever since he first read *Catcher* at the same age.

After all, this is the book that the amazed New York policemen found him quietly reading outside The Dakota when he had thrown down his gun immediately after killing Lennon – with the inscription inside the cover written by Mark: 'To Holden Caulfield from Holden Caulfield. This is my statement.' In his prison cell awaiting trial, he maintained: 'The reason I killed John Lennon was to gain prominence to promote the reading of J. D. Salinger's *The Catcher in the Rye*. I'm not saying I'm a Messiah or anything like that. If you read the book and if you understand my past . . . you will see that I am indeed "The Catcher in the Rye" of this generation.' Millions of people have heard those words spoken in Mark's flat, emotionless voice, only slightly tinged with a Southern accent, in Kevin Sim's British television documentary *The Man Who Shot John Lennon*, transmitted on both sides of the Atlantic in February 1988.

This has become one of the accepted – and I believe profoundly erroneous – motivations for the murder. *Catcher* is a very impressive book. It is required reading in many American schools as a prime example of the country's mid-twentieth-century literature. 'A crusade against phoniness,' one American critic has called it. The character of Holden, driven to near-despair by what he sees as the pervading hypocrisy of the adult world, has struck a chord with untold numbers of young readers in both Britain and America. Perhaps that is why it is one of the most banned books by local ordinances in some parts of the United States – just because it is so dangerously subversive for receptive young minds.

But that does not alter the fact that, until shortly before the murder (as we shall see later), Mark seems to have forgotten all about the fact that, in his teens, he had read the book. Despite the hordes of journalists from all around the world who descended on Decatur after Lennon's murder, and the many telephone calls that must have been made to local 'stringers' in nearby Atlanta by anguished news editors attempting to cover every possible angle of the story, not one of Mark's ex-schoolmates or teachers has ever been quoted as saying anything about the book or Mark's alleged involvement in it, let alone his identification with its main character.

The only reference to *Catcher* that I have found is not by a schoolfriend but by Vince Smith, a senior official at the South De Kalb YMCA, in his contribution to Kevin Sim's documentary. He said he 'knew Mark quite well' and continued: 'He tended to have grand ideas, passions, that would stick with him – then one day they'd be gone and another one would come by. I felt that the *Catcher* business was one of Mark's passions. I didn't see anything in there that made me think it a more serious passion than another book. In fact, I figured that maybe next week he'd have another book that he'd be trying to get everybody to read. He certainly didn't seem like Holden Caulfield to me.'

Albert Goldman in his biography of Lennon takes a view fundamentally out of line with the evidence:

> Just as Thomas a Kempis titled his famous work of devotion *The Imitation of Christ*, so Mark David Chapman might have titled his autobiography *In Imitation of Catcher*, for from the age of eighteen [in fact, sixteen], when he discovered this famous rendering of modern youth, Chapman had discovered one similarity after another between his life and that of Holden Caulfield.
>
> At first glance the parallels between the fictitious preppy from a classy WASP family . . . and the suburban mall-boy . . . are far from obvious. But if you scrape off the surface and focus on their core personalities and the cardinal episodes of their lives, you soon see why *this book became Chapman's private Bible* (my italics).

I do not see that at all – even apart from one essential difference between Holden and Mark, ignored by Goldman: that Holden was very close to his younger sister Phoebe and wanted to protect her in particular from the world's 'phoneys', whereas Mark was never close to his younger sister Susan who, like his parents, has never even chosen to visit him in prison.

If one is going in for supposition, I prefer to speculate on the possibility that, knowing that Mark had, like many other young Americans, been impressed by reading *Catcher* at a formative stage in his mid-teens, those who programmed him to shoot Lennon as the ultimate 'phoney', worked assiduously at putting into his mind the conviction that he was, in some twisted way, the real-life embodiment of Holden, the fictitious young crusader against 'phoneys'. What better 'split-personality' could you have for the victim of your programming? I say 'victim' for, if I am right, Mark David Chapman is in many ways as much the victim of those who wanted to kill John Lennon as Lennon himself.

The third popular misconception about Mark in much of the published material is that he was 'a loner', someone who found it difficult to make friends and preferred a solitary existence.

Again, this is moonshine, with no sound basis in fact and all part of the general 'lone nut' image. His mother, in the only interview she has granted (to Jim Gaines for *People* in 1987), is quite adamant: 'I've seen him described as being a loner. Are you kidding? He had lots of friends. I never had to tell him to go out and play. And when he was inside he was always on the couch talking to me. I was the one who wanted to be the loner.'

And so it has been throughout his life: with the exception of the occasional person in Hawaii who has spoken about his personality during the build-up to the murder, the remarks are generally of the same kind and generally very flattering: 'Mark was an out-going, good humoured, optimistic guy . . . Mark was – is – a gentle, compassionate man. He never lost his temper that I saw. Never violent . . . I remember Mark as one of a crowd who used to meet before school in the woods by the tennis courts to talk, maybe smoke a joint. He was really into music.' And so on.

He could always talk easily to women, young and old. He had 'the chat' and never had any problem in picking up girls, even in the street, and persuading them to come out with him or have a meal with him. He even did so when hanging around outside The

Dakota, with a gun in his pocket, waiting to kill John Lennon. Up to the last minute, he was not 'a loner'.

He had two teenage romances while still at school: first, with a girl who took part in Kevin Sim's television documentary and afterwards gave an interview to the British *Woman's Own* magazine but only on condition that her real name was not revealed. A slight whiff of hype is in the air since it was claimed that, if her real identity were known, she might be shot by an angry Lennon fan – which seems more than a little far-fetched. Even so, her words seem genuine enough: 'All the girls liked him. He was attractive, warm and friendly, and he sang and played the guitar beautifully.'

More significant was his relationship with a girl named Jessica Blankinship, whom he met when they were both around seventeen and members of the same prayer group. They were to remain close friends for four years. At one time they were in love with each other, and she was to have a great influence on him.

She is married now, with children of her own, and has always refused to give any interviews – as did her parents until I sat down with them in late May 1988. 'There was nothing devious about Mark,' says Mrs June Blankinship. 'Everybody liked him. He used to come over to our house all the time, eat and sleep there as a friend of the family. So we had a personal loss when it all happened, like one of our kids.'

Yet neither romance was sexually fulfilled. Of course, these were both respectable Christian girls in the South in the early 1970s but, even so, Mark does not seem to have been all that interested in physical involvement with the opposite sex.

But two things are clear: one, his passion for, and remarkable ability to get on with, children – 'No one was better with kids,' according to the YMCA's Vince Smith; and, two, his capacity for deep, meaningful friendships with men, especially with those a little older. 'I needed emotional love and support. I never ever got that,' he told Dr Lee Salk in prison about his childhood. 'I think my life shows that I was always trying to get it with older males; my friends were always at least two years older, and I maybe looked upon them as father figures.'

Dr Salk also quotes Mark describing a fantasy involving his father: 'I was going to break into his house, and get him in his room alone, and put a gun to him and tell him what I thought about what he had done to my mother, and that he was going to pay for it – and then I was going to blow his head off!'

This combination of mother-love and father-hate is almost textbook for men who are drawn to other men, whether they know it or not, whether they like it or not, whether they are, in fact, bisexual or homosexual. The youth with the shining apple cheeks and the nervous smile in Mark's graduation yearbook photograph was already on the way to being a highly complex individual.

8

Mark and the YMCA

Mark had not done well enough in his grades at Columbia High to go straight on to university, as many of his contemporaries did. But then he did not really want to. He had other ideas for his future.

Soon after May 1973, he left home – never again to live with his parents in their shady corner house on Green Forest Drive – and went with a friend, Michael MacFarlane, up to Chicago. The aim: to find fame and fortune as, of all things, a comedian.

'Michael was a brain but he was arrogant. He wasn't as amenable as Mark was,' said Mrs June Blankinship in May 1988. 'They went to two separate high schools but were in the same youth group at our church in Decatur. That church, under its pastor, the Rev. Charles McGowan, was the drawing card: kids came to it from all over. We had a fantastic youth group. I don't think Michael was a member of the YMCA.' 'He wasn't a YMCA person!' interrupted her husband Harold at this point.

'Anyway, they got an apartment together and Mark lived up there for several months. Mark was not steadily employed all that time, and his other plans did not work out.' He came back on his own to Decatur and, the last that Mrs Blankinship heard, Michael MacFarlane was in California studying to be a writer. I have telephoned him there but all he says is: 'I really don't want to get into this. I would rather not talk about Mark Chapman. I did not see him in Chicago in the first week of December 1980. I didn't live there then. I haven't seen him since the early 70s.'

The night that the news of Lennon's murder burst upon the United States, Mrs Blankinship had a phone call from MacFarlane in California: 'He was weeping on the phone. He was just devastated. He said that sweet guy could never have done that. It's not in his body to do that, not in his make-up.'

But, back in the mid-summer of 1973, how was Mark to cope with life? His first girlfriend who took part in Kevin Sim's 1988 television documentary under a false name said in her subsequent interview in *Woman's Own*: 'When Mark came back from Chicago he was a different person. His bubble had burst and the little world he had built for himself wasn't perfect any more. Whereas once he had been very strong – he'd supported me when my parents split up – he was now insecure.'

He turned for help to the one organization that had always given him support and hope: the YMCA. Says Tony Adams, then still executive director of the South De Kalb 'Y' (he has now moved on to Thomasville, North Carolina): 'He was a young man of moods, of ups and downs, and when he had a down he always returned to the "Y" for pumping up again. He thought the YMCA represented a lot of good in his life. He felt he always had the "Y" to fall back on.'

So, encouraged by Tony Adams, he opted for a full-time career on the permanent staff of the organization – but that meant he would have to go to university. All senior posts were only available to university graduates with a four-year degree behind them. Mark enrolled at the De Kalb Junior College, on a transitional two-year course, to get his grades up to university entrance level.

In the meanwhile, Adams put him back onto the temporary pay-roll as a counsellor on South De Kalb 'Y's' summer camp, a post he had held for at least two previous years. There was no problem about that for he was undoubtedly quite marvellous with children. He was like a modern Pied Piper of Hamelin: he never talked down to kids, he never was superior, he genuinely liked them.

If, for example, he sent them out looking for watermelons, he would make it exciting by saying they were searching for dinosaurs' eggs. They called him Nemo, after the captain in Jules Verne's *20,000 Leagues Under the Sea*. 'He was a great story teller, and the kids loved him,' Vince Smith has said.

The following summer, in 1974, they made him assistant director of the summer camp. Tony Adams has explained why: 'He had real leadership qualities. He was a very caring person. Hate was not even in his vocabulary.' After his experimentation with drugs, 'he felt like the Lord had touched him, that he had turned his life around. He wanted to prove that he was a good person, that there was no bad person inside of him.'

As Mark later said while awaiting trial: 'Jesus Christ came into my life. I was just nothing but a dope head and I asked Christ to come into my life and he came. . . . I felt forgiven of all my sins and felt like my life was headin' on the right track again. I read the Bible and I worked in inner-city Atlanta with kids that you just wouldn't believe.'

But it did not last. As was to prove the pattern of his life, Mark, amenable and soft but also a creature of moods, could not *without direction or control* maintain a steady course. He saw a lot of Jessica Blankinship. They prayed together, they went out together, they had fun together – but he still had to look elsewhere for fulfilment.

After the murder, Tony Adams explained to a reporter from the *Chicago Tribune*: 'College didn't work out. Mark wasn't below average or anything like that, but he had trouble applying himself to his schoolwork. He had a lot of disappointments in his life.'

Pushing twenty and itching to wander, Mark turned – as ever – in early 1975 to the YMCA for help. And here at this stage, bearing in mind what later happened to John Lennon and the strong probability of a continuing link between the 'Y' and the CIA, things really do get very interesting:

The year before, in 1974, the American YMCA had started a non-profit programme called ICCP/Abroad, an International Camp Counsellor Programme. It still flourishes today and, in the words of its latest brochure, 'works to further international peace and understanding through person-to-person contacts in youth camps around the world. It is an opportunity for you to inexpensively get to know people, values and customs of another country. Working side by side with other local young men and women as counsellors in a camp (or camp-like setting), you will have the chance to gain the kind of cultural understanding that few tourists can. You will also give the children at the camp a first-hand experience with an American as opposed to the image they often have through TV and the movies.'

If duly approved by both ICCP/Abroad's New York head-quarters and the relevant foreign YMCA authorities, all this is – and was in Mark's time – available for only $100 application fee plus minimal transportation costs (in fact, waived in Mark's case). Plus the youngster earns money into the bargain!

On 25 February 1975, Mark filled out his application form, and mailed it to New York. Although, as we have seen in Chapter 2, nothing survives of Mark's involvement with the YMCA in their central archives at the University of Minnesota, Bonnie Mairs of the New York headquarters of ICCP/Abroad has been good enough to dig out for me this application form, although everything else appears to have been lost.

It provides fascinating information. Everybody who has written about Mark or Lennon's murder to date has said that, in June 1975, Mark visited Beirut, Lebanon, for the YMCA – which is true and bizarre enough anyway – but his form shows that his first choice was even more strange: the Soviet Union! Why would this nineteen-year-old religious and vehemently anti-Communist Southerner, who had never before been out of the United States, opt to go to Russia of all places and, in the words of the form, 'represent the YMCA while a camp counsellor in the Soviet Union and share my experience with YMCAs and camps upon my return to US'? Mark admitted that he could not speak a word of the language but undertook to 'engage in Russian language study before departure to USSR'; and he had actually gone to the trouble of provisionally enrolling himself on a course at Georgia State University from 25 March to 6 June.

This projected trip was a special exchange and, in the end, Mark was rejected because, as Bonnie Mairs says, he 'was young and did not speak the language'. No one to whom I have spoken in Georgia, Chicago, New York or Honolulu who knew Mark has been able to give me any answer as to why Mark wanted to go to Russia in 1975. No one I have spoken to even knew about it.

One is only left with speculation, and one thinks: would not this eager, young, intense American have been an absolutely marvellous spy for the CIA in those Brezhnev years long before the *glasnost* of Mikhail Gorbachev? He would not have been the first American student recruited by the Agency to bring back information from behind the Iron Curtain. As we have already seen in Chapter 2, eight years earlier, in March 1967, *Ramparts*

Magazine had exposed the scandal of the CIA's use of students to gather information for them abroad. What could be more attractive or exciting to the dispirited, unhappy Mark than to be offered the opportunity to spy for his country for a while in the mysterious land of the Soviets and render service to 'one nation under God', as the US Pledge of Allegiance has it?

If the Russian trip was not to work out, then Lebanon, in the summer of 1975, would also have been a very useful country to which the CIA might have wanted to send Mark – but for a totally different reason than just gathering information. The late Mae Brussell, the avant-garde radio commentator on world events in Carmel, northern California, was adamant that the agency maintained training camps for assassins there at that time. She has actually named to me a prominent Palestinian in Lebanon and a leading rival of Yasser Arafat's Popular Liberation Front (PLO) as the main local political figure on the pay-roll of the agency then organizing such camps.

Even if this is too over-blown a view of CIA immersion in 'international assassination teams', to use her phrase (and it will be remembered that in Chapter 2, Daniel Sheehan of the Christic Institute was speaking about one such actual training camp in Hawaii that the institute's investigation had uncovered), there can be no doubt that violence-wracked Lebanon would have been an ideal place to 'blood' any would-be, programmed killer.

CIA involvement in the country, at the absolute centre of the volatile Middle East, goes back to at least 1952 when, according to William Blum's *The CIA: A Forgotten History*, it played a role in the Christian leader Camille Chamoun's election as president. Again in 1957, the agency 'furnished generous sums of money to Chamoun to use in support of candidates in the Chamber of Deputies June elections who would back him and, presumably, US policies'.

But that was in the days when the troubled country had at least some semblance of central government. As over the next three decades the rich Christian minority increasingly lost their political and commercial ascendancy over their Moslem compatriots, CIA involvement became ever more feverish and active. As Bob Woodward has written in his *VEIL: The Secret Wars of the CIA*: in the mid-1970s 'the CIA maintained a large presence in Beirut, the crossroads of the Middle East, the most Westernized of the Arab capitals, teeming with intrigue, as powerful and wealthy Lebanese travelled the region, providing good intelligence about less accessible Arab countries'. Many others believe that the CIA's Beirut station was far more than just an intelligence outpost, however valuable.

The ICCP/Abroad had a vastly more important and popular programme going on in Jerusalem than ever their local Moranite Christian representative Ghassan Sayyah could mount in Beirut. In fact, only one young American flew with Mark to join Sayyah – who still, even today, bravely hangs on to his office in the partly destroyed Lebanese capital.

Surely a young Southern Christian like Mark would have been more interested in visiting the Holy Land and working in the very city where Jesus Christ lived so much of his life and died than this semi-heathen modern township? 'That's a very good point you've got there. I never thought of it before,' said Harry Brunger, now representative to the UN World Alliance of YMCAs, but then a senior YMCA official overseeing the 'Y's' work in Lebanon, sitting back in his comfortable armchair at the Yale Club, New York, in June 1988. 'Why did Mark, whom I remember when he was out in Beirut, choose Lebanon? I have no idea.' When I put to Brunger that one would have thought that Mark, 'as a nice Christian lad from Atlanta', would have surely have preferred to go to Jerusalem, he agreed: 'Yes, that would have been normal.'

Tony Adams is equally baffled as to why Mark chose Beirut (which he would have had to do; he would not have been sent there without his having specifically requested it). 'Who knows? I have no earthly idea. It is beyond my comprehension. I agree with you. I would have thought he would have preferred Jerusalem.'

Whatever the answer may be, he was not in Beirut for long – less than a month, in fact. The country's second Civil War – it is now knee-deep in its protracted Third – had been simmering since April 1975 when over thirty women, children and elderly people had been killed when a busload of Palestinian and Lebanese families had been ambushed by gunmen in the Beirut suburb of Ain-Remaneh. Mounting bloodshed flared into full-scale war in late June 1975 – soon after Mark and his solitary young companion arrived at Gassan Sayyeh's office. This is Mark's own report to the

South De Kalb YMCA's board of management in October 1975 on his time in Lebanon, it has never been published before:

> Arriving in Lebanon in mid-June, Martin Andrews (an ICCP worker from Michigan) and I were taken to the YMCA youth hostel by Mr Ghassan Sayyah (director of the Beirut YMCA) on what we thought would be a three month International YMCA experience. But due to the countries [*sic*] political and religious unrest, our experience was shortened.
>
> We were to work as camp counselors in Camp Faris, a beautiful resort area in the mountains of Beirut and during the first week to prepare for our work, we went sight-seeing and worked at the Beirut YMCA telephoning families about the activities that were being offered. Then in a matter of days, the entire city was one big blasting zone, in which mortar fire and rapid machine gun sounds could be heard echoing in the streets. All vital communications were cut off for nearly a week and it seemed the 'roller coaster' effect of these outbreaks cancelled Camp Faris. Soon afterward, Bonnie Claire (another ICCP worker) and I were to leave Beirut, leaving Martin behind to fly to Cyprus to begin a non-Y refuge job there. The latest word is that the Beirut YMCA has been closed and activities are at a standstill.
>
> Returning to Atlanta, I felt discouraged but thrilled to have had an overseas experience and to see and learn so much.

His time in Beirut, however brief, had a profound impact on Mark. On the surface, while there, he struck Harry Brunger as 'just like any other kid in the "Y" from the United States. As I remember him he had a nice, calm pleasant sort of personality. Not attractive particularly. A young man who looked as if he was interested in doing good things.' He then paused and added: 'It wasn't surprising that he liked young people: in that day and age, we didn't expect every male that dealt with kids to be some homosexual guy who was trying to pervert somebody. We didn't think much about it in those days. It may have been happening but we didn't make a legal thing out of it, as we do now. It wasn't something that entered our mind.' He brought up the subject – unprompted. One wonders why?

June 1975 seems to have been the first time that Mark heard

gunfire, the whizzing of bullets, bombs bursting nearby and the screams of people in pain and dying. It etched deep into his consciousness. This 'gentle' man, who hated violence, came back from Beirut with a cassette recording that he had actually made of the barbarous sounds of warfare. He played it time and again to anyone in Atlanta who would listen. Says Harold Blankinship: 'He played us this recording he had made in his hotel room at the YMCA in Beirut of all the fighting going on. You could hear the shooting, etc. That could have affected him. He was real up-tight about it, I know that.'

Whether intentional or otherwise, Lennon's future killer had, indeed, been 'blooded' in war-torn Beirut.

But, for the moment, there he was: back in Decatur, out of work, staying again with friends, dropped out of junior college – what could he do next? He turned for help, as before, to Tony Adams. 'Tony asked me to help him,' says Bonnie Mairs, 'and we really did feel responsible for Mark after all that had happened.' The YMCA was then setting up services at a resettlement camp for Vietnamese refugees in Fort Chaffee, Arkansas. So she contacted the newly appointed director, thirty-five-year-old David C. Moore, who readily agreed to take Mark on and, over the next five months, the two men became roommates and firm friends.

Moore, now a pastor in his home town of Chicago (where Mark once briefly visited with him during his time at Fort Chaffee), has always said to many different journalists, and to me, only the very best possible things about Mark – both about his time at Fort Chaffee and generally as a person. 'I have just recently re-established communications with Mark at Attica Prison,' he told me in June 1988, 'and I am not prepared to say anything that might endanger that. Nor would I want to. The fact is I value his friendship, always did and always will. The Mark that I knew was this protective, loving, nurturing person that abhorred violence.'

I will let Mark himself speak of his time at Fort Chaffee, of what it meant to him – and of the resolve that, with David Moore's help, he then made for his future life of service within the YMCA movement. It is in part of his hitherto unpublished report to the South De Kalb YMCA's board of management in October 1975 (supplied to me by David Moore):

But Beirut was not the end. The YMCA in New York had felt responsible in some way to me for the disappointment that had occurred and in two weeks I was flown to Ft. Chaffee, Ark. to assist Mr Dave Moore (Director) in the Refugee program for the Vietnamese. The position was as an Area Coordinator in a seven block section of the actual refugee area. In charge of roughly fifteen Vietnamese volunteers and one American assistant, my job was to provide physical and leisure time activities to the (then) five thousand refugees in my area. What a blessing to work with these wonderful and truly talented people. If I could write of all the experiences and life-changing incidents that have happened, it would take hours and many pages.

The work has been long and hard. Sometimes a seventy hour week is not surprising to the area coordinators here. Also during this experience, I received a chance to attend the International Division Conference held in Houston, Texas. These conferences are held twice yearly and hold meetings that benefit everyone. I went representing you, the South Dekalb YMCA Board. Attending region meetings and meetings concerning the Far East were great experiences and when leaving Houston, I realized that the 'Y' has many programs throughout the world in eighty-six countries!

In talking with Dave Moore and considering the possibilities, I am giving serious thought to a career with the International Division of YMCA. In January, I'll be returning to school and finishing up those college years. Then hopefully a World Service Program position abroad for the next two years. I want to personally thank all of you for your help in giving me the opportunity to work with the YMCA and to serve on the South Dekalb Board of Management . . . a genuinely concerned and forward moving group of people.

A recording still exists of his voice at that time ringing out clearly over the camp radio: 'My name is Mark Chapman and I came to work at Fort Chaffee about three months ago. It's so good to work closely with the Vietnamese people and to exchange culture and ideas.' He was in his element again: striding around the camp in his Todd Rundgren T-shirt, playing with the children and organizing their games while their parents worked out their future. But, as with his YMCA time in Beirut, there was a possible

– people like the late Mae Brussell would say, 'certain' – CIA undertone. For who were these refugees that poured into the United States in April 1975 before and after the fall of Saigon, the South Vietnamese capital?

Of the estimated 120,000 people who were lucky enough, with American help, to get out of their country, some were undoubtedly those who simply did not want to live under the Communist Vietminh regime from North Vietnam. But many were those who, in some way, had supported the American cause or been otherwise actively involved in bolstering up the puppet South Vietnamese government of President Nguyen Van Thieu. The CIA had been operating in Vietnam since before 1954, when the old French colonists finally beat a retreat. Thereafter, it was the agency, under its legendary local chief General Edward Lansdale, the real-life model for the principal character in Graham Greene's novel *The Quiet American*, who led a campaign of military and psychological warfare against the Vietminh – until 1965 when President Lyndon B. Johnson sent in hordes of young US soldiers, marines, sailors and airmen to augment the struggle to preserve this endangered outpost of American influence.

Once his successor, Richard Nixon, had been forced, both by defeat in the field and mounting protest at home, to halt all offensive military operations against North Vietnam by the Paris Agreement of January 1973, Thieu had only been able to cling on to power by means of his own straggly army and with the essential continued support of the CIA and of the many 'front' organizations backed by CIA funds. However, in late 1974, the US Congress, sickening of this seemingly never-ending involvement with South Vietnam, halved financial aid to the beleaguered country. Thieu's regime was left like a rotten apple hanging on a tree branch just waiting to be picked whenever the Vietminh chose to launch one last powerful attack. In the spring of 1975, they did – and the regime collapsed.

It was against this context that the mass evacuations took place. All American civilians in the country fled by President Gerald Ford's order, including Mark's Fort Chaffee boss, David C. Moore, who had only arrived in Saigon eight days earlier to head the local YMCA. As many South Vietnamese as could use influence, money or strong-arm tactics to get out also scrambled on to the departing boats and planes. There could well have been more than a whiff of the CIA hovering over at least some of the inmates at the camp at Fort Chaffee with whom Mark was happy to 'exchange culture and ideas'.

And could not the very fact that he was there at all have been some kind of looking after its own by the agency after its grievous mistiming in Beirut?

Whatever the truth may be about that, as 1975 drew to a close, all looked really well for Mark. He had found work that he loved, he had made up his mind – seemingly definitely – on his career structure and his relationship with Jessica Blankinship had entered a new phase of closeness and commitment. In October, she had visited him at Fort Chaffee where David Moore had cooked dinner for the three of them. 'She was a lovely girl,' he told two reporters from the *Chicago Tribune* after the murder. 'When Mark and Jessica were together, he acted like a little kid with her. He was full of laughter and practical jokes. He had a wonderful laugh.'

The two agreed to enrol together at the beginning of the next year at Covenant College, a strict Presbyterian educational establishment in Tennessee, where Mark would take a four-year degree and at last qualify for a permanent life with the YMCA.

In early December 1975, the Fort Chaffee programme was running down. Nearly all the camp's eventual 29,000 refugees had been placed in the homes of sponsoring families – and Gene Scott, by then Mark's closest friend, drove in to take him back to Atlanta. This is not his real name and I do not propose to give it; for several people to whom I have spoken in Decatur and elsewhere believe that the two men, who have known each other since Columbia High School days, have complex undertones to their apparently still-continuing friendship. Certainly Mark idolized Gene, older by a few years and a handsome Rambo-like character who has never married: he is today a Georgia sheriff's officer. As we shall see later, he was to be the man who gave Mark the hollow-point bullets, not knowing (as he said) that he would then use them to shoot John Lennon.

A few weeks before Gene's arrival, Mark and David Moore had been driving by a pick-up truck that had a hunting rifle hung up in a rack behind the driver's seat. This was by no means a rare sight in Arkansas. But Mark had reacted angrily: 'That's disgusting! Why do we have to have so many guns in America?'

And now this tall, good-looking man was driving a 1350-mile round trip to collect him – with a white-handled revolver in his gear.

'As soon as Gene arrived, Mark's behaviour changed,' a co-worker told journalist Craig Unger for his article in *New York* magazine in June 1981. 'Mark cleaned his nails for Gene, he put on his clean clothes for Gene, he made telephone calls for Gene. And there was Gene's gun. Mark was so non-violent. He hated guns. I still remember them sitting in the office of the YMCA centre at Fort Chaffee, playing with this gun, looking at it, talking about it. It just wasn't like Mark. They started rough-housing, then Gene gave Mark this look. He froze.'

'We don't know much about Gene, except that he's a bad influence,' says Mrs June Blankinship. 'He came to the house several times and we tolerated him for Mark's sake only.'

Rev. Charles McGowan, the pastor at Mark's church in Decatur, describes him as 'kind of a mysterious character'. David Moore is more reticent: 'I met him. I just thought they were very good friends. I don't know who influenced whom.'

Whatever the truth may be, this is the man who drove Mark back to Atlanta to stay with him in his bachelor flat – until he went off with Jessica to Covenant College.

9

Lennon Marks Time

If 1975 was ending for Mark on a note of cautious hope, for Lennon the bells were pealing chimes of pure happiness.

On 7 October of that year, his hard-fought struggle to remain in the United States had ended in the assurance of certain victory. The US District Court of Appeals quashed the deportation order made against him, and opened the path for a new review of his application for permanent residency – with a clear indication of its own view on the matter. 'The Court cannot condone selective deportation based upon secret political grounds,' said the presiding judge. Stated the court's written judgement: 'If in our 200 years of independence we have in some measure realized our ideals, it is in large part because we have always found a place for those committed to the spirit of liberty and willing to implement it. Lennon's four-year battle to remain in the country is testimony to his faith in this American dream.'

He did not actually get his precious green card number A17-597-321 until the following June (together with the news that he could apply for full US citizenship in 1981); but that was now merely a formality.

Nor was that the only reason for a new contentment in his life.

On 9 October, two days after the court's decision, and on Lennon's own thirty-fifth birthday, Yoko gave birth to Sean Taro Ono Lennon. 'I feel as high as the Empire State Building!' exclaimed the new father.

But Yoko was forty-two. It had not been an easy pregnancy, and she had had three earlier miscarriages. They had often proclaimed their views on absolute equality between the sexes, so now she told Lennon: 'I've carried the baby and brought him into the world.

111

Now it's your turn to look after him.' He could not have agreed more. The timing was perfectly right. For the last two years, ever since they had moved into The Dakota, had not been good ones: he needed a time to withdraw from the world and find himself again – and there could be no better way than by devoting himself to the young son they had both been longing for in the home that was by now already so precious to him (the year before, they had bought their apartment on the seventh floor from the late Robert Ryan's estate and had started their process of buying a total of five apartments in the venerable block).

What had gone wrong since June 1973? It had been a powerful combination of almost everything: the continuing battle with the authorities, a falling off in the quality of his work and problems in his marriage.

The deportation struggle was not just a case of frequent visits to his attorney Leon Wildes and going to court often. The unrelenting pressure from the FBI's harassment had not lessened. For instance, on 21 September 1973, the Special Agent in Charge (SAC) of the FBI's New York office sent his director a coded teletype stating that a review of their records 'failed to indicate that Lennon or premises in which he had proprietary interest have been subjected to any lawful electronic surveillance'. What on earth did that mean? A 'failure to find evidence of' some undesirable fact is American officialdom's favourite phrase when it does not want to commit itself to a positive denial. Lennon was convinced he was still under strenuous observation; and the New York SAC was in any event only speaking for his own bureau. He was silent as to what the CIA or the Immigration and Naturalization Service (INS) were – or were not – doing.

In the following month, Lennon sued the INS under the Freedom of Information Act demanding that it affirm or deny that it had violated the law by its activities – and he made public this damning INS memorandum, entitled 'The Supervision of the Activities of Both John and Yoko Lennon', sent from 'Supervisor, Intelligence Division, Unit 2' to 'Regional Director, Group 8':

Their relations with one (6521) Jerry Rubin, and one John Sinclair (4536), also their many commitments which are judged to be political and unfavourable to the present administration. This was set forth to your office in a previous report. Because of this and their controversial behaviour, they are to be judged as both undesirable and dangerous aliens.

Because of the delicate and explosive nature of this matter the whole affair has been handed over to the I&N Service to handle. Your office is to maintain a constant surveillance of their residence and a periodic report is to be sent to this office. All co-operation is to be given to the I&N Service and all reports are to be digested by this office.

Can you imagine what 'constant surveillance' means in terms of your everyday life, knowing that you are always been watched by unfriendly eyes, your every movement monitored? It must have been appalling for Lennon and Yoko.

Liberal Americans may have been scandalized by this new revelation of what was going on in their country, but the authorities seem not to have been in the least deterred. A year later, in October 1974, Lennon was swearing an affidavit: 'I respectfully urge that the cause of justice will be advanced by permitting me to demonstrate that my case has been selectively prosecuted in a discriminatory manner; that I have been the subject of illegal surveillance activities on the part of the government; that as a result my case and the various applications filed in my behalf have been prejudged for reasons unrelated to my immigration status.'

He may, indeed, have loved America, but they were certainly making it difficult for him to remain living there.

On the artistic front, the mists were also rolling in. In November 1973, he issued *Mind Games*, his first solo album since the album *Imagine* over two years earlier. It had a certain modest success; no Lennon album could be a complete failure but it showed grievous signs of jaded creativeness. As even his sympathetic biographer Ray Coleman admits, '*Mind Games* has several pleasant tracks – notably the title song – but it suffers from too many mid-paced rockers and lacks his usual lyrical inventiveness. The old radical Lennon had gone. . . . The love poet of *Imagine* had gone. . . . Lennon sounded listless and uninspired.'

There was a remission of sorts with the single 'Whatever Gets You Thru The Night' and the album *Walls and Bridges*, both released in September 1974. Both were huge commercial successes but neither really fulfilled him. 'Whatever Gets You Thru The Night' was his first (and only) number 1 solo single since the break-up of the Beatles but its bitter-sweet melody sounded as if it could have been written by Paul McCartney, and Ray Coleman quotes Lennon's own wry comment on the best-selling new album: 'It was . . . the work of a semi-sick craftsman. There was no inspiration and it gave an aura of misery.'

The truth is· that Lennon *was* miserable at the time. He was knee-deep in the famous 'lost weekend', his own phrase for those disastrous fifteen months that he spent away from Yoko in Los Angeles between October 1973 and January 1975. In the *Playboy* interviews recorded in September 1980 and published soon after his death, both gave fundamentally the same explanation (but viewed from their different stand-points) of this major crisis in their marriage:

Yoko: 'By then it was getting obvious to even the most unworldly couple that the world didn't really want us to work together. John wanted to insist on it. It was not only bad, it seemed, for John's career but in a way I lost my career. I mean, I could do something as Mrs Lennon but I really lost my identity as Yoko Ono. . . . I said to John we're both still young, and we have a beautiful future. Why kill it by trying to be together? Let's give ourselves a chance and see what happens.

'I said, "Look, why don't you just go to L.A. and have fun. And leave me alone." I just wanted to think straight because I couldn't think straight anymore.'

Lennon: 'She literally said, "Get out!" and I thought, "Okay, okay, I'm going." I hadn't been a bachelor since I was twenty or something, so at first I thought, whoopee! . . .

'And then I woke up one day and thought, What is this? I want to go home. But Yoko wouldn't let me home. That's why it was eighteen months [in fact, fifteen] instead of six. Because we were talking all the time on the phone and I kept saying, "I don't like this, I'm out of control, I'm drinking, and I'm getting into trouble, and I'd like to come home." She's saying, "You're not ready to come home." Okay, back to the bottle . . .'

Everyone knows the story of those hard-drinking, time-wasting, stupid months in Los Angeles consoled by the young May Pang, their secretary whom a thoughtful Yoko Ono suggested that he take along. It was a dissipation of his talents – but it also served a purpose. As Elliot Mintz, a Los Angeles-based media consultant and a long-standing friend of both of them, told Andrew Solt in January 1988 for the film *Imagine: John Lennon*, 'The lost weekend was a combination of remarkable party, an exercise into the depths of foolishness, and I think John's last effort to assert his manhood. It was his departure from his youth, to becoming a man, to wanting to be with Yoko, to having a child. Some people have bachelor parties, John had a lost weekend.'

The simple truth was that it taught Lennon that he could not work or live without Yoko Ono. It was a great love story; even if, as Yoko herself said, 'Neither of us was an angel,' soon after Albert Goldman's biography *The Lives of John Lennon* appeared in August 1988 to cause so much unhappiness. In an interview with Francis Schoenberger in the early spring of 1975 but not published until October 1988 in the magazine *Spin*, Lennon said: 'I just walked in and thought "I live here; this is my home. Here is Yoko, and here is me . . .`."'

The following month Yoko became pregnant and they seemed on course for straightening out their lives – except for the still-continuing deportation proceedings. 'Why do you think the immigration people are making it so difficult for you to stay here?' Francis Schoenberger asked him. Lennon's reply was battle-weary: 'It keeps all the conservatives happy that they are doing something about me and what I represent. And it keeps the liberals happy that I am not thrown out. So everybody is happy – but me! I am still being harassed.'

Asked if he felt he was being used, he said: 'Yeah. It keeps all the other pop stars in line. In case they get any ideas about reality. Keep them in their place. They also hassle Paul, George, Mick Jagger . . . obviously Keith Richard.' Why had they not got David Bowie in their sights? 'They probably just think he's something from the circus! He's never been busted and he didn't get mashed up with lunatics like Jerry Rubin. And Abbie my boy Hoffman.'

At that low ebb in his political fortunes, he obviously felt used by those two as well. 'I never see them. They vanished into the woodwork. . . . Jerry has been nothing but trouble and a pain in the neck since I met him. I decided, as he didn't lead the revolution, I decided to quit answering the phone.'

In June 1975, he was telling Pete Hamill for *Rolling Stone* that he was 'jumpy' and 'nervous' even 'commenting on politics'. He said he was 'sick of being in crusades'.

Then came his great victory in the US District Court of Appeals and the birth of Sean. After that, he could not get out of the active world fast enough. He rushed through an album of his best work since the break-up of the Beatles (*Shaved Fish*) and announced his temporary withdrawal from public life. He was going to be a house-husband and look after his new son's early years, while Yoko handled their business affairs.

As he later told Barbara Graustark of *Newsweek* in September 1980, in his first interview when this period was over:

The mind is cluttered. You can fake it and be a craftsman and put out paintings if you're Picasso, or records if you're a pop singer. And you might get away with it. And the business will let you get away with it. And the public will let you get away with it. You know, inside. So in order to get that clear channel open again I had to stop picking up every radio station in the world, in the universe. So my turning away from it is how I began to heal it again. I couldn't see the wood for the trees. Or I couldn't hear the music for the noise in my own head.

It was not an abdication from the real world but rather a retreat into it.

It is these next five years of Lennon's life that most come in for attack in ex-Columbia University English Professor Albert Goldman's lurid biography. In 1984, Ray Coleman's biography, written with Yoko's encouragement, gave what one might call the 'official' view of this vital period so close to Lennon's sudden death:

His attention to Sean was total. The baby was fed, washed, bathed, dressed and taught to read by him. He hated changing his nappies but he did it all the same. No babysitters were needed. When Sean was about six months old John saw a pimple on him. Agitated, he went right round twenty offices and domestic staff forbidding them to give Sean sugar of any kind in his diet: 'Sean may not have come out of my belly but I'm gonna make his bones.'

And Coleman backs up this picture of ideal contentment – and commitment – with a quotation from Elliot Mintz: 'I remember reading that Brian Epstein once said he was happiest when the four Beatles and he were in a room together, without anyone else, before a concert. For me, during those five years, John and Yoko and little Sean together as a family in The Dakota embodied everything that was special between lovers.'

You could argue that both Coleman and Mintz, as long-standing friends of both Lennon and Yoko, were biased and to a certain extent interested parties. They could also, of course, still be telling the truth as they saw it.

As against that, Goldman states:

By 1978 Lennon had ceased to resemble himself. Wasted by dieting, fasting and self-induced vomiting, he weighed only 130 pounds. Totally enervated by lack of purpose and exercise, he rarely left his bed. Drugged all day on Thai stick, magic mushrooms, or heroin, he slept much of the time and spent his waking hours in a kind of trance. Though he kept up the pretence of running the house and taking care of Sean, he was so zonked out that his presence in the apartment was hardly noticed. People who worked for the family would say, 'Is there a real John Lennon?'

Which version of the man's final years is the right one: Goldman's or Coleman's – which basically is the same as everybody else's apart from Goldman and corresponds with the picture painted by Lennon himself in his interviews in the autumn of 1980? In a sense, you could argue that it does not matter for the purposes of this book. This is an investigation into the circumstance of his murder not the manner of his living. Whatever the truth may be about this period so close to his death, does not alter the vital fact that, if there was a conspiracy to assassinate him, it would have been grounded in the public perception of him and not upon the inner reality of the man.

After all, the last-but-one document in my swadge of papers from the FBI's file on Lennon is dated 7 July 1976, when his deportation battle was well over and he had already been retired from public life for the better part of a year. Yet it still apparently contains such sensitive material to the official mind that, when it was released eleven years later, in September 1987, the entire text was massively blacked out – except for one little inked phrase in the margin overlooked by the bureau's censor which shows clearly that a copy had gone to the CIA.

So the agency was still interested in Lennon, even if Goldman is right and the singer *was* already on the way to spiritual and physical self-destruction.

And we have already seen, back in Chapter 5, that the very last page of the FBI swadge, dated 13 August 1976, from the bureau's New York office states:

> No investigation should be conducted concerning subject but your sources should be alerted to the subject's presence in the area covered by your office. Any information developed indicating activity outside the scope of the intended purpose while in the United States should be promptly furnished to the bureau.

Richard Nixon was no longer even president then; it was Gerald Ford. But the FBI and the CIA were still keeping their tabs on Lennon, even after he had been granted his green card and was in seclusion. They were doing this because he was perceived by the outside world to be in perfect health and in full command of his senses: not spending his waking hours 'in a kind of trance'.

Yet one still needs to examine the issue of Lennon's condition in the years of his house-husband period, not only out of respect for his memory but also because of the need to assess all the relevant facts about his murder. If Goldman's account is correct, then it really is the most pathetic irony that anyone should have felt it necessary to conspire to remove such a zombie-like figure from the world: he surely posed a threat to no one except possibly to himself. On the other hand, if Goldman is wrong, it makes the tragedy of 8 December 1980 even greater.

There can be no doubt which is the answer.

The Goldman book received predominantly scathing reviews both in Britain and the United States, although that did not prevent its apparently being a huge commercial success in the United States, less so in Britain. The British reading public were perhaps more affected by the critics' strictures and by other such factors as Paul

McCartney's and Elton John's call for everyone to boycott the book and Cynthia Lennon's dismissal of its author as 'a vulture', not to mention her son Julian's description of it as 'Crap, lies and untruth. The whole thing is just sickening.'

Both Jon Wiener in the *Los Angeles Times* and David Fricke and Jeffrey Ressner in *Rolling Stone* brought out the fact, ignored by Goldman, that two of his most important sources for the two last – and 'worst' – years might have had highly suspect testimony. One was Fred Seaman who, in 1979–80, had been Lennon's gofer and a trusted employee at The Dakota. Goldman did not tell his readers that the New York publishers Simon & Schuster refused to release Seaman's own book on Lennon written after the murder and sued him for $500,000, because they had 'grave doubts about the veracity and source of the book's contents'. Furthermore, in July 1983, he was put on probation for five years for second-degree grand larceny after having pleaded guilty to stealing his late employer's personal diaries, unreleased recordings, stereo equipment and other personal effects. When Simon & Schuster cancelled his book, he began collaborating with Goldman.

The other alleged ex-Dakota intimate much relied upon by the worthy ex-professor was Marnie Hair, a neighbour of Lennon and Yoko's. She was quite vocal on Lennon's more bizarre antics. But again Goldman did not think fit to inform his readers that Hair sued Yoko for $1,500,000 in 1983 after her daughter was injured in an accident at Yoko's house on Long Island – and had to settle her claim for a mere $18,000 paid by insurers into a trust fund.

It was predictable that Yoko herself, in interviews in the press, on radio and on television, both in the United States and in Britain, would say how much she had been hurt by the book, how untrue it was and what a false picture it painted of her late husband. But I was personally most affected by the contribution of Sean Lennon, then only twelve years old, to the debate. Early in the book, at page fifteen, Goldman writes: 'If in a rare access of parental affection he takes Sean on his knee, John will make sure to set the child facing away from him so that the boy will not have the opportunity to paint a wet, smacky kiss on his father's face.' Sean's comment (to Elliot Mintz on a Westwood One Special aired on the Los Angeles radio station KMPC-FM in September 1988): 'I'd kiss him, I'd sit on his lap – all the time – any way I wanted to. What he writes is just stupid. Dad was a great person as a father. He did twenty years of fathering in the five years that I knew him.'

But the *coup de grace* to the credibility of this part of Goldman's book is given by Goldman himself. He begins page 605 with the bold paragraph that I have already quoted about Lennon by 1978 having 'ceased to resemble himself', with the specific assertion halfway through the text: 'He rarely left his bed.' Yet on the very next page, describing Lennon's visits to the Caribbean and Japan that self-same year, appear these passages:

> . . . in the spring of 1978 Yoko . . . took the whole family to the Caribean Club on Grand Cayman Island . . . After arriving in a Learjet from Miami, the Lennons settled in a private cottage on the beach, where they enjoyed a sunny vacation until it was time to fly to Japan for their summer vacation . . . Every day (in Japan) John swam in the hotel's splendid pool, often with Sean . . . For the rest he doubtless enjoyed his daily naps and his health food meals, which alternated with visits to fine restaurants, where he sampled the delicacies of Japanese cuisine, including Kobe beef, which was one of John's favourite dishes in Japan . . . He also bought a lot of clothes, including silk kimonos, Japanese footwear, and other items of Oriental apparel, which he mixed tastefully with his Western costumes.

In my view, little credence can be put upon Albert Goldman's account of Lennon's house-husband years. The man whom Mark David Chapman shot was not a drug-wrecked shadow of his former self.

In truth, Lennon was growing in stature in the five years 1975–1980. He devoted himself to Sean while Yoko took over the financial and business side of their life (and with her natural skill, perhaps inherited from her banker father, made them even richer); but his mind was also developing. Norman Seaman, an old friend who got his nephew Fred his job as Lennon's gofer, told David Fricke and Jeffrey Ressner for their *Rolling Stone* article that he frequently went with Lennon to the theatre in the late 1970s. 'We spent a very exciting evening with Carly Simon and James Taylor at a Merce Cunningham one performance,' he said. 'We talked for hours, everyone hanging on every one of John's words. And they are not exactly people who are easily impressed.

'He was educating himself in that period. When he was in [his bedroom], he wasn't zonked out at all. He'd be all hopped up to talk about philosophy. He had a tremendous gift for gab. He wasn't zonked out on drugs. He wasn't anorexic. That's all bullshit.

'He was a more fully developed mature person at the end of 1980 than he had ever been in his life.'

Robert Hilburn, pop music critic of the *Los Angeles Times*, commenting on what he calls Goldman's 'suspect' biography, confirmed this warmth and awareness of Lennon: 'Over the course of more than a dozen encounters from 1973 to 1980 (both formal interviews and casual dinners), Lennon was as engaging as anyone I've met in rock. Unlike pop stars who are often guarded or overly calculating during interviews, he seemed uncommonly open and real. He was invariably warm, invigorating, candid and fun – and almost never pretentious.'

He could still be capable of the old 'bed-ins' kind of foolishness. In May 1979, he and Yoko ran a long 'love letter' to their fans as a paid advertisement in New York, London and Tokyo: 'Sean is beautiful. The plants are growing. The cats are purring. More and more we are starting to wish and pray . . . Wishing is . . . effective. It works . . . Magic is real. The secret of it is to know that it is simple, and not to kill it with an elaborate ritual which is a sign of insecurity. We love you.' Even the loyal Jon Wiener comments: 'Almost everybody shrugged. Those who still cared about John were appalled.'

But his heart was in the right place. For all the vast wealth that Yoko accumulated, with their four other apartments bought in The Dakota; four farms purchased in the Catskill mountains, Virginia, Vermont and upstate New York; 250 heads of prize Holstein cattle; a stunning weekend home on Long Island over-looking the Atlantic; a beachfront mansion in Florida and a 63-foot ocean-going yacht, he somehow remained loyal in his own mind to his basic principles. In his *Playboy* interview in September 1980, he was to say: 'In the late 1960s and 1970s I dabbled in so-called politics more out of guilt than anything. Guilt for being rich, and guilt thinking that perhaps love and peace isn't enough and you have to go and get shot or something, or get punched in the face, to prove I'm one of the people.'

Unknown to the general public, he and Yoko in 1979 gave

$100,000 to set up a non-profit organization they called the Spirit Foundation to donate money to charitable groups in New York. Most of the groups helped abused children, orphans and the poor but a grant of $1000 went to a campaign to provide the city's policemen with bullet-proof vests. Lennon's sheer joy and gratitude at living in the Big Apple and in his apartment at The Dakota, now extended to include the whole seventh floor, had not abated.

During the house-husband years, he and his family travelled a lot – especially to Japan, where he immersed himself in an entirely new culture and he even took on the daunting task of trying to learn Japanese.

But he was perhaps at his happiest in New York itself, walking the streets without molestation or wandering in Central Park with Yoko or Sean – or dropping in on about four afternoons a week to Vincent Urwand's Cafe La Fortuna at 69 West 71st Street, one block away from The Dakota. There he would sit, have a *cappucino*, smoke a Gitane cigarette, read a newspaper or chat to any cordial person who happened to be there. 'He was a lovely man, a marvellous man,' remembers Urwand's Italian wife, Alice. In her cosy little coffee shop, where they sell coffee, hot chocolate and delicious pastries, photographs of long-dead and half-forgotten Italian opera singers line the rough red brick walls – except for a corner near the Espresso machine, where hangs a photograph of Lennon, Yoko and Sean. 'Yoko gave us that as a present, because she knew how much John liked coming here,' says Alice Urwand.

In the shop window of the West Side Pharmacy just round the corner, on Columbus Avenue, a photograph of Lennon is displayed to this day. 'He was a good guy, a friend. He'd come in here just like anyone else,' explains the owner.

Yet despite all this quiet contentment, one thing was missing. Four months after Sean had been born, Lennon's recording contract with EMI/Capitol had expired and he had not renewed it. For the first time in fifteen years, he was not tied to a recording deal. Effectively, he had walked away from making music. For nearly five years, he had not written any songs. He had not even listened to any contemporary rock. He was a musician without music.

Then, in July 1980, while holidaying on their yacht with Sean in Bermuda, with Yoko back in New York, he walked into the Forty Thieves Disco on the island. 'Rock Lobster', a track by the new wave group B.52's, was playing. Its sound reminded him of Yoko's music of ten years earlier. He called her excitedly the next day. 'They're ready for you this time!' And that meant *he* was ready to come back as well. They would do an album together. The songs began pouring out of him 'like diarrhoea', as he later told Barbara Graustark. He would call 'Mother', his Freudian nickname for his wife, and sing them to her over the telephone. She would write a song in reply. Within two weeks, they had twenty-two songs between them – nearly enough for two albums, not just one.

By now, he even had the title: 'I was walking in the Botanical Gardens in Bermuda, taking Sean and the nanny and the household, my little kitchen entourage,' he told Barbara Graustark. 'We all went to lunch and I looked down and there was this flower.' It was an orchid, and its name was 'Double Fantasy'.

On 12 August 1980 a press release announced that Lennon had come out of retirement and that he and Yoko were working on a new album. Immediately the news flashed around the globe. Lennon was back where he belonged: making music and bringing his voice to the world.

10

Mark's Life Changes

For all his hopes of success, Mark did not do well at Covenant College, the strict Presbyterian establishment in Tennessee where he and Jessica had enrolled. In fact, he only lasted one semester there.

Mrs June Blankinship says: 'He was there after the first of the year 1976 and through the spring. I think the trouble was that he needed the college to go further with the "Y", that was his ambition; but he got up there and began to exhibit emotional problems. I don't want to talk much about it but he and Jessica did seek the counselling of one of their professors.

'Some of the newspapers tried to say that he flunked out but Jessica said he did not. She said that his grades were not all that bad.'

But whatever they were, they made this moody young man give up all hope of a degree and, with it, a career in the YMCA. 'I wasn't enough of a Christian,' Jim Gaines quotes him as saying. It also cost him any chance of a lasting relationship with Jessica Blankinship. She still remained very fond of him, but she did her best to make it clear to him that they had no future as a couple.

What to do? Mark fell back, as ever, on the YMCA, even though he had blotted them out as a long-term prospect.

But now even that temporary shelter did not suffice. Within a month of taking up his usual mid-year job as assistant director of the South De Kalb YMCA's summer camp, he walked out after losing his temper with a parent of one of the campers. That door was also now closed to him.

He had to earn money, so what did he do – this young man who everyone says until then was known for his non-violence

124

and his abhorrence of guns? He got a job as an armed security guard. It was Gene Scott's suggestion. And, in a sense, why not? The two men were sharing an apartment, they were close friends, Gene wore a gun to go to work as a sheriff's officer; there could have been no good reason why Mark should not do the same as a security guard. But it does seem a strange choice of occupation for this devout, God-fearing Southerner who only a few months earlier had been fulminating at David Moore when they had seen that Arkansas hunter's rifle stacked behind the driver's seat in a pick-up truck. 'That's disgusting! Why do we have so many guns in America?' he said.

He certainly had an aptitude for the job. He went on a pistol-training course at the Atlanta Area Technical School. He needed to score 60 out of 100 to pass, and notched up an impressive 88. Natural ability – or had he perhaps been a little helped by his 'blooding' in Beirut the previous year?

Mrs Blankinship says: 'That summer, after he went into being a security guard, living with Gene, his personality began to change. He became quickly angry – just a trigger! He could just explode, and so then's when we began to be concerned, really concerned, about him. But we didn't know what to do with him. He claimed that his parents had more or less kicked him out. They had gone and built another house and didn't, I understand, even build a room for him – that's what he told us. We didn't know for sure. There are always two sides to every question.' (In fact, David Chapman, in one of his rare comments to the press, told a reporter from the *New York Times* soon after the murder that his son had not lived at home since his Columbia High School days when he was 'industrious, cheerful, likeable'. 'He hasn't been a member of the household since he was seventeen or eighteen,' he said.)

The next thing the Blankinships knew was that Mark had left Atlanta for Hawaii. 'I was stunned,' says Mrs Blankinship. 'We didn't know why. That was the worst thing. I couldn't figure it out.' Says her husband Harold: 'He did not come to say goodbye. We did not know he was gone until somebody told us. It didn't sound like the boy we knew.'

Why did Mark uproot from his nearly native soil in Atlanta, sell his car and most of his other personal belongings and fly off halfway round the world to that exotic cluster of islands in the middle of the Pacific Ocean? 'To kill himself,' says Jim Gaines in

People magazine in both 1981 and 1987. 'Nonsense!' David Moore told me in May 1988. 'It was quite the opposite. To start a new life. I had been through Hawaii myself to kind of "de-compress" on my way back from Saigon and I had talked about it a lot to Mark at Fort Chaffee, and I think he was also impressed by the Asian quality of serenity and calmness that he had witnessed among the refugees at the camp.' Hawaii is geographically and, in many ways, spiritually closer to Asia than to the mainland United States, although it was annexed by the US in 1898 and became the fiftieth state of the Union in August 1959.

To be fair to Jim Gaines, Craig Unger in *New York* magazine in June 1981 also quoted an unnamed friend of Mark's as saying that Mark told him 'he went there with the idea of killing himself. He said that was his biggest dream'; and many other journalists have given the same reason. But the explanation that he gave at work was simply that he had always wanted to go to Hawaii. Interviewed in May 1988, a woman colleague in ARC Security Inc.'s office in Atlanta, who would only give her name as 'Mary', laughed outright at the suggestion that he had gone to Hawaii to kill himself. 'No! That's a funny one! He did his job, gave nobody any problems. He was an alright guy. He did not strike me as the sort of person who would go off and kill himself. No way! He never said anything that would make me think he intended to do anything like that.'

Perhaps predictably, the late Mae Brussell in Carmel had an alternative theory: 'There are mind control places in Hawaii. There are hospitals there where it would be very convenient for that sort of thing to be going on. There are a lot of military and naval bases in Hawaii where we send all kinds of people to do all kinds of secret things.'

She could have been right, she could have been wrong. She could give me the same of no single hospital to support her charge. But the fact remains that in recent times the islands have always had a strong US military and naval presence. Around Honolulu alone, the state capital on the island of Oahu which is the most populated of the seven inhabited major islands, there were in 1976–77 no less than seven major military and naval bases, including Pearl Harbour itself.

But, of course, the islands are also one of the most beautiful places in the world, visited by millions of tourists every year seeking sun and paradise for a short while. Others come for a longer time, because they are ordered to, as part of their job: 'Hawaii is a very transient place,' a local inhabitant told me in September 1987. 'It's not only the military – and they move around a lot – but it's the corporate people as well. This is a stopping station on the way up the ladder. You prove your worth here and they move you on up back to the mainland.' Still others come to the islands for good, searching for a peace and a serenity they cannot find at home.

One can only make one's own assessment into which of these two latter categories Mark fits: working under orders programmed into his brain or seeking internal peace running away from his problems, his family, perhaps even Gene Scott. Whatever the answer, it was to Honolulu International Airport that Mark flew in January 1977.

As with every other major project in his life, he started off with great hopes and in high style. He did not book into one of the many cheap hotels in Waikiki, the tourist section of Honolulu, but selected the stately Moana Hotel, one of the oldest and loveliest, right on the beach with a breath-taking view of flat-topped Diamond Head Mountain to the left and the shimmering coastline of Oahu Island to the right.

For a brief while, he gave himself a holiday, sipped Mai Tais in the hotel's Banyan Court and went on many of the cheap tours and excursions that are always available to the tourist. But then it began to pall. What was he wasting his money on? As anyone who has been there will know, Waikiki may be fun if you are in holiday mood, with money to burn and you like drinking a lot of Mai Tais. But it is not the real Hawaii: it is like any other international mass tourist centre – and, if you are on your own and uncertain, it can be very depressing. Especially when everyone around you is having a really great time – or at least loudly telling themselves that they are.

After his initial splurge, Mark had to count the pennies. He moved out of the Moana and into Honolulu's YMCA hostel.

But that did not make him feel any better. It was, as always, scrupulously clean as well as being cheap – but he did not even have the brashness of the large hotels and crowded bars to take him out of himself. He telephoned home to Jessica telling her how miserable he was. She was still fond of him, felt sorry for him. She told him to come back to Atlanta.

And, using up even more money, that is what he did. But that also did not work out. He was only back home for a very short while: Jessica's parents did not even know he was in town. As soon as he realized that Jessica wanted him back because she thought it was best for him and not because she thought it was best for *them*, he once again boarded a plane and flew back to Honolulu. And to the YMCA hostel.

It was *then*, and not earlier, that he first seriously thought of suicide. He realized that he needed help, and he picked up the telephone to a suicide hotline. They said he should go to the Waikiki Mental Health Clinic – and he did. Anne Jones (that is not her real name – according to her, she asked Jim Gaines not to quote her by name but he still did in his first article in *People* in February 1987 and she does not want a repeat of the publicity that it caused her) is the psychiatric social worker who dealt with him there: 'I only knew him for about two to three weeks in that summer of 1977,' she told me, when we spoke at length in September 1987. 'But it was very spotty and very intense at the same time because we were working on a crisis basis.'

What was wrong? 'He was depressed and had a lot of concerns about making a new life in Hawaii, finding a job, making a living – Hawaii is an expensive place to live – and about his girlfriend Jessica. He was putting more on the relationship than I believe was there. He was hung up tremendously on this girl and she had rejected him right along but he wasn't seeing that.

'The trouble with Mark was that he had to do the right thing, you know. He was almost like one of those kids from upper middle-class families that have to do the right thing. "I do everything one's supposed to do but things still don't turn out right." They can't understand it! That was Mark's attitude – and one of the things that hadn't turned out right was Jessica. He really wanted this girl and why didn't she want him? He did all the right things, he bought her roses – and I can't remember what else he said he did – and still she wouldn't have him. I'd say: "Mark, these things happen, you know. Get on with your life" – but he couldn't get off that.'

Okay, but not every love-lorn young man ends up shooting John Lennon. There must have been other things bugging him?

'Yes, of course, there were! The Jessica thing was only part of it. He was very unhappy. He told me about his episode with drugs in high school, his relations with his family, his YMCA camp days.' And Beirut? 'Yes, he told me about that too; but that was different. *He was proud of that, very proud.* (my italics) That was a period when he had done well. People thought well of him. That was very important to him.'

(But work this out: why should he have been so 'very proud' of his Beirut trip, if all he had done was go there and then have to scurry home within a month because of the civil war? There was nothing particularly commendable in that. Or was his attitude a Freudian acknowledgement that he had, in some way, proved himself in Beirut, so that 'people thought well of him' for what, as a virtual trainee, he had accomplished there?)

At first, Anne thought Mark needed to be hospitalized. She actually took him along to a private hospital in Honolulu, where he could have been treated on state welfare, but it was very crowded and they did not have a bed. She did not want him to go to the large impersonal state-run hospital that was available, so they agreed – and he was leaving all the decisions to her – that they would see how he went with anti-depressant medication and therapeutic sessions with her. He was happier not going into hospital because he was doing day labour work, to earn some money, and he did not want to let his employer down – 'There, you see, always wanting to do the right thing!' says Anne.

But then she came into work one morning at the clinic, and found Mark sitting waiting for her with a burnt hosepipe in his hands. He told her that on the previous evening he had driven a hire-car over to the deserted north side of the island, fitted the hosepipe from a vacuum cleaner to the exhaust tube, fed it back into the car, then got into the driving seat and turned on the ignition with all windows and openings closed as tight as he could – shut his eyes and waited to die. But all that happened was a Japanese fisherman knocked at the window, thinking he had fallen asleep with the engine running. Mark could not understand it: why wasn't he dead yet? He got out of the car and saw that the hot exhaust had burned a hole in the hosepipe.

'This poor kid can't even kill himself right,' Anne Jones thought to herself.

There are two kinds of suicide attempts: those where the person really means to kill himself and those where he only half means to do so. He is really trying to call attention to himself. It is a cry for help. 'That is what Mark's was,' says Anne. 'As he was telling me about the whole malarkey where he got the hosepipe through the open hatchback door of the car and tried to seal up the gap with towels and things, I knew that even he must have realized it really was not going to work.'

Still, she was not going to take any chances. She put through a call to the Castle Memorial Hospital at Kailua on the other side of the island, where she knew they had just opened a new health services unit and they said they would be happy to take him in. So far they only had three patients in the unit. Anne drove him over at once – and, in the car, for want of anything else to talk about, they talked about their favourite types of music. Anne told him she preferred classical music. He said he liked modern music – 'but he did not mention the Beatles or John Lennon'.

The Castle is a private hospital but Mark's fees were paid by state welfare and he was given every attention. Anne went to his first case-conference and they all seemed very pleased with him. Mark himself told her how much happier he was, and insisted on showing her around. 'He seemed to be doing very well,' she emphasizes, and this is important for what happened later: 'I never detected one whiff of psychosis in him.'

And this was so at Castle where, as they later told Allen Sullivan, the New York County Assistant District Attorney (but have never made public to anyone else), they diagnosed him as suffering from severe depressive neurosis but did not find him to be psychotic – i.e., labouring under a mental illness. Nevertheless, ever since he killed Lennon he has consistently and inaccurately been described in the media as 'an ex-mental patient'. He was not. That is one more myth about this case.

In fact, he made such good progress that he was out of hospital in only two weeks. But he had proved so popular there, and he so much preferred the peace and tranquillity of the small town of Kailua and its surrounding area that he made a major decision. Kailua is only sixteen miles from Honolulu and easily reached by the fast-moving Pali Highway that cuts the island in two; but, as I have seen for myself, the Kailua region is in another world where, on the other side of the Koolau tree-covered mountain range, even the weather is different – milder and more relaxing. So Mark did not go back to Honolulu. He moved into a small apartment at 112 Puwa Place on the modern Aikahi Gardens Estate on the outskirts of Kailua, an idyllic spot nestling calmly between hills and ocean.

And here at once there is a mystery that has never before been revealed. His Hawaiian driving licence that he had on him when he was arrested for Lennon's murder gave his address at the date of issue as 112 Puwa Place, and I have checked for myself that it was issued on 29 July 1977. This is fine. It would more or less tie in with when he came out of hospital and oriented himself to living on that side of the island.

Furthermore, postal records show that nearly two years later, in May 1979, Mark moved to another address in Kailua. That was the home of Rev. Peter Anderson, the pastor of Mark's small Presbyterian church, and his wife Martha. This again causes no difficulty: I have been told that for a while before his marriage in June 1979 Mark took a room in the Andersons' house. I cannot give more details as Mr Anderson has refused to talk to me about Mark: 'As a pastor, I don't discuss with anyone people that I already know,' he said over the telephone.

But what is strange is that, after the murder, the *Honolulu Star-Bulletin*, after saying that Mark's driving licence showed that in 1977 he had been living at 112 Puwa Place, continued:

The owner of the apartment said Chapman lived there with a woman and three young children, possibly her sisters. The apartment had been rented by the woman's mother, the owner said.

The landlord said Chapman, the woman and children lived there about six months and 'skipped out in April' this year [1980] with the rent unpaid, leaving the place in a mess. It took $2000 worth of clean-up to get the place back in shape.

She said the electricity bill had not been paid, and the tenants had spent that last month in the apartment without electricity.

Now what on earth is that all about? How does that tie in with Mark's life on the island so far as we have always known it? Of course, it does not. Local journalist Walter Wright says that he and his colleagues 'spent hours' trying to trace this woman and her young sisters and to follow up the landlord's story but in the end came to the conclusion that the whole thing was a mistake. 'It must have been another Mark Chapman,' says Wright.

But this does not make sense either. If it was another 'Mark Chapman' who lived at 112 Puwa Place, why did *our* Mark Chapman give that as his address when applying for his Hawaiian driving licence? Furthermore, Mrs Jean Capotani, who later worked in the management office of the Aikahi Gardens Estate, has been kind enough to check the records for me. She writes that, although 'they show nothing on Mr Chapman's stay here,' the postman – who, alas, did not deliver mail to the estate in the late 1970s – has told her that 'he still gets mail for "Mr Chapman" now and then.' This must be 'our' Mr Chapman because the postman also told Mrs Capotani that 'Mr Chapman's parents-in-law still live in Kailua,' which Mr and Mrs George Abe, Gloria's parents, indeed do. Furthermore, Mrs Capotani writes that her son has told her that the Aikahi Gardens 'Mr Chapman' worked at the Castle Hospital. And there is as I have already said, the unrebuttable fact of the Aikahi Gardens in 'our' Mark's driving licence.

Mark worked at the Castle from August 1977 to November 1979, first as a maintenance worker then promoted to the customer relations department, where his supervisor Paul Tharp said he displayed 'a remarkable gift towards graphics, particularly in the area of printing'. Like almost every other employer Mark ever had, Tharp found him an 'outgoing type' and an 'excellent employee': those are the words he later used to Walter Wright.

In the quiet atmosphere of the hospital and in that more serene part of the island, he seems at last to have got over his obsession with Jessica Blankinship. He found a new girlfriend, a psychiatric nurse at the Castle, and when, after four months, that friendship ended, he transferred his affections to another local girl working at the hospital, on the catering staff. This time, alas, she was a little like Jessica – she was wary of him, put off by his persistence and his excessive devotion.

In December 1977, his parents visited him and it was a good time for all three of them. Mark could show off his new stability, and at last it seemed as if they could stop worrying about him. In any event, now they had their own problems: soon after returning to Atlanta, David and Diane Chapman began divorce proceedings after twenty-four years of marriage. Towards the end of 1978,

Diane returned alone to the islands to live and Mark found her an apartment near to his own.

But before that, in the summer of 1978, Mark did something else which – like the episode in Beirut – seems out of the ordinary. This young man in his early twenties, with very restricted financial resources, went on a journey around the world.

Why on earth did the twenty-three-year-old Mark, at last beginning to get his feet firmly on the ground, with a job where he was content and got on well with everyone, suddenly take it into his head to go off around the world – which few people are lucky enough to do even in their retirement after having worked for over forty years? We shall probably never know the real reason. All that Jim Gaines says in his three articles in *People* magazine in 1987, written with Mark's full cooperation, is: 'In 1978, buoyed by a loan from the hospital's credit union, Chapman decided to see the world.'

Let us pause for a moment to consider the cost of all this. I have tried to check with the credit union at the Castle as to whether they did, in fact, lend Mark the money with which to make this trip – for which the airfare alone would have set him back well over $1000. Quite properly, they have refused to release any information on the ground of confidentiality. But is it really likely that they would have financed this ex-patient and new junior employee in their maintenance department, for, of all things, a trip around the world? Where was the collateral? What guarantee did they have that he would even come back? He had only been in Hawaii just over a year when he began planning the trip, for in a letter to David Moore in April 1978, he was already referring to his having arranged 'loaned money'.

So who really made the loan: the Castle's credit union or – directly or indirectly – the CIA or some front individual or organization? And, if it *was* the Castle, who put up the collateral or gave his written word to secure the loan for this impecunious, young newcomer to the islands? These are fair questions, but we have no answers and they query received wisdom about this whole trip.

At all events, on 6 July 1978 Mark took off from Honolulu to Tokyo on the first lap of a six-and-a-half week journey that would take him on to Seoul, Hong Kong, Singapore, Bangkok, Delhi,

Israel, Geneva, London, Paris, Dublin, Atlanta and then back to Honolulu. There was – perhaps significantly – a high YMCA element in the whole operation. Armed with a signed letter of recommendation from David Moore, who was then stationed at the Geneva office of the World Alliance of YMCAs, he stayed at 'Y' hostels around the world. He had written to Moore requesting such a letter because, 'meeting people would not only give me a real feel for these countries but . . . would help me financially'. But would it not also be a marvellous cover for making useful contacts with CIA representatives and others around the world? Or perhaps it was a sort of bonus for doing well as a promising recruit in the service of the agency? Whatever the explanation, Moore's letter of recommendation written on official writing-paper appears to have meant so much to Mark that it was one of the items he left out on display in his hotel room two years later for the New York police to find after he had killed Lennon. This is what Moore wrote:

TO WHOM IT MAY CONCERN

This is to introduce Mark Chapman, a staff member of the US International Division of the National Council of YMCAs. Mark was an effective and dedicated worker at the refugee camp in Fort Chaffee Arkansas following the mass influx of refugees after the change in governments in Indo-China in the spring of 1975. Mark was also the youth representative to the Board of Directors of the YMCA in his home town in Georgia. Mark will be visiting YMCAs in Asia and Europe and we look forward to his visit here in Geneva. I can commend him to you as a sincere and intelligent young man. Any assistance that you can give Mark during his travels will be greatly appreciated by this office.

The trip was exhilarating and exciting. He took many photographs and slides. He was even still nattering away about it at lunch to two girls he picked up outside The Dakota over two years later on the day of the murder. He saw Moore in Geneva, and the older man still has a vivid recollection of that night in his apartment overlooking Lac Leman when his mother had gone tactfully to bed early and he and Mark talked until the dawn. 'He told me about his problems with his love life,' says Moore, 'and his rejection by Jessica. He said that he felt that academically he could not make it, that college was not for him and that, therefore, a career with the YMCA was not an option for him. But then at the same time he said that he was enjoying what he was doing at the hospital in Hawaii, that he was very intrigued with this new girl he had met at the travel agent's who had arranged this tour for him – and that he intended to try and see more of her when he got back.

'He also told me that he had attempted suicide, which really surprised me. I didn't think he had those kind of emotional problems. But at the end of it all my impression was that he was regaining peace and contentment, and looking forward to the future.'

Yet, as so often with Mark, there was an undertow to everything else going on. In London, he went to see the Andrew Lloyd Webber-Tim Rice rock opera *Jesus Christ, Superstar*, in itself a strange thing for a deeply religious fundamentalist Christian to do when his Presbyterian local church under Pastor Peter Anderson, in the words of the *Honolulu Star-Advertiser*, 'placed emphasis upon the infallibility of Scripture, Christian education and evangelism'. This was perhaps doubly so when one considers that the seat-prices for this smash-hit at the West End's Palace Theatre were not cheap and Mark was supposedly a young tourist counting every penny.

But what is perhaps of greater significance for an understanding of Mark's true personality, is that afterwards he went round to the stage door to congratulate one of the main performers – and two years later, when Mark's photograph appeared in all the newspapers, he recognized him and said to Paul Baden, also in the show: 'You know, I always thought he was gay. There was just something about him.'

Gay, bisexual or simply in inner turmoil sexually, when he got back to Hawaii Mark did, indeed, pay court to Gloria Abe, the twenty-eight-year-old Hawaiian-Japanese travel agent whom he had told David Moore about at Geneva. She converted from Buddhism and joined his church. They saw a lot of each other. In January 1979, walking along the beach at Kailua, he paused and wrote in the sand: 'Will you marry me?' 'Yes,' she wrote in reply. They hugged and he carried her piggy-back down the beach.

They were married on 2 June 1979 at the United Methodist

135

Church in Kailua, some two miles down the road from the Castle Memorial Hospital. It was not their ordinary church but a larger one with beautiful grounds: Pastor Anderson, however, officiated. 'That happens all the time,' I have been told. 'It's because our grounds are so lovely. We often have weddings here from people who belong to smaller churches.' At that time, Pastor Anderson's fledgling Presbyterian church only had twenty-seven members and met in a local school for lack of its own building.

The *Honolulu Star-Bulletin* was later to quote a husband and wife who went to the wedding as saying that it was a somewhat strange affair, with Mark clearly running the show. 'He was sorta domineering and would tell Gloria what to do,' the man said. 'One funny thing I noted,' commented his wife, 'was that Mark would not allow any chairs. He didn't want anyone sitting down.' In accordance with his particular church's strict Presbyterian views, no liquor was served at the wedding reception for the 100 or so guests – who included both Gloria's parents and Mark's mother, but not his father (who had by now remarried).

After the murder, some reporters claimed (and Dr Daniel Schwartz, principal psychiatrist for the defence, suggested) that Mark married Gloria because, like Yoko, she was of pure Japanese blood and he already saw himself as another Lennon. This is unfounded surmise. Shy, retiring Gloria, to be dominated throughout her marriage by her husband (she still pays a yearly pilgrimage to visit him in Attica Prison), is the absolute opposite of tough, independent Yoko as a person. She is much more the prototype of the classical Japanese wife, submissive and ever pliable to her husband's changing moods.

Indeed, she has consistently remained loyal to Mark ever since the day of their wedding. But 'you've got to remember,' says Ruth Brilhante, who worked with her at Waters World Travel Agency (now closed) that arranged Mark's world trip, 'that Gloria is an Oriental and was brought up not to question too much what her husband did or decided to do.' Mark quickly established an ascendancy over her. Says Ruth: 'He was very finicky, very possessive. Gloria was a very dedicated travel agent who would put in a lot of overtime – as I do – you can't just walk away from making a reservation because it's 5 o'clock or whatever; and he did not like that. He would be outside waiting for her and that would make her nervous. She'd say: "I've got to go. I've got to go. Mark's outside!"'

She did not have to say it for long. Within two months, Mark had persuaded her to give up her job at Waters World Travel, where she had been since she graduated from Kailua High School eight years earlier, and take a job at the Castle Memorial Hospital, working in the accounts department. At about the same time, after a jealous row with a neighbour who had whistled at Gloria, who was petite and not unattractive, Mark insisted on their moving out of their homely local apartment – and crossing back over the Koolau Mountains into Honolulu. They took a $425-a-month apartment on the 21st floor of an ultra-modern building at 55 Kukui Plaza near the city's Chinatown. Then, to make Gloria even more cut off from her family and old friends, he insisted on selling their car as an economy measure: they both had to commute every day by bus to the Castle Hospital.

Now a brief new passion came into Mark's life: art. Pat Carlson, a Texan who then worked in a Honolulu gallery but who has since, like so many others, moved on back to the mainland, later told a local reporter that in September 1979, Mark came into her gallery, with Gloria and his mother. 'He said they were very interested in buying art, or at least he seemed very interested in looking at it.'

The following month, Mark bought a Yamagata lithograph for $300. Then he became fascinated with Salvador Dali and bought a golden wall plaque of his *Lincoln in Dalivision*, with $5000 he borrowed from Gloria's father – only to change his mind almost at once, borrow another $2500 from his mother (whose divorce settlement had just come through) and trade in the Dali for a $7500 lithograph of Norman Rockwell's *Triple Self-Portrait*. (I have taken the facts of these two loans from the second of Jim Gaines' articles in *People* in February 1987.)

Pat Carlson reckoned that this intense period of artistic curiosity lasted for about six months: from September 1979 to January 1980. 'He was as obsessed as anyone you could imagine. He would go from gallery to gallery. He would call me three or four times a week to talk about his art. He didn't just ask questions, he did a lot of investigative work, making long distance calls and writing letters all over the United States. He really became an authority.'

Then just as quickly he lost interest. He had other things on his mind. He had a row with the head of nursing at Castle because someone else had got a promotion that he thought he was in line for, and walked out of his hospital job – although Gloria still remained in hers. He looked around for other work, and found it difficult to find. Six days before Christmas 1979, he was right back where he had been in the summer of 1976 in Atlanta: he was forced to take a job as a security guard, although this time unarmed. He went to work at a Waikiki vacation apartment complex at 444 Nahua Street, just behind all the tourist hotels.

Fue Liva, then thirty-one, was chief security officer at the complex. Now he says that he does not want to talk about Mark: 'No one could understand why he did the murder. I've forgotten all about it but whatever I said in the newspapers at the time is OK.' What he said at the time to the *Honolulu Star-Bulletin* was that he became close with Mark when they worked together. He was a 'very dependable person' but someone with his share of problems: involved in drugs when growing up, involved in a 'religious organization', not getting along with his family – 'his last word from his sister was "Mark, go to hell!"' He also told the local newspaper that he once visited Mark's home in Kukui Plaza: 'He liked music. He had a few records in his apartment – but I didn't see any Beatles.'

Much was later made in the press about Mark's undoubted feud with the local Scientologists' headquarters at 447 Nahau Street, opposite from where he worked. Dennis Clarke, then Scientologist spokesman (they have since moved), has been quoted many times as saying that the phone would often ring and a voice would whisper: 'Bang, bang. You're dead!' The clear implication is that the voice was Mark's and that it was also Mark who beamed loud Beatles music across the street to try and disrupt their activities. But the *Honolulu Star-Bulletin* reported that Mark was not alone in his hostility to that questionable outfit's local activities. Three other men were also harassing the Scientologists at that time, as many a deeply involved fundamentalist Christian might have done.

In fact, according to the precise language of Honolulu Police Captain Louis L. Souza, Mark objected to 'the manner in which they were acquiring their financial funds from prospective members of the church'. Come to think of it, one does not have to be a deeply involved fundamentalist Christian to object to that.

Thinking back later, nearly two months after Mark quit his

work to murder Lennon, Clarke told the newspaper that the whispered phone calls had stopped when Mark left 444 Nahua Street — but it was never proved that the threatening voice was Mark's, with his slight but distinctive Southern twang. It could have been any one of the other three men.

Yet undoubtedly as the hot Pacific sun of August came to the islands, Mark was going through some kind of inner crisis. He nearly walked out on his $4 an hour job because there had been a break-in at 444 Nahua Street and he thought that his employers held him to blame. He was upset and angry about it. Fue Liva had to talk to him 'like a brother', to persuade him to stay on. But he transferred to the maintenance division rather than continue as a security guard.

It was clearly a difficult time for him. And now an ominous new factor came into his life: he became interested in *The Catcher in the Rye*. We do not know why. We do not know if anyone suggested it to him and, if so, who. *Catcher* is a book that most people read once in their life in their teens — and that is it. Why on earth, seemingly out of the blue, did Mark suddenly get so involved in a book that, like most of his generation of young Americans, he had already read before at school nearly ten years earlier?

Whatever the reason, whoever his controller may have been (if he had one), however the message was got through to him (it could even have been by a phone call or the suggestion of a 'friend'), he threw himself spiritedly into the book. He bought two paperback copies, one for Gloria and one for himself. He even called himself 'a twenty-five-year-old Catcher'.

Strange timing — for, by August 1980, the battle lines in the upcoming US presidential elections in November had been clearly drawn. As far back as the end of May, Ronald Reagan had been assured of a convention majority as Republican candidate and, although the Democratic convention did not take place until August itself, Jimmy Carter, the incumbent Democratic President, had also long been certain of his party's nomination.

Furthermore since the middle of June, Reagan had overtaken Carter in the Gallup and other polls and at the beginning of August his ascendancy peaked to an all-time high. Apart from

139

two brief intervals, he was to remain consistently ahead, albeit by only a slight margin, until voting day itself.

So is it absolutely too far-fetched to contemplate that there may have been a connection between these two events: Reagan emerging as front runner in the election stakes and Mark now picking up *Catcher* again – with the further coincidence of Lennon striding back with renewed vigour into the Hit Factory in Manhattan to record his come-back album *Double Fantasy*? If *Catcher*, with its explosive effect on Mark, was, indeed, the trigger for his programmed mind serving to put him 'on alert' in case of call, it all does seem to come together with remarkable neatness.

11

Countdown to Murder

August 1980 was one of the most fulfilling months in Lennon's life. Not only was he back working again, but working with a new excitement and a new feeling of commitment. He did not even have a deal with a record company: as we have seen in Chapter 8, he had not renewed his old EMI/Capitol contract when it had expired in early 1976, he and Yoko were making this album just for themselves. They were entirely their own bosses, a novel situation for a pair of rock singers. They were going to make the record first – and then choose the label under which it would go out. They knew there would be no shortage of companies ready to assume that role.

It was a marvellous position to be in: all the joys of artistic creation with the assurance of a major commercial success into the bargain. No wonder he was happy. As biographer Ray Coleman has written: 'John was in superb mental and physical shape for the recording sessions' at the Hit Factory Studios on New York's West 54th Street. In under three weeks, everything was accomplished – with spare tracks left over for possible future singles and the better part of a second album (which eventually was released as *Milk and Honey* in 1984).

But this had not been achieved without a measure of self-sacrifice so far as his close relationship with his young son was concerned. He explained to an interviewer: 'I hadn't been in the studio for five years, and Sean was used to me being around all the time. But I started to work, and I got back on a night schedule. And then one day he said, "You know what I want to be when I grow up?" And I said, "No, what's that?" He looked me right in the eye and said, "Just a daddy." And I said, "Uh huh, you don't like it that I'm working now, right?" He said, "Right." I said, "Well, I'll tell you something, Sean, it makes me happy to do the music. And I might have more fun with you if I'm happier, right?" He said, "Uh huh." And that was the end of that.'

Elliot Mintz several times visited the *Double Fantasy* recording sessions and gave Ray Coleman this account of their setting: 'Yoko made it very clear to everyone that there was to be no alcohol or drugs of any kind during the making of that album. When it was time to break for dinner she had exquisite servings of fresh *sushi* delivered to the studio for the musicians and crew. A large colour photograph of Sean was taped over the television screen that faced the mixing console. There were dishes of raisins and sesame seeds placed around the control room. An assistant set up a small room with an interior look that resembled one of the rooms in The Dakota. Some pieces of furniture and art were placed in there so they would both feel comfortable and at home during the breaks.'

The songs produced in this eminently civilized ambiance had a somewhat varied reception from the critics when eventually the album came out: Robert Christgau in *Village Voice* found them for some reason 'basically sexist' while Simon Frith called them 'comfortable and happy' and Stephen Holden dubbed the album as a whole 'a pop fairy tale of perfect heterosexual union'. Listening to the tracks now, they have an almost elegiac sub-tone, from the quiet cadences of 'Beautiful Boy, (Darling Boy)' and the near-despair of 'I'm Losing You' to the serenity of 'Watching The Wheels' and the poignant irony of '(Just Like) Starting Over', the lead track and separately released as a single.

Most of Lennon's seven songs on the album (Yoko also had seven) had been written while he was still on the yacht in Bermuda, before he even set sail for the return to New York. The fresh inspiration after his five years within himself simply flowed like water from a spring; but this is his much better analogy, given in his interview to Barbara Graustark for *Newsweek* in September 1980:

Newton would never have had the apple fall on his head and conceive of what it meant had he not been sitting under the tree. Day-dreamin'. So for me, it's the same with music. The real music comes to me, the music of the spheres, the music that surpasses understanding, that has not to do with me, that I'm just a channel. . . . So for that to come through, which is the only joy for me out of the music is for it to be given to me and I transcribe it like a medium. But I have nothing to do with it other than I'm sitting under this tree and this whole damn thing comes down and I've just put it down. That is the only joy for me.

But, with his new awareness, he was not only thinking musically but politically. Also in September, he gave a second major interview linked to the publicity for *Double Fantasy*: to David Sheff for *Playboy* magazine. His message was now no less intense than in the turbulent days of the early 1970s, but far more mature:

We're one world, one people whether we like it or not. . . . We can pretend we're divided into races and countries and we can carry on pretending until we stop doin' it. But the reality is that it is one world and it is one people. . . .
   Leaders is what we don't need. We can have figureheads and we can have people that we admire and like to have standing up and all that. We can have examples. . . . But leaders is what we don't need. It's the Utopian bit again. We're all members of the conceptual Utopia. So let's not go round and round it. It's one world, one people, and it's a statement as well as a wish.

What is even more significant, especially if one is thinking of why anyone with an extreme right-wing kind of mind would want to kill him, is what he said to Sheff about his song 'Revolution' recorded back in 1968: 'The statement in that was mine. The lyrics stand today. They're still my feeling about politics: I want to see the *plan*. That is what I used to say to Jerry Rubin and Abbie Hoffman. Count me out if it's for violence' (in fact, this is not necessarily true for his views of nine years earlier). 'Don't expect me on the barricades unless it is with flowers. As far as over-throwing something in the name of Marxism or Christianity, I want to know what you're going to do after you've knocked it all down. I mean, can't we use some of it? What's the point of bombing Wall Street? If you want to change the system, change the system. It's no good shooting people.' This was the voice of maturity.

The new Lennon was a far more persuasive left-winger than the old. As a rallying-point for protest, his credibility had grown over the nine years since the 'Free John Sinclair Rally' at Ann Arbor in December 1971. Now he was potentially far more powerful – and far more dangerous.

By contrast, the second half of August and the whole of September 1980 continued to be a bad time for Mark.

He was not really happy in his job. He felt even worse off, doing less satisfactory work, than in Atlanta before he ever came to Hawaii: what had he achieved in the past four years? It seemed precious little. He was now even questioning his firm religious faith: 'It was kind of ironic that I could encourage my wife and give her specific directions as to how she could grow in her Christian faith and commitment in terms of reading the Bible and studying the Bible,' he later told Rev. Charles McGowan, his former pastor at his South De Kalb Presbyterian Church; 'and at the same time *I* wasn't doing it!'

The Catcher in the Rye that he had just again read for the first time in six years began to exert its baleful influence. If his controller was triggering him into action by suggesting that he re-read this book, he could not have chosen a better fictitious character for Mark to identify with than young Holden Caulfield. Not only did Holden's relationship with his non-interfering mother and coldly distant father strike chords in Mark's own childhood, the book as a whole seemed almost written for the purpose. Soon after its original publication in the summer of 1951, Ernest Jones, Sigmund Freud's student and eventual biographer, had described it in a review as 'a case history of all of us'. It was, he wrote, 'not at all something rich and strange, but what every sensitive sixteen-year-old since Rousseau has felt, and of course what each of us is certain he has felt.'

When Mark himself was sixteen, he had been too juvenile to appreciate it, too involved in the circumstances of his own young life; but now, nine years later, its effect was almost instant. It was not only Holden's almost pathological dislike for 'phoneys', it was also his ambivalent attitude to violence that rang bells for Mark. If anyone had tried to trigger him on a James Bond or modern-day Rambo sort of character, they would have got nowhere. Pseudo-macho aggressiveness, or even the real thing, was not Mark's style. He was the young man who vacillated between revulsion at the Arkansas hunter's rifle stacked at the back of a truck driver's cabin when he was out with David Moore and engrossment with Gene Scott's white-handled revolver when he came to collect him at Fort Chaffee. By temperament, Mark was contemplative and introspective rather than a dynamic man of action. He was nearer in feel to the self-doubting Hamlet, compelled almost despite himself to kill his uncle and avenge his father's 'foul murder' than to being a sort of real-life version of Charles Bronson in some *Death Wish* kind of movie, killing people almost as if he enjoyed it.

The imbalance in the psychological make-up of immature sixteen-year-old Holden Caulfield exactly suited the temperament of bewildered, unhappy twenty-five-year-old Mark Chapman. Nowhere is this better exemplified than in the passage towards the end of *Catcher* when Holden, visiting his beloved young sister Phoebe's school in an abortive attempt to talk to her, sees the words 'Fuck you' written on a wall: 'It drove me damn near crazy. I thought how Phoebe and all the other little kids would see it, and how'd they wonder what the hell it meant, and then finally some dirty kid would tell them . . . I kept wanting to kill whoever'd written it. I figured it was some perverty bum that'd sneaked in the school late at night . . . and then wrote it on the wall. I kept picturing myself catching him at it, and how I'd smash his head on the stone steps till he was good and goddam dead and bloody. But I knew, too, I wouldn't have the guts to do it. . . . That made me even more depressed.' But a few lines later, despite his fears, he erases the offending 'Fuck you.'

That was exactly the way Mark would soon respond to his 'special mission to kill John Lennon', a phrase he later used to his ex-pastor, the Rev. Charles McGowan. Like Holden, Mark would also show anger, determination, then doubts followed by fear, anxiety – and finally definitive action: 'rubbing out' John Lennon.

Albert Goldman, with his normal confidence, boldly asserts in his biography: 'In mid-October 1980 Mark David Chapman read an article in *Esquire* titled "John Lennon, Where Are You?" The piece was slugged: "In Search of the Beatle Who Spent Two Decades Seeking True Love and Cranial Bliss Only to Discover Cows, Daytime Television, and Palm Beach Real Estate . . ."

After he read that piece in *Esquire*, Mark David Chapman knew whom he must kill.'

The article by Laurence Shames, a New York-based journalist, is indeed a scathing indictment of Lennon. Shames wrote how he went in search of 'a man who had always taken chances . . . who by his unflinching slit-eyed stare, by his appalling honesty, had shamed the world into examining itself . . . who had always shot his mouth off,' etc. etc. He claimed that he would have found instead 'a forty-year-old businessman who watches a lot of television, who's got $150 million, a son whom he dotes on, and a wife who intercepts his phone calls. He's got good lawyers to squeeze him through tax loopholes, and he's learned the political advantages of silence. He doesn't do anything ridiculous any more.' And so on, and so on.

Despite Goldman's firm statement that it was this article that sparked Mark's murderous interest in Lennon, Jim Gaines in his four articles on Mark in *People* in 1981 and 1987, does not even once mention it. In fact, that issue of *Esquire* did not come out in Hawaii until at least 20 October and not 'in mid-October', as Goldman says, while Mark himself has told Kevin Sim, the British television documentary film maker, that (although not included in Sim's programme) he did indeed read Shames' article – but only after he was on the plane bound for New York to kill Lennon. Steve Spiro, the New York policeman who arrested Mark, told me he was '95 per cent sure' that Mark had told him he bought the magazine when he was already actually in New York.

However, the power of the printed word is so great that in October 1988 Yoko announced that she and Sean were going to spend most of the next few years in Europe, partly out of fear that a reader of Goldman's book might react to her as violently as Goldman claimed that Mark had reacted to the article in *Esquire*. She repeated that Goldman's biography should not be taken seriously 'at all' and called it a 'vicious, inaccurate character assassination' but his assertion that her husband's killer had been motivated by the *Esquire* article would seem to have got to her. 'It was a nasty one,' she said before leaving for Switzerland where she was going to stay near Sean's boarding school. 'We laughed it off at the time but forty-five days later John was killed.' Such is the power of legend based on imagined fact.

In truth, Mark had got Lennon mentally in his sights weeks

before Laurence Shames' article appeared. And it was a book, not a magazine feature, that did the job.

Just as he had suddenly become involved again, in August 1980, with *The Catcher in the Rye*, he equally suddenly and mysteriously thereafter recovered interest in Lennon whom, as with Holden Caulfield, he had not thought about for nearly the past ten years. I can be specific about the chronological order, *Catcher* and then Lennon through another book, because of this vital piece of hitherto unpublished cross-examination on 24 August 1981 when Mark was finally sentenced in New York's Supreme Court for Lennon's murder. This part of the proceedings was not open to the public but a written record of the cross-examination appears in the prosecution's confidential brief in Mark's subsequent appeal that has been made available to me by Allen Sullivan, the Assistant District Attorney in charge of the case.

Sullivan is cross-examining Dr Daniel Schwartz, the principal defence psychiatrist:

Q   As a matter of fact, did you learn that [Chapman's] interest in John Lennon largely stemmed from his reading of a book in Hawaii during either September or October of 1980?
A   Yes.
Q   Have you ever read that book?
A   No.
Q   Have you ever seen it?
A   No.
Q   Or any copy of it?
A   No.
Q   Did you learn that the defendant said that at or about the time that he was reading that book he felt, 'Gee, wouldn't it be funny, wouldn't it be a kicker if I killed John Lennon?', said that to himself, words to that effect?
A   I believe so, yes.

If *Catcher* was the trigger in Mark's programmed mind alerting him to the danger of the world's 'phoneys', then this unnamed other book – perhaps suggested to him by his controller? – pointed him in the right direction. I can name the book. It was Anthony Fawcett's *John Lennon: One Day at a Time*. Although it was written by someone who was clearly an admirer of Lennon, it also showed the style and wealth in which he lived – and, paradoxically in the circumstances, how he had retired from active involvement in radical politics in the face of the Nixon administration's concerted efforts to deport him. Gloria Chapman told Jim Gaines that, after Mark had brought this book home from the public library and read it, he 'would get angry that Lennon would preach love and peace but yet have millions'. It completed the job started by *The Catcher in the Rye*.

Mark was clearly going through torment. He told his perplexed wife that he was thinking of changing his name to Holden Caulfield. On 10 September he actually wrote to a schoolteacher friend named Lynda Irish, who had moved from Honolulu to New Mexico: 'I'm going nuts.' He drew a picture of Diamond Head Mountain with the sun, moon and stars above it and signed the letter: 'The Catcher in the Rye, Mark.' (Three years earlier, soon after he had arrived on the islands, he had had his long psychiatric sessions with Anne Jones, but she does not recall his ever having mentioned the book. 'It was certainly no big deal for him then,' she says.)

Something was afoot. He called Pat Carlson and told her he wanted to sell his treasured Norman Rockwell lithograph for $7500. He said he knew that was what he had paid for it not all that long before but he 'badly needed the money'. Her gallery was not interested in buying it and she could not find anyone else, but somehow Mark found his own purchaser: a Honolulu public relations executive named Craig Travis who negotiated on behalf of his uncle, a collector in California. 'We had a drink and struck up a deal', during an initial meeting between Travis, his uncle and Mark at the Waikikian Hotel in September, Travis later told the *Honolulu Star-Bulletin*.

Mark, for some reason of his own, wanted the matter finalized quickly. In the first week in October, he started calling Travis at work, saying he wanted to know where the cheque was because he really needed the money. 'He was very insistent and I had to keep reassuring him,' Travis said.

On 10 October Mark and Gloria brought the lithograph to Travis' home and Travis handed over a cheque for $7500. 'I just thought he was a very nice, sweet guy who was very thankful he was able to sell the painting. He kept saying he really needed the money,' Travis recalled.

But why did Mark need the money, and what was the extreme

urgency? If Jim Gaines in *People* in 1987 is right, none of the $7500 was really his anyway: it belonged to his mother ($2500) and his father-in-law ($5000) for the money they had loaned him to buy the lithograph in the first place. There is no indication that either of them were pressing him for the return of any loan and it is perhaps significant that, in all of Gaines' three long *People* articles in 1987, written with Mark's full cooperation and after many hours of long interviews, there is not a single mention of the sale of the Rockwell lithograph, the $7500 he then received – or how Mark ever got the money to make his eventual two journeys to New York to kill Lennon. Why this gap? Why is not Mark more forthcoming?

It does not make any kind of sense – unless perhaps Mark misled Gaines in their long discussions in Attica Prison. For there is another possible scenario: Pat Carlson has a different version of the financial set-up. After the murder she told James Dooley of the *Honolulu Advertiser* that Mark's mother and Gloria's parents had each contributed only $2500 to make up the original $5000 which Mark had paid for the Dali work – and that he had found the extra $2500 he needed for the Rockwell by borrowing that amount from a credit union.

If this is right, then we can well understand why Mark 'really needed money' in September–October 1980: he needed to get his hands on so much of the cash tied up in the lithograph as was available to him. From Allen Sullivan's cross-examination of Dr Daniel Schwartz, one learns that Mark paid off his mother her $2500, gave back the credit union *their* $2500 – *but hung on to his father-in-law's $2500.*

And why did he so urgently need this money? It could be because the seed had already been planted in his mind by the *Catcher* novel and Fawcett's book that he might be needed for his 'special mission' to murder Lennon. The meaningful stages of his programming as the singer's assassin could now have started.

Perhaps that is why Mark even years later did not tell Gaines the full facts about the money to buy the Rockwell – or that he later sold it and did not repay his father-in-law. His controller would have wanted to cover his tracks and make the decision to kill Lennon seem as last-minute and as unplanned as possible.

On Thursday 23 October 1980, Geffen Records released Lennon's new single, '(Just Like) Starting Over',) and on the very same day, at 3.00 p.m. Hawaiian time, having come on duty at 6.00 a.m., Mark walked out of his job at 444 Nahua Street. He signed himself off, not in his own name, but as 'John Lennon'. This has made many commentators on the case maintain, taking their tune from psychiatrists consulted by the press and later Dr Schwartz himself, that Mark had by then come to believe that he had really become Lennon. That Lennon had taken over his personality.

This is untrue. Completely apart from the fact that, as we have seen, Mark had not for years, if ever, been a specific fan of Lennon and had never shown any tendency to identify with him, this theory ignores the vital circumstance that Mark did not merely write the name 'John Lennon' on the time sheet, and leave it at that. He immediately scrawled it out with an angry double line through it. He was not saying: 'I am John Lennon' but 'John Lennon, you are a write-off. I am going to kill you!'

It was a declaration of intent to commit murder.

After the breakup of the Beatles, John Lennon asserted his new freedom and used his fame as a Beatle to support political causes in the United States. These included a "Freedom Rally" held in Ann Arbor, Michigan, in 1971 to free John Sinclair from drug charges. Sinclair was, in the early 1970s, a hero for the New Left. Though Lennon was unaware of it at the time of this particular concert, FBI agents were secretly taping everything Lennon said or played onstage. John Lennon had come under "top secret surveillance."
(Retna Ltd./Joseph Sia)

Mark David Chapman was "like any other of the 300 young men and women of the 'Class of 1973' of Columbia High School in the comfortable middle-class suburb of Decatur." (See page 81.) *(AP/Wide World Photos)*

The creative partnership, John Lennon and Yoko Ono. *(Photo David Redfern/Retna Ltd.)*

Chapman with an unidentified Vietnamese child during a Vietnamese relocation effort in 1975 at Fort Chaffee, Arkansas. A tape still exists with Chapman's voice over the camp radio: "My name is Mark David Chapman and I came to work at Fort Chaffee about three months ago. It's so good to work closely with the Vietnamese people and to exchange culture and ideas." *(AP/Wide World Photos)*

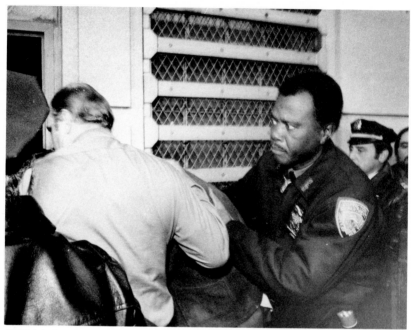

With his head covered, Mark David Chapman is led from the New York City Police's 20th precinct on the Upper West Side on December 9, 1980. *(AP/ Wide World Photos)*

The entranceway into the Dakota became a shrine to Lennon in the days following his assassination. Hundreds of thousands of fans sent flowers and letters of support from all over the world to pay their respects to the slain musician. *(Photo by Michael Kagan/Retna Ltd.)*

One of the many organized vigils during the week of December 8, 1980, in Central Park. Vigils were held in public parks and town squares across the United States. *(Photo by Gary Gershoff/ Retna Ltd.)*

L. Sooza of Honolulu Police who checked out Chapman's airline ticket. *(Photo from author's collection.)*

The prophetic signature. Joe Bustamonte, Chapman's former supervisor, holds up the entry sheet for the workers at Waikiki Condominium. Chapman's signature read "John Lennon," which he then crossed out. *(Photo by Ken Sakamota/Black Star.)*

Chapman holds his copy of *The Catcher in the Rye* in court. Note Chapman's haircut after shaving his head in jail. *(Sketch by Ida Libby NBC-TV via AP/Wide World Photos)*

Chapman with Attorney Jonathan Marks and Judge Dennis Edwards on the bench. *(Sketch by Ida Libby NBC-TV via AP/Wide World Photos)*

12

Anti-Climax

If you want a third party to commit a murder for you, there
are three ways of going about it. Either you hire a professional
assassin, a hit man, who accomplishes his job with cool, quick
professional efficiency, often already sitting comfortably on the
plane flying out of town before the body has even been discovered,
or you put some non-professional up to it, by playing on whatever
emotions are available to you – jealousy, hatred, thwarted love,
resentment, envy, call it what you will. Or, if the stakes are really
high and you have the resources, you programme him to commit
your crime by mind control.

Why one method rather than the other, the amateur as against
the professional? Because that way you avoid any awkward questions. If Lennon had been gunned down by a professional killer, the
whole world would have known: such swift expert assassinations
carry their own individual hallmark. It would have been obvious
what had happened and, with Lennon's history of anti-government
radical political activity, there would have been an explosion not
only of anger but also of in-depth investigation – by the world's
press if by nobody else – into what exactly had happened.

But if you programme an amateur to do the job, a so-called 'nut',
very few questions are asked. Almost everyone easily accepts that
in this crazy world one more crazy man has done a crazy deed.
So that even eight years later, so knowledgeable a television
commentator as Mike Wallace can still call Mark inaccurately 'a
deranged fan'.

Yet there is a flip side to this, another side of the coin. Just
because you have chosen a non-professional killer, there will be
hiccups along the way. Mistakes will be made. You will have to

151

keep your tabs on him, and sometimes even give him a gentle nudge back on course. But, provided you have chosen your man with sufficient care in the first place, and you are prepared to monitor him and be patient, at the end of it all you will get what you want: the elimination of your target – and the whole world will think it is the work of one more lone 'nut' or 'a deranged fan'.

Amazingly, no one seems to have paid any particular attention at the time to Mark's bizarre way of signing off work. Asked why he was quitting, he had told his friend Fue Liva that he had 'personal problems to settle' and he told Joe Bustamente, the building manager at 444 Nahua Street, no more than that he 'was going to London to take a trip' – but no one seems to have bothered to query his sign-off entry, so different from his normal routine 'Chap'.

It was only when Mark's replacement, twenty-six-year-old Michael Bird, heard on the radio on the night of the murder that Lennon had been killed by a 'Mark David Chapman from Hawaii', that he realized belatedly that the sign-off 'John Lennon' might have had sinister undertones. 'At the time, I just thought he was playing a game,' he explained to a local reporter.

But, when he got to work on the day after the murder, he went immediately to the security office and, when he *then* saw the entry, he 'just went numb'.

Captain Louis L. Souza of the Honolulu police says: 'Chapman is not insane. I am not a physician but I had been eighteen years in the service then, and I wouldn't consider him a nut. I believe he was well aware of what he was doing in relation to John Lennon's death. His actions here to my investigation didn't find that he was "nuts" (the quotation marks are Souza's). To me, he was a slightly below-average guy – no more than that. If you were rating him from one to ten, I would say a four.'

If someone with that slightly limited intelligence plans and executes a murder, he will very likely do it in the same stop-start, imperfect way that Mark did. Three days went by after he left work without his apparently doing anything really at all. Jim Gaines paints a word picture of him in *People* in February 1987 'sitting naked, rocking back and forth at the controls of his stereo and tape recorder, splicing together his reasons for killing John Lennon from the lyrics of Beatles songs, the sound track of *The Wizard of Oz* and quotations from *The Catcher in the Rye*.' His source is presumably Mark himself in Attica Prison. Whether or not accurate, it is certainly not dynamic.

However he may have spent the previous three days, on the morning of Monday 27 October 1980, Mark walked into J&S Enterprises Ltd, a gunshop in a dingy little shopping cluster in midtown Honolulu. 'Buy a Gun and Get a Bang out of Life!' said the sign over the door. He had come to this establishment just down the street from the city's police department (and Captain Souza's present office) to buy the weapon with which to kill John Lennon. From the scores of guns on display (the shop closed a year later, partly because of bad publicity over the Lennon murder), Mark selected a five-shot, two-inch barrel Charter Arms Undercover .38 Special revolver at a price of $169 (£70.40). The model is still a best-seller today throughout the United States but inflation has had its inevitable effect: it now sells at $195.

The legal procedure could not have been simpler. Mark did not even have to wait fifteen days for a really thorough nationwide computer check of police records, as in other US states. The transaction was completed within an hour.

He picked out his gun and a counter-clerk gave him its exact description and serial number, 577570. Then he walked round to the nearby police station, housed in an old department store building, and presented himself at the firearms window, next to an escalator formerly used by eager shoppers. He showed his driver's licence and Social Security card as identification and filled out an application form for a police gun permit. After giving his address, date of birth and other personal details including business 'None' and occupation 'None', he signed the form under five lines of close-printing confirming that he was not under criminal indictment and had never been convicted of a felony, that he was not a fugitive, not addicted to drugs or stimulants, had never been committed to a mental institution, had not been discharged from the armed forces less than honourably, was not an illegal alien and had never renounced his US citizenship – and he handed it back through the window. A clerk then ran a brief computer check to see if he had a criminal record in Hawaii or was wanted as a fugitive nationwide. On satisfying himself that Mark was in neither category, he handed him his police permit – clearing him to become one of the 16,000 to 20,000 people who legally purchase handguns in Honolulu every year.

Mark then went back to J&S Enterprises, showed the counter-clerk his permit, filled out an identical form for the US Alcohol, Tobacco and Firearms Bureau, handed over his $169 – and walked out of the shop with his gun. 'He didn't do anything weird or peculiar,' Steve Grahovac, the shop's owner, said afterwards. 'If they do anything whippy, we won't sell them a gun. I've got six kids.'

Next, Mark bought his ticket for New York: a one-way ticket – not a return, you will notice – for Newark, New Jersey, New York's third major airport after Kennedy and La Guardia and easily linked to the city by subway. He was to fly in two days' time.

What explanation did he give to his wife Gloria? He told both her and his mother that he needed to sort himself out for a while, and that was why he was going to New York. The submissive Gloria asked no questions but Diane Chapman, when they had lunch together on the day before he left, said she did not like the idea of his going off to New York on his own and what was all this nonsense about wanting to change his name to Holden Caulfield?

If a programmed Mark had, in fact, been put on alert by his controller in August and pointed in the direction of Lennon in the following month, it seems as if the order 'alert' had now been changed to 'action stations' – albeit at Mark's own somewhat erratic pace.

Before Mark had even left his apartment to have lunch with his mother on that Tuesday, 26 October, television sets in 60 million American homes had been tuned to a programme beamed from an old convention hall in Cleveland, Ohio, at 6.00 p.m. East Coast Time (eight hours ahead of Hawaiian time). It was the Carter–Reagan presidential debate, the only one of the campaign. It consumed ninety minutes of prime time and attracted about 100 million spectators, the largest political audience yet in American history. It augured well for Reagan's eventual victory in the voting that was to take place eleven days later: as a *Washington Post* team of political journalists were to write in their book *The Pursuit of the Presidency 1980*, published in the following year, 'Reagan infused the occasion with a style, a presence, a grandfatherly sense of dignity and kindness that evoked sympathy among millions of Americans. . . . Intellectuals were fixated on the fact that he was "not with it" in terms of Eastern sophistication: he was a square; he was not one of them. The American masses reacted quite differently. The opinion polls revealed that he had come through quite well, that he had, in fact, won the encounter in the minds of most Americans.'

The groundswell that was to sweep Ronald Reagan into office, though hesitant at first and still not totally assured of victory, was now well under way. The polling trends were favourable to Reagan. As the *Washington Post* team has written, 'More importantly, the calculations of electoral votes strongly indicated a Reagan victory.' The water was coming to the boil.

If John Lennon were to be eliminated by some kind of 'preemptive strike', before he had properly got his own act together to make a full return to public life, now was the time.

Mark really was the most amateurish of assassins. He must be the only murderer in recent history who buys the murder gun – but not any bullets to go with it! This never appeared in the press in the months and early years after the murder: indeed, I was the first to reveal it in the London *Daily Express* in 1985 at the early stages of my research for this book. My source was Allen Sullivan himself.

Mark went to the bother of telephoning the authorities at Honolulu airport to check that he could perfectly easily take both firearms and ammunition with him on the flight to New York, with absolutely no problems under Federal law, so long as he filled out a form and the firearm and ammunition were separately packed and stored in the hold with the rest of his checked-in luggage. The only difficulty, for obvious reasons, was that he could not carry a loaded firearm with him in the passenger cabin. US gun laws may be lax but they do not positively encourage armed hijackers. But Mark still had not bought any ammunition along with his pistol because he believed – totally inaccurately – that bullets might prove dangerous in flight because of the pressurized air in the plane.

This proved to be a serious mistake.

For when he went into a gunshop in New York to buy ammunition, he found that his whole journey was pointless. Despite the Big Apple's reputation as one of the most dangerous cities in the world, local firearm legislation has made it impossible for anyone to buy live ammunition across the counter except if he holds a New York City gun permit. The gunshop salesman to whom Mark showed his Hawaii state gun permit just laughed. It would not have been worth his licence to comply with the angry and baffled would-be assassin's request.

So what did Mark do? He went back home to Atlanta – and Gene Scott.

In an attempt to explain Mark's surprising flight down to Atlanta within days of arrival in New York on his murder mission, earlier writers have had to seek the answer in conjecture. Craig Unger in *New York* in June 1981 wrote that he was 'seeking solace from his torment'. Jim Gaines in his first article in *People* in the same month wrote: 'As if seeking to re-connect one last time with his past, he flew to Atlanta and made the rounds of old acquaintances.'

The truth is much more prosaic. As Allen Sullivan, sitting back in his office high above Manhattan, says in his laconic way: 'He went to get the bullets.' And, with Gene Scott's help, he did. He flew down to Atlanta on Friday, 7 November for the weekend and stayed with Gene.

As a sheriff's officer, the country equivalent of a police officer, Gene found no difficulty in helping Mark get the bullets he needed, even though technically Mark would seem to have been committing an offence against paragraph 16-11-28 of the Georgia State Law Code of 1981 by even carrying his unloaded pistol about with him without a licence obtained in Georgia or in an adjoining state. Nor was Mark content with any ordinary kind of bullets. As Allen Sullivan was later to bring out in his cross-examination of Dr Daniel Schwartz, the defence psychiatrist who gave evidence at Mark's sentencing hearing, he insisted to Gene that he did not want reloads or old ammunition but only reliable fresh bullets – and specifically hollow-points. In Britain, they are called 'dum-dums' and are notorious for doing the most damage to their victims. Having helped Mark get these extra-deadly bullets, that are incidentally standard police issue in some parts of the United States, Gene obligingly took his friend out into nearby woods and helped him get back his marksman's eye at target practice.

What on earth is Gene's explanation for all this? He told Wesley Nunn of the Georgia Bureau of Investigation shortly after the murder that Mark had told him about his mistake in thinking he could get ammunition in New York and explained that he wanted a loaded weapon as protection for himself against street muggers while staying in the city. Interviewed in May 1988, Nunn said: 'When we interviewed Gene, he was I guess shocked by the whole thing. It was almost like pulling teeth, he didn't want to talk about anything. I guess he was very scared of us. He understood the magnitude of what had happened. He was scared of being a police officer, having the bullets and going out shooting with the guy. He gave me the box of bullets he had purchased to go out with Mark to practise shooting out of which Mark took five or six bullets back to New York with him.

'You ask was Gene under suspicion. I don't think he was really under suspicion. He was looked at as a very potential witness: getting the bullets, helping him shoot the gun, directing him in this type of gun, how to handle it and that.

'After interviewing Gene, I don't think that he actually knew or had any idea that Mark was going up to shoot John Lennon. But I'm sure after it all happened it struck him: "I helped him shoot John Lennon. Am I in trouble?"'

For his part, Allen Sullivan accepts Gene Scott's explanation. Back in 1985, he told me that Mark's story of needing a loaded gun with which to defend himself against potential muggers on the streets of New York was 'just the sort of reason for carrying a loaded gun in this city that someone from the South would find no difficulty in accepting'.

Gene would not talk to Kevin Sim's television documentary team and, when I tried to interview him in May 1988, I got absolutely nowhere. I phoned him at work and asked if he would agree to meet me. He refused but in a brief conversation he confirmed that he saw Mark in November 1980 and that he seemed exactly the same as usual: 'perfectly alright', 'the same as ever'.

His manner was brusque: to be fair, I had phoned him out of the blue. So I only had time to ask him two further questions. Here they are and his answers, written down by me as soon as I replaced the receiver:

Q Did Chapman give you any explanation for wanting the bullets or getting his marksmanship sharpened up?
A No. Do you think he told me he was going to kill John Lennon?
Q Did he give any explanation for being in Atlanta?
A Not that I recall – but what do you want? This was eight years ago!

157

Then I said: 'Thank you, Mr Scott,' and he said: 'OK' – and that was it. I was not able to ask him why both he and Mark told the police about the New York muggers as an explanation for the ammunition or ask what he and Mark had talked about during their weekend together or put a host of other questions to him about their long friendship.

Meanwhile, on Tuesday, 4 November 1980, three days before Mark flew down to Atlanta to spend the weekend with Gene, Ronald Reagan had been elected president by a landslide. Not only did he carry forty-four of the fifty states and win 489 electoral votes but his victory covered the whole political spectrum. The Republicans took over control of the Senate after twenty-six years of Democratic rule, they gained more than thirty seats in the House of Representatives and they added another four state legislatures to their tally. If Richard Nixon had stood as Republican candidate, he would almost certainly have been returned to power despite what many liberals considered the shame of Watergate. Reagan was a good substitute. His policies were likely to prove even more to the right. If Lennon had lived into his years of office, his voice would have been raised loud in protest – as a naturalized US citizen, which he was due to become in 1981, probably even louder than in the earlier days of Nixon.

Before Mark had come down to Atlanta he had spent just over a week in New York, in his normal style of plush spending followed by penny-pinching.

As upon arrival in Hawaii three years earlier, he had first booked into a luxury hotel, this time the Waldorf-Astoria on Park Avenue. It was his first visit to New York and, with the better part of $2500 in cash in his billfold, he enjoyed himself to the full – despite the disappointment about his not being able to buy any bullets. He enjoyed the hotel's efficient room-service, he went to the theatre, he took a girl he picked up to the Empire State Building and toured the other sights; he even went on the Circle Line boat trip around Manhattan Island. You might have thought he was a tourist, not an assassin thwarted in his mission.

Then, as in Hawaii, after a few days he moved into a YMCA hostel, this time the Vanderbilt branch on 224 East 47th Street. He was not there long, for he was to go to Atlanta on the Friday but, as Allen Sullivan later brought out in his cross-examination of Dr

Daniel Schwartz, 'he was upset with the homosexuals there'. One wonders why that was so important to him, especially when, as we shall see later, that did not stop him booking into another 'Y' hostel on the West Side of town closer to The Dakota when he returned to New York the following month. Poor Mark, he seems still not to have been able to make up his mind whether he was repelled by manifested homosexuality or intrigued by it.

The impression left upon his friends after his weekend in Atlanta was uniformly favourable. Both his Columbia High School chorus teacher Madison Short and Paul Visscher, a former classmate, told Craig Unger that he was 'the same old Mark'. He telephoned his ex-high school girlfriend 'Judy Williams', now married, to tell her that he too was now married and briefly in town. 'His voice was excited, so much had happened to him,' she later told Simon Kinnersley, her *Woman's Own* interviewer: she agreed to see him – but then stood him up. 'For that she felt guilty – eternally as events were to now unfold,' wrote Kinnersley.

'The Woman Whose Snub Drove Chapman To Kill', screamed a *New York Post* headline after Lennon's murder over a news-story that Jessica Blankinship had refused to see him during this trip. That was totally untrue: they *did* spend time together – as her parents have told me. For Mark made a point of visiting her parents' house. Apart from a brief meeting when he came by Atlanta on his way back to Honolulu at the end of his world trip in the summer of 1978, he had not seen them since he had originally left for Hawaii. Now they found him 'just old friendly Mark'.

Mrs June Blankinship, who says that she still cannot accept that the man she talked to had come down to Atlanta to get the bullets with which to kill Lennon, gives this vivid word picture of Mark's time in their house. It most certainly does not read like a murderer-in-waiting – nor did it sound like that when she was talking and my tape recorder was quietly whirring. I print it almost verbatim as it gives a unique insight into Mark in his native Southern habitat:

It was November 8, 1980. On the previous night, our daughter Jessica had had her tonsils out. Mark called and wanted to speak to her. He had earlier telephoned and talked to Aunt Sugar, Harold's mother. She was an old lady in her eighties who had lived with us for ten to fifteen years. Mark knew her very well.

When I got back from the hospital, she tells me that he called and was in town. Shortly after we got in the door, he calls and talked with me and wanted the telephone number of the hospital and so forth. So I gave it to him though I said she should not be talking because of the operation and he said, 'No problem! I'll do the talking!'

Next afternoon we came home from the hospital with her. He came bringing a little flower arrangement – which is very typical, very thoughtful. He chatted with her for a long, long time. They went through old pictures together and then he decided he had spent enough time. He didn't want to tire her, so he came into the kitchen where Harold's mother was drinking a cup of coffee.

He propped up against the sink and I did too, and we talked about everything. Like 'Why didn't your wife come?' And he said, 'She wouldn't like the cold weather,' but that was vague and I said, 'Are you heading back for Hawaii now?' and he said 'No.' He was going to New York and I took this to mean he was going up East to see his grandmother. I knew he had a grandmother up there someplace. . . . We used to tease him about being a Yankee!

That reference to a grandmother 'up East' has a relevance that we shall need to return to later. But June Blankinship continued:

I was stunned by Mark's appearance. He did not look like the boy that we had known. He was taller. In fact, he said to me rather devilishly: 'Don't you think I've grown taller?' and I thought he had perhaps lifts in his shoes or something. I didn't bite on his question because I figured it was a gag he was going to pull on me.

I said 'I believe you're certainly bigger,' because he *was* heavy and Mark had never been heavy. He'd always had a round face but not heavy like he was. He did not really have a good colour either but that was just a mother thinking. And so we chatted back and forth.

Then came a remarkable conversation about the ethics of aborting an unborn baby or the mercy killing of an adult, and remember that this was a man who had probably by then already obtained the bullets with which to murder Lennon:

> He began talking to me about our church and the fact that our church is taking a very specific stand against abortion. He said 'I just think it's wonderful that the church is taking this stand. I agree with it wholeheartedly.' He said that the next thing, if you kill unborns, is that you'll be killing people that are in your way. And I said: 'That's true. The next move is euthanasia. All I'd have to do would be to decide that Aunt Sugar is in my way and I'd just get rid of her because she's bothering me.' And he agreed.

Gene Scott had driven Mark over and gone for a walk while Mark chatted with his old friends. So now Mark said: 'I guess I've kept Gene waiting long enough. I'd better go.' Mrs Blankinship said: 'Keep in touch, Mark, and let us hear from you.' Mark said he would. She reached up and kissed him and he went out the door. 'And that's the last we heard until my daughter ran in a month later to say the radio just said a "David Chapman" shot John Lennon and she said: "Could that be Mark?" And I said: "Surely to God no!" Now I say to you: I don't believe that Mark did it. It was terrible. It was the Devil!'

GBI investigator Wesley Nunn sent to the New York police after the murder a photograph taken by one of Mark's local friends of his farewell group at Atlanta airport on the Sunday evening. 'They looked like any other group of friends saying goodbye to someone who had paid a visit back home,' he says. 'No one got the impression that he was contemplating anything like murder. He was not distressed or wild-eyed. He was just the same old Mark Chapman.'

But later that night, on arrival back in New York, with the bullets safe in his luggage, he did not go back to the city's East Side but checked into the Hotel Olcott at 27 West 72nd Street, less than 200 yards down the road from The Dakota – and Lennon.

That same Sunday, 9 November 1980, the 'Arts and Leisure' section of the *New York Times* carried some wry, urbane new photographs of Lennon and Yoko taken by Jack Mitchell, a leading New York photographer who had been working on assignment for the newspaper and for *Dance Magazine* for many years. They were part of the publicity for *Double Fantasy*, due to be released in eight days. They show a couple clearly in total command of themselves and their lives: a determined and wise-eyed Lennon, his hair flecked now with grey and wearing a polo-neck sweater and blue jeans, stands beside a pert Yoko, gamine in skin-hugging designer jeans, V-neck sweater and woollen scarf tied with mock casualness round her neck while a cap perches jauntily on her head.

They had not been happier for years. Both were keyed up by the almost instant success of the single '(Just Like) Starting Over' released the previous month. They were heavily involved in interviews and photo sessions for *Double Fantasy*'s imminent release. They had had a marvellous double birthday celebration for Sean's fifth birthday and Lennon's fortieth birthday on 13 October. The whole world lay before them again. They were, indeed, both 'starting over'.

During November, Lennon's mind buzzed with new projects looking beyond *Double Fantasy*. He was thinking of an album in the New Year with Ringo Starr and a re-recording of some of his old standards. There was the possibility of his own commercial recording studio. He was elated that Yoko was also planning a new recording future based on some of her unused tracks from the *Double Fantasy* tapes. They were out nearly all the time: either over at the Record Plant Studios on West 44th Street supervising the transfer of *Double Fantasy* cuts into singles format or around town promoting the album itself, or talking about projects – or living. As Bob Gruen, a well-known New York photographer specializing in musicians, has said of this period: 'John seemed like a new man. He hadn't been drinking or abusing himself, and he had learned a lot about nutrition. He seemed more confident and had great joy and respect for life.'

Towards the end of the month, they did a combined video and photographic session, linked to *Double Fantasy*'s release, starting off in Central Park and ending in a gallery in SoHo in which a large loft had been decked out like a white bedroom. Allan Tannenbaum, the New York-based photographer who took the pictures, wrote three years later, in *John Lennon Summer of 1980* edited by Yoko: 'Throughout a long night of costume changes and retakes, John alleviated the tedium with his ever-witty stories and jokes. We talked easily about everything from commercials to sailing, everything but Beatles. I never felt I was in the presence of John Lennon – Famous Beatle. Just John Lennon – Great Guy.'

If this sounds too fawning, there is, as so often, Albert Goldman to paint a different picture. 'Glumly John lay down on the bed naked, embracing Yoko from the side,' he writes. 'Unsatisfied, [the director] instructed Lennon to mount Yoko, a position he was obliged to hold for the next half hour while he conferred with Yoko about camera angles. Meantime, the still photographer, Allen Tannebaum [sic] circled the scene restlessly, taking scores of shots.'

However 'glumly' Lennon may have got on the bed, there is nothing glum about the five photographs from this sequence shown in the *Summer of 1980* book. In fact, if the sheer pleasure shown on Lennon's face in one of them is anything to go by, for Goldman to be right, Lennon would have had to be an even better actor than he was a musician. And Tannenbaum relates how, when he showed Lennon the pictures on 30 November 1980, Lennon's comment was: 'You know what I like about these? You really show how beautiful Yoko is.'

Unknown to Lennon, he was then living on borrowed time for Mark had already made two botched visits, with loaded gun, to The Dakota to kill him.

On the morning of Monday, 10 November 1980, Mark walked down the road from the Hotel Olcott and joined the normal small group of tourists and fans hanging around outside The Dakota. He was there most of that day and returned the next, but there was no sign of Lennon or Yoko. Finally, he summoned up courage to ask Jose Perdomo, the senior doorman, where they were. 'They are out of town,' replied Perdomo. He will not talk about the murder and it is difficult to tell whether the Lennons were really out of town or whether this was the experienced Perdomo's standard ploy in deterring troublesome hangers-around.

But it was enough to throw Mark, in inner torment anyway, into deep depression. What was he going to do? He had no idea when the Lennons would return. Had he come all this way and spent so much money for nothing? It was at this stage, thwarted and angry, that Mark thought briefly of killing some other public figure – not Lennon.

Both Jim Gaines in *People* in February/March 1987 and the *New*

York Post in late June 1981, after Mark had pleaded guilty and before he was due to be sentenced, have made public the fact that Mark had a list of other famous people he might kill.

But they fail to make clear these three significant factors:

(1) There is no evidence whatsoever before Mark's arrest of any such list. In nothing that anyone has ever quoted him as saying before he was arrested is there any indication of wanting to kill anyone but Lennon. The possibility of him killing other celebrities only arises from what he said to the police and to psychiatrists *after* he had killed Lennon. There is nothing at all to substantiate any such intention prior to 8 December 1980.

(2) Neither Gaines nor the *New York Post* makes the point that, even on the basis of Mark's own post-arrest testimony, he considered killing someone other than Lennon *only during this first abortive visit to New York and after he had found that Lennon was 'out of town'*. This was when he was at his lowest ebb and felt that he had to kill someone famous – almost anyone – to make the whole sorry mess in which he had landed himself seem worthwhile. This vital timing shows clearly from the transcript of Allen Sullivan's courtroom cross-examination of Dr Daniel Schwartz, the principal defence psychiatrist, when the court was in closed session with the public (and press) locked out.

(3) The names in the list, as published by Gaines and, as varied in the *New York Post*, are fascinating. I have an authoritative list. It was given to me by Steve Spiro, the New York policeman who arrested Mark and was the first to talk to him. It contains only four names: TV talk show host Johnny Carson, TV commentator Walter Cronkite, actor George C. Scott and Jacqueline Kennedy Onassis. Both Gaines and the *New York Post* agree about Johnny Carson: in fact, that is the only name given by the newspaper. But Gaines calls the list 'a long one' and says it includes, apart from Carson, George C. Scott and Jacqueline Kennedy Onassis, Hawaiian governor George Ariyoshi, Paul McCartney, Elizabeth Taylor – and, of all people, Ronald Reagan. His sources are apparently the reports filed by the several defence psychiatrists and psychologists repeating what Mark told them in prison. In my view, very little credence can be put on this 'long list' to which incidentally Gaines does not refer at all in his earlier article in *People* in June 1981.

One must remember that the psychiatrists' and psychologists' reports date from a time when Jonathan Marks, the defence attorney, was quite properly doing his best to build up a picture of an insane killer to support a defence of criminal insanity. Mark was going along with that, and it was a case of, the 'madder' he was, the better. What better way of showing everyone he was 'mad' than for him to have a whole selection of would-be victims to choose from? It should also not be forgotten that, if Mark was indeed programmed to kill Lennon and Lennon alone, it would probably have been part of his programming that he should name to the doctors as many other proposed victims as possible. There could have been no better smoke-screen to mask his real purpose.

Mark was so low and depressed when he was at the Hotel Olcott that he once again contemplated suicide. He took himself off to the Statue of Liberty. There were not many visitors around at that time of year. He waited until he was alone, then he took out his loaded gun and held it to his head.

But he did not pull the trigger. 'I could not think of anything to write in the suicide note,' is the mundane (and hardly believable) explanation he gave to Dr Daniel Schwartz, as later given in evidence by Schwartz at Mark's sentencing hearing. Back at the Olcott, he telephoned Gloria in Hawaii and told her: 'I've won a great victory. I am coming home. I'll tell you about it when I get there.' He flew back to Honolulu – throwing away, as he later told Dr A. Louis McGarry, a prosecution psychiatrist, his copy of *The Catcher in the Rye*.

Lennon had won a few more weeks to live.

PART THREE

THE MURDER ITSELF
(November to December 1980)

13

Journey to Murder

Mark's return home to Honolulu was far from triumphant. He was depressed and miserable, consumed with feelings of failure. He told Gloria the truth about his visit to New York: that he had gone there to kill John Lennon – but he claimed that 'her strong love' had saved him.

Albert Goldman paints a picture of Mark's condition at this time, absolutely consistent with the 'lone nut' image that every other writer and commentator has taken as his basic premise. He writes: 'For the next three weeks he did nothing but watch television. During this period he had two hallucinations which he interpreted as divine messages. Walking past a plaque on his wall listing the Ten Commandments, Mark saw the Sixth Commandment, "Thou shalt not kill", leap forward. Another day, while watching a cartoon, he suddenly spied the same phrase on the screen.

'By late November Mark was telling Gloria that it was time he grew up. He was a married man now and ought to be able to support a family. What he needed to do first, however, was to go off by himself for a while, to think things over. He had decided to return to New York. She needn't fear that he would do anything wrong. He had thrown the gun and the bullets into the ocean.

'At the same time he called the Waikiki Counselling Clinic, where he had gone before when he felt suicidal.'

The ex-professor has a nice turn of phrase but this account is flawed with three almost certain inaccuracies and also suffers from the defect of being based on Mark's own unverifiable statements in prison. From the sources that he gives at the back of his book, it would seem that Goldman himself never visited Honolulu for his research and, of the twenty names that he cites as the basis of information for this last section of Lennon's life, not one person lived or worked in Hawaii or knew Mark Chapman: they all have to do with Lennon.

Goldman expresses his indebtedness to Craig Unger, the writer of the article in *New York* magazine in June 1981, who later 'abandoned his efforts to turn his material into a film and shared it with the author of this book', and to Jim Gaines who 'published his findings in *People* in 1987'.

If this is so, they have led him into error. Amid the heated prose of Goldman's account, there are only three solid facts: as to one, he is contradicted by another source and two have no basis in reality.

First, Goldman's confident assertion that Mark told Gloria he was going back to New York, albeit not to kill Lennon. At a press conference in Honolulu that Brook Hart, her attorney, called on 10 December 1980, Hart, with his client sitting beside him, said: 'She knew he was going on an airplane. She knew he was going somewhere, but she didn't know precisely where he was going.' Interviewed by me in September 1987 in his office, full of law books and potted plants, he said that he still stood by every word of that. Yet Goldman does not even mention the press conference or what was then said on Gloria's behalf.

The two facts that are provably wrong are both contained in these words in Goldman's text: 'For the next three weeks [after Mark's return from New York] he did nothing but watch television. . . . At the . . . time he called the Waikiki Counselling Clinic.'

For a start, Goldman has not even got the name right: it was the Waikiki Mental Health Clinic. But, far more important, Mark was *not* back in Hawaii for three weeks before he called a clinic, and the clinic was anyway *not* the Waikiki. If Goldman has got those two substantial facts wrong, how much reliance can one place on his acceptance of Mark's prison cell descriptions of his so-called 'hallucinations' given at a time when he was setting up a defence of 'criminal insanity'?

Janice Wolf was, in November and December 1980, a staff writer on the *Honolulu Advertiser*. She was an experienced journalist and, when interviewed in September 1987, she had moved on to the responsible post of administrative director of Hawaii's state courts.

Her integrity and ability are unassailable. Under a joint by-line with her colleague, Walter Wright, the *Honolulu Advertiser* ran a story on 13 December 1980 detailing Mark's efforts to seek help from the Hawaii state mental health system in the previous month. Wolf and Wright were specific in the result of their researches: 'A state clinic . . . refused to see him, referring him instead to Catholic Social Services. On 20 or 21 November, CSS made a 26 November appointment for him.'

So it is impossible for Goldman to be correct. If Mark mooned around his apartment watching television and having his two hallucinations for three full weeks before making his phone call and the phone call itself took place on a date just before 20 or 21 November, when he actually called the CSS, that would mean Mark had returned unfulfilled to Hawaii from New York on about either 30 or 31 October or 1 November. But this is nonsense. Four pages earlier in his own book, Goldman gives the date – quite correctly – of Mark's flying to New York in the first place as 27 October. Furthermore, on that very same page, Goldman also gives the date – again correctly – of Mark's weekend visit to Atlanta to get the bullets as being Saturday and Sunday 8 and 9 November. It just does not gel: Goldman is correct on page 674 with his dates – which means he cannot be right with his 'three weeks' story on page 678.

Furthermore, as we shall see, Mark did not call 'the Waikiki Counselling Clinic where he had gone before', as Goldman says; he called the Makiki Clinic. They sound and write very similarly but they are two separate clinics and the fact that Mark called one rather than the other may well be significant.

The sad reality for Mark was that, within less than a week of his return from New York, he was right back to where he had been in the summer of 1977: telephoning a local mental health clinic for help. Yet here at once there is a mystery: why did he not call the Waikiki Mental Health Clinic where psychiatric social worker Anne Jones had been so helpful to him three years earlier? Anne cannot understand why he called the Makiki: was he really seeking help or was the whole thing a charade? 'Why didn't he call me, if he thought so highly of me?' she says. 'I was shocked at that because I feel that if he was really seeking help, he would have called *me*. The Waikiki had moved its location by then but he could easily have found me.'

The irony, as we have seen, is that the Makiki Clinic did not want to talk to him at all. They referred him to the Catholic Social Services – even though Mark, with his fundamentalist upbringing, was far from being a Roman Catholic. Why did the Makiki turn him away? It seems that, although, like the Waikiki, it was a state clinic available to all in its area, it concentrated less on direct work with patients and more on indirect work, such as lectures and dispensing public information.

As Janice Wolf and Walter Wright reported, Mark called the Catholic Social Services on 20 or 21 November, and spoke to a social worker who offered him an appointment for that very day – but Mark backed off and said it was not that urgent. He made an appointment for nearly a week ahead: on 26 November; but why was he seeking help anyway? Was it to cope with an intense inner battle as to whether or not to kill John Lennon? Was it to try and stop himself being taken over by the spirit and personality of Holden Caulfield? Or was it rather a desperate attempt to get some kind of help because his controller was making his life impossible, exerting immense mental pressure on him for having returned from New York with his mission unaccomplished and Lennon still very much alive?

Whatever the truth, Mark did not get the assistance or counselling he needed. But it is perhaps difficult to fault the CSS social worker who got the call. All that Mark told him, according to the organization's executive director when talking to Janice Wolf after the murder, was that he 'was concerned about his unemployment and the slight depression he was in'. He sounded depressed and under stress but he 'was coherent and mentally alert'.

He apparently did not sound like someone who was going to go out and shoot himself – or anyone else. He did not seem to think it was urgent. So why should the social worker do more than merely make an appointment for later?

But when Mark did not show up on Wednesday, 26 November, the social worker then got concerned. He telephoned Mark's apartment on the Thursday and Friday and on 1, 2 and 5 December of the following week; but he got no answer to any of those five calls. In itself, this poses another little mystery. Interviewed in September 1987, Janice Wolf said: 'I remember the CSS people telling me that they didn't think it was urgent but the curious thing is, if they thought it wasn't urgent and only offered their caller an appointment several days later, why did they get so worried when he did not turn up and phone him practically every day thereafter?' One possible answer, of course, is that perhaps they realized they had made a grievous miscalculation. Her sombre view is that this perplexed and troubled young man 'slipped through the cracks of the state mental health system'.

Eight months later, in August 1981, soon after Mark had been sentenced, she filed another story in her newspaper that Dorothy Lewis, a psychiatry professor at New York University and one of the medical experts for the defence, had said the day before: 'I think the killing might have been aborted' if Mark had received proper help from the local mental health clinics at that time. Perhaps yes, perhaps no. Professor Lewis is the only psychiatrist who used the graphic term 'command hallucinations' in her report to defence attorney Jonathan Marks on Mark's condition. Was she perhaps hinting that Mark might have been trying to get away from the pressures of those constant commands to kill in his head – or from the person or persons who were putting them there? In June 1988, I tried to interview Professor Lewis in New York but she said she could not talk to me because of her understandable – but frustrating – duty of confidentiality to her ex-patient.

Janice Wolf, in September 1987, had another nugget of information about this period that is intriguing and possibly significant. She told me that, when she was working on the story, she had received information from a professional source, whose reliability she had been unable to confirm, that in the months prior to the murder, Mark had been having private sessions with a local psychiatrist (she gave me his name) who had given him the remarkable advice: 'Act out your fantasies!' Is that a proper thing for a psychiatrist to tell his patient – or had Mark's controller called in extra help?

Mark was not an automated robot. He was a complex, highly strung and emotionally tense human being. Were those who wished to see John Lennon dead having trouble with their wavering non-professional hit man? Could they keep him safely on course?

In truth, it would seem that Mark continued to vacillate almost right up to the last minute when he actually pulled the trigger. But he was like a fly caught in a web spun by a spider more powerful and intelligent than himself. Try though he may to escape, to seek refuge in his wife's love or the counselling of experts, inexorably he was being drawn to that final encounter at the entrance to The Dakota. He could not escape his destiny – or the manipulation to which he was being subjected.

A few days after the murder, while being held in Rikers Island Prison awaiting his preliminary court appearances, he was to describe this period to the Rev. Charles McGowan, his ex-pastor from South De Kalb who had flown over a thousand miles from his new ministry in Alabama to give him comfort. Confused and frightened, Mark opened up to his former mentor. 'I would say he was very lucid, very rational,' McGowan later told an *Atlanta Constitution* journalist. 'He had a clear memory of everything he had done. And he said, "Although I understand what I've done, and although it was well planned by me, I do not understand why I did it . . ."

'He said it was a struggle and that he went through a torment. He said, "I've been through a torment for the last two or three months, and it's a struggle between good and evil and right and wrong . . ."

'He said, "I just gave in. It was almost as if I was on some kind of special mission that I could not avoid."'

It is difficult to think of wording more appropriate for someone who, despite all his efforts to fight against it, was being relentlessly programmed to kill. To follow through his 'special mission'.

Every account to date of Lennon's murder, from newspaper reports at the time through Craig Unger's and Jim Gaines' intervening magazine articles to Albert Goldman's biography in August 1988, including even my own version in the *Daily Express* in 1985, has Mark landing in New York on Saturday, 6 December 1980 on his second and final journey to kill Lennon, having flown overnight from Honolulu changing planes en route at Chicago. That is, in effect, the official version: a determined assassin flying halfway across the world to stalk his victim with gun and ammunition stowed safely in his luggage, and the whole venture financed unknowingly by his compliant wife with a new $2500 loan he had persuaded her to take out from her employer's credit union.

It is a coherent picture and a simple one. Get your act together: your gun, your bullets, your money, your resolve – and get on a plane.

But I am now convinced that it did not happen like that.

United Airlines, then and now, have no direct flights from Honolulu to New York. You have to fly by way of Chicago, changing planes at that major hub of mid-American air travel. I fully accept that Mark landed at New York's La Guardia Airport on Saturday 6 December on United Airlines Flight 904 from Chicago – but he had not flown overnight from Honolulu changing planes en route at Chicago. On the contrary, he had started his journey earlier that morning at Chicago where – and this has never before been published – he had spent the previous three days.

Unlike the official version, I believe that he did not leave Honolulu on Friday, the day before, to fly on a connecting flight to New York to kill Lennon. He left Honolulu on the previous Tuesday to fly to Chicago. That was his destination. When he left Honolulu, he had no firm intention of flying on to New York and of killing Lennon. It was only in Chicago that he formed that intent or was finally programmed to that effect – and remember that, on his return to Hawaii the previous month, he had thrown away his 'trigger' book, *The Catcher in the Rye*. That episode in his life was supposed to be over.

I am sure that there are three missing days in Chicago, from 2 December to 5 December. They are denied by the New York County District Attorney's office but I believe that is when and where Lennon's fate was really sealed. Whatever the truth may be about conspiracy or mind control or programming, those three missing days exist and they have been covered up by the authorities – or *for* the authorities.

Why am I so confident of this? It is a tangled story but, at the final untying of the knots, there is no other conclusion to which one can come.

We start with Captain Louis L. Souza of the Honolulu police, who carried out the local follow-up investigation after the murder for the New York authorities. In September 1987, he told me that he had established beyond doubt that, on 28 November 1980 (two days after Mark had not kept his appointment with the social worker from the Catholic Social Services), Mark bought

WHO KILLED JOHN LENNON?

a United Airlines 'special fare' ticket number 24-65607-252 for $459.86 for a return flight out of Honolulu. Captain Souza told me the name of the United Airlines agent, Steve Maruyama, who had sold Mark the ticket but admitted: 'I don't have his address and I didn't interview him because my only concern at the time was to establish that Chapman acquired an airfare out of the state and the ultimate location.'

Captain Souza does not seem to have been bothered that that 'ultimate location' was not New York but Chicago. For Mark did not buy on 28 November 1980 a ticket for United Airlines Flight 2 at 6.10 p.m. on Friday, 5 December for New York connecting with Flight 904 out of Chicago on the Saturday morning. He bought a return ticket for United Airlines Flight 2 at 6.10 p.m. on Tuesday, 2 December for Chicago with a return flight from Chicago at 11.20 a.m. on Thursday, 18 December – and that was all. It was purely and simply a visit to Chicago. I at once queried the date '2 December' as against '5 December' with Captain Souza and, with my tape recorder openly in use on his desk, he checked his original report to the New York authorities lying in front of him and said: 'No, the date was 2 December.' I later called him back on the telephone specifically to see if he had checked out with United Airlines at the time that the ticket had, in fact, been used by Mark on 2 December and he said that the airline had confirmed that to him when he was preparing his report. I made a note of his reply immediately after I put down the telephone.

Unfortunately, none of this can be confirmed now by the airline because, as Robert Morgan of their consumer relations department told me at United Airlines headquarters outside Chicago in May 1988, all records and tickets are destroyed after two years and they do not even have available now the timetable or fare-structure on which they were operating back in November/December 1980.

Surely Gloria Chapman can help? She must know which day her husband left Honolulu, the Tuesday or the Friday. Jim Gaines in *People* in February 1987 has her sitting in a taxi with Mark going to the airport to see him off on what Gaines calls a 'rainy Friday afternoon'. He does not specifically quote Gloria as to the day of the week or the date.

But on 10 December 1980 the *New York Post* printed a news-story by Sam Rosensohn and David Seifman that 'last night' Gloria had said 'her husband had left Hawaii eight or ten days ago to go to New York'. Alright, she is quoted as giving New York as Mark's destination but the date, working backwards, would be almost exactly 2 December. 'Eight or ten days' before 10 December would put Mark's departure at between 30 November and precisely 2 December. In any event, no way could it be so recent as the afternoon of 5 December, 'rainy' or otherwise.

I have been unable to check it out with Gloria Chapman for myself. She has three times refused to see me: once over the telephone when I called her at work from New York in 1985 and twice by not answering letters requesting an interview. There is no more I can do.

So we would seem to be stymied. But I do not think so. I have in my possession a photocopy of an air ticket that the New York police found in Mark's hotel room on the day following the murder. It formed part of a 'display' of his personal effects that he left out for them to discover when he left his room on the morning of 8 December to walk up to The Dakota and kill Lennon. It is a remarkable document for it is in every respect the same United Airlines return ticket that Captain Souza told me about, the same number (24-65607-252), the same date of issue (28 November 1980), the same return date from Chicago to Honolulu (18 December) but *not* an outward departure date of 2 December. The date looking inexorably up at one is 5 December!

This document does not make any kind of sense. Allen Sullivan, in his cross-examination of Dr Daniel Schwartz on Mark's sentencing day putting the prosecution's case to him for his detailed comments, made great play of the fact that Mark 'pre-arranged, made reservations and booked all the way through to New York by a variety of airlines to go through at a cheaper rate'. With all respect to Sullivan, that is nonsense, for I hold a photocopy of Mark's baggage claim check that he also left out in his hotel room. It is a United Airlines tag and it says: 'Destination LGA, Flight 904. To ORD Flight 2.' Translated from airline jargon, that means that Mark's luggage first went from Honolulu on United Airlines Flight 2 to Chicago's O'Hare Airport and then direct through to La Guardia Airport on United Airlines Flight 904. In other words, it is, in effect, saying that Mark did what the prosecution said he did: he flew straight to New York from Honolulu by way of a connecting flight at Chicago. *But both flights were United Airlines flights*, so Sullivan's point about making reservations on different airlines 'to go through at a cheaper rate' simply does not stand up. It is balderdash.

Furthermore, if Mark really was trying to keep his expenses down – despite the $2500 loan he had talked his long-suffering wife into taking out from her credit union at the Castle Hospital and the Bank of Hawaii Visa Card that he had on him – then, as Robert Morgan at United Airlines headquarters confirms, it would have been stupid for him to buy a 'special fare' rate ticket to Chicago and then some other kind of United Airlines ticket on to New York. Said Morgan in May 1988, 'It *can* be cheaper to take out a "special fare" return ticket than a full fare one-way ticket, if you do not intend to return to your original point of departure. A "special fare" return fare can, after all, cost less than a full fare one-way ticket. If Chapman when he bought his ticket in Honolulu intended going on right through to New York, it would have been cheaper for him to have bought a "special fare" or some other discount fare right through to his farthest destination, New York. Once you break a journey, that in itself makes it, by however little an amount, that bit more expensive.'

So, therefore, even if Mark was trying to save money, as Sullivan said in court, that does not explain why he did not simply buy a discount return fare right through to New York, without all this Chicago twaddle. It would still have been cheaper than buying a one-way full fare, even if he had no intention of using the return half because (as actually happened) he was going to give himself up to the police. Indeed, a travel agent in Honolulu has confirmed to me: 'It would have been cheaper to fly return to New York with a stop-over at Chicago than buy a return fare to Chicago and from there get a return – or single – fare to New York.'

Furthermore, as anyone who has ever booked air travel to several onward destinations will know, your batch of tickets will give on each one *all* the destinations, with the airline staff merely peeling off the ticket applicable to their section of the journey. My photocopy of United Airlines ticket number 24-65607-252 only has Honolulu and Chicago on it. There is no mention whatsoever of New York.

The implication is obvious. When Mark bought his Honolulu–Chicago return ticket from United Airlines agent Steve Maruyama on 28 November 1980, he had absolutely no intention of flying on to New York and killing Lennon. I accept that he must have taken his gun and ammunition with him but who knows under what pressure he was labouring? The fact remains that he did not buy a ticket to New York in Honolulu. The decision to fly on to New York – and use the gun – was only taken in Chicago where I am convinced he bought his ticket for New York.

Yet someone 'doctored' the United Airlines Honolulu–Chicago–Honolulu ticket that he left out in his New York hotel room. Someone also 'doctored' the United Airlines baggage claim check accompanying that ticket to make it look as if he had started his journey in Honolulu on the Friday with the baggage going straight through to New York. It could have happened before Mark set out his 'display' in his hotel room prior to the murder *or at any time afterwards*. Since at least the beginning of the 1970s, the New York police has had close ties with the CIA. As far back as 17 December 1972, the *New York Times* revealed that the agency had secretly provided training for fourteen local police officers. A CIA spokesman admitted that other American police departments had also received 'similar courtesies' but he would not specify how many. When New York congressman Ed Koch, now the mayor, pressed for further information, the CIA's Legislative Counsel, John Maury, himself a former station chief in Greece, told him that 'less than fifty police officers all told, from a total of about a dozen city and county police forces, have received some sort of agency briefing within the past two years.' How convenient for the CIA to have such useful friends in 'about a dozen' of the nation's major cities! It must be comforting for senior officials at agency headquarters in Langley to know that they can pick up the telephone at any time and have a receptive police officer at the other end of the line, ready to give whatever commands are necessary to comply with their wishes. After all, what is a little forgery between friends? One would have thought that falsification of documents was one of the easiest things that Langley could have asked for, if they had not already done the job themselves before Mark even left his hotel room.

Incidentally, why did he only leave out his Honolulu–Chicago return ticket and not also the used part of the ticket that had actually brought him from Chicago to New York? Could it be because it would have shown it was purchased in Chicago and not Honolulu and, with typical CIA bungling, they only realized that at the last minute?

Anyway, what did happen to that Chicago–New York ticket? And was it single or return? No one has ever told us. I wonder why.

The fact remains that the New York police have in their files a United Airlines numbered ticket with a departure date from Honolulu of 5 December and Captain Souza has in his office in police headquarters in Honolulu a copy of his report in which the ticket with the same number has a departure date of 2 December. If I had not walked into that office and started questioning Captain Souza, this discrepancy would never have come to light.

When I pointed it out to Allen Sullivan over the telephone in New York in June 1988, he point-blank refused to dig out the information from his files to establish exactly when Mark did leave Honolulu. 'I have four drawers full of papers and I am not prepared to undertake the work to sort it out,' he said. I persevered with Gerald McKelvey, special assistant to the New York County District Attorney, trying to obtain a copy of a sixteen-page chronology of Mark's movements that Sullivan had told Justice Dennis Edwards on Mark's sentencing day had been compiled by his office – but, on 23 June 1988, McKelvey wrote me: 'I am sorry to tell you that it appears that the sixteen-page chronology that we had worked up on the movements of Mark David Chapman cannot be located in our files.' I can only hope that other important documents from major cases are kept more carefully. Meanwhile, one more piece of vital documentation – like so much of the FBI and CIA files on Lennon and the YMCA's central record on Mark Chapman – is not available to public scrutiny.

McKelvey added: 'Allen Sullivan told me that reconstructing the chronology now would be an enormous undertaking.'

Perhaps. But why on earth has it gone missing? It would answer a lot of questions if, even at this late stage, it could be found. McKelvey explained: 'The case, as you will recall, had been closed for many years and the exhibits – what would have been the exhibits had there been a trial – stored away.' One wonders why. If we are ever to begin to know the truth about the murder of John Lennon, Allen Sullivan and his colleagues should either have a really good look for it or set about the 'enormous undertaking' of reconstructing this mysteriously missing prime exhibit forthwith. Justice demands no less.

Reverting to Chicago, there was a perfectly legitimate acceptable reason why Mark would want to visit that city in early December. You will not find it mentioned in Goldman's book or by Craig Unger or Jim Gaines. I only came across it myself by chance: going into a travel agency in Kailua in September 1987 looking for someone who might have known Gloria Chapman, I lighted upon Ruth Brilhante, who used to work with her at the now-defunct Waters World Travel and has remained friends with her ever since. She also knew Mark and was reminiscing to me about him: 'When we heard that Mark had shot Lennon we could not believe it. Not only because we could not believe he could do a thing like that but because we did not know he was in New York. We all thought he was in Chicago. That is where he had gone to take his grandmother home after she was visiting out here.'

I could not believe it. But I checked in the local newspaper files to see if there was any reference to a visiting grandmother in either the *Honolulu Advertiser* or the *Honolulu Star-Bulletin*, and I found this clear reference in a report by Beverley Creamer and Walter Wright in the *Honolulu Advertiser* for 10 December 1980:

> Mrs Chapman . . . was also in seclusion yesterday at the home of a friend. She spent the afternoon resting and trying to understand and comprehend what happened.
>
> 'It was a total shock,' said the friend.
>
> Her initial concern was for Mark's grandmother, who had been visiting the island recently from her Chicago home. Mark returned with her to the Mainland last week and apparently went to Chicago with her before he went to New York.

This last paragraph was gold dust! I asked Beverley Creamer, who wrote that part of the story, for her source: the name of 'the friend', anything. She did her best to help. She looked up her old notes at home, she searched through her records – 'but it is, after all, nearly seven years ago. I just cannot find anything. I didn't invent the story, I assure you. I know I got it from someone who I had no reason to believe was not telling the truth but I just cannot remember who! I don't know how many hundreds of stories I have filed since then.'

When I was in Honolulu in September 1987 and later in May 1988 in Chicago, I tried to trace Mark's grandmother in the Chicago region but it was a daunting task. Some 3.5 million people live in the Chicago metropolitan area and I was not even sure of her full name or whether she was his maternal or paternal grandmother. Without any help from Mark and his family, and with even Ruth Brilhante not answering a letter asking for further information, I have been unable to trace her nearly eight years after the event. She may have moved or sadly she may no longer be living.

There is, however, confirmation of her existence in Chicago in December 1980 from another journalist writing in a newspaper several thousands of miles away from Honolulu. In an article appearing on the same day as Beverley Creamer and Walter Wright's article, 10 December 1980, in the *Atlanta Constitution*, staff writer Bill Montgomery, reporting from Honolulu, wrote:

> Chapman apparently used more than $2000 borrowed from the Castle Memorial Hospital credit union to finance his trip to the mainland this week. He was supposed to be visiting his grandmother in Chicago before going to New York.

In addition to these three totally independent sources putting Mark on a plane to Chicago involved with his grandmother (either taking her back there or visiting her there) and not flying to New York to kill Lennon, I give you these three other pieces of information for you to evaluate:

(1) Allen Sullivan's cross-examination of Dr Daniel Schwartz confirms, in effect, that Mark had a grandmother of whom he was very fond. For Sullivan asked Dr Schwartz if, when Mark was about sixteen, he had sold his entire record collection, which included some Beatles, for $15 in order to finance running away from home. Dr Schwartz agreed. 'He went to Miami for two weeks' – and the only person living in Miami at that time whom the troubled teenager knew was his beloved grandmother.

(2) Mrs June Blankinship, interviewed in May 1988, talked, as we have seen, about a 'Yankee' grandmother 'up East'.

(3) Anne Jones, interviewed in September 1987, specifically recalled: 'Mark had a grandmother somewhere in the mid-West' – which is the region dominated by Chicago.

Returning to New York in June 1988, I wanted to talk to Allen Sullivan about all this. He had been very generous with his time on two earlier visits in 1981 and 1985 so I called him up. But now he said that he simply could not spare the time to see me. This was now a very old case which had long been closed. 'What about Chapman telling a friend in Honolulu [Ruth Brilhante] that he was taking his grandmother back to Chicago?' I asked in our brief telephone conversation. 'Yes, we know. It was a lie,' was all he said.

Ex-twentieth precinct lieutenant of detectives Arthur O'Connor has done his best to be helpful but he has not really been able to take the matter any further. When we spoke over the telephone in June 1988 setting up our meeting for a few days later, I explained to him about the United Airlines ticket and the grandmother in Chicago but, when we met, all he could say was: 'I have racked my brains about Chicago and couldn't come up with anything. I don't remember the grandmother or anybody else or anything coming up in connection with Chicago with Mark Chapman, in conversation with him or anything. I have no knowledge of Chicago.'

But he also added: 'As far as you are trying to build up some kind of conspiracy, I would support you in that line. Like I said originally over the phone, if this gentleman [Mark] wanted to get away with it, he could have got away with it. There was the subway across the road and no one around to stop him. If there is a conspiracy, it would never have been investigated and no conspiracy was investigated to my knowledge, and it would have come to my attention if it had.

'You've got to understand the human element involved. You're so happy to "ground" the case, you don't want to open Pandora's box because, you know, with investigations, one thing leads to another and another and another; and you have resources and manpower and money involved. And you have another human reaction – laziness!

'There *could* have been a conspiracy – but it was hallelujah! to get this one "grounded". You say you've got a copy of the ticket that got him to Chicago. Did I have any evidence of how he got from Chicago to New York? From memory, no! – and nobody cared to pursue it. I was not aware of that Chicago ticket and, if I had been aware at the time, I honestly tell ya: "So what?

The case is grounded. A man acknowledges his guilt, he pleads guilty. That's it!" If there is conspiracy, I have no information of a conspiracy nor did I look for such information.'

You cannot be more honest than Mr O'Connor. I cannot take it any further. David Moore, Mark's old friend from Fort Chaffee who had helped him with a letter of recommendation on his world tour in 1978 and with whom he then stayed overnight in Geneva, was in December 1980 living in Chicago. He was in charge of a YMCA hostel there. Did he see Mark in Chicago that first week in December 1980? 'No, I didn't,' he told me in May 1988. But he also said that, even if Mark were merely stopping over on the Saturday morning at O'Hare Airport in transit to New York, as the official version has it, he would have expected him to call him just to say 'hello', however early in the day it was. Mark could easily have called: he had Moore's address and telephone number. Mark's plane from Honolulu (if he caught it) would have landed at 6.05 a.m. He would probably have had at least an hour to make his connection but Moore says that he did not call – 'which, if he was at O'Hare, surprises me'.

Also consider this: if Ruth Brilhante and Beverley Creamer are right and Mark did take his grandmother back to Chicago, he would surely have never left her alone at O'Hare Airport at 6.05 in the morning after a long flight from Honolulu and, even if he was going on to New York, quickly kiss her and run off to make his connection? Does that sound like a loving grandson? The odds are that he would not have let her make her own way home across the vast distances of that extremely spread-out city. Even if he *was* going on to New York, he would first have seen her home and then got a plane later that day to the Big Apple.

But the baggage tag so conveniently left out in his hotel room for the police to find has him flying on by direct connection on Flight 904 to New York. It simply cannot be.

This whole ticket and tag affair does not hang together. To my mind, there can be no real doubt that Mark *was* in Chicago for three days before he flew on to New York. He *did* take his grandmother back. He *was* intending to use his return ticket for 18 December. But something happened to him in Chicago. Someone got hold of him. Someone got him back on course.

Someone put murder yet again powerfully and dominatingly into his mind.

He had left Honolulu as Mark Chapman. He flew out of Chicago to New York as Holden Caulfield. His 'special mission' to assassinate John Lennon had entered its final stage.

14

Prelude to Murder

Lennon spent the last two weeks of his life working flat out, and enjoying every minute of it. 'Kiss Kiss Kiss', which was the other side of the single '(Just Like) Starting Over' that had been released in late October, had got a lot of rock club, new wave-type of exposure. So Yoko had suggested that they take 'Walking on Thin Ice', one of her unused tracks from their mammoth recording session in early August, and turn it into a six-minute 'discoesque' number specifically for that market. Lennon threw himself into the project with all his newly refound enthusiasm.

With something of a sneer, Goldman has him 'spending the last two weeks of his life labouring day in, day out to make this track a big hit for Yoko'.

Lennon *was* working at full pelt, but it was not only on Yoko's one-track. The two of them had already started work at the Record Plant on *Milk and Honey*, their projected successor album to *Double Fantasy*. They had already got half the basic tracks from their over-production for the earlier album. They intended releasing it in the following year after a world tour to promote *Double Fantasy*. In the end, Yoko could only bring herself to put out a reworked version in January 1984. But now, as Jay Hastings, the bearded young front desk clerk at The Dakota, told Ray Coleman: 'At the beginning of December 1980, John was particularly "up". He was going back and forth two miles to the studio most days with Yoko, leaving late afternoon and returning between 10.30 and 11.30. I'd listen out for the slam of their black limousine door. I could always tell his walk as he bounded up the steps into the hallway.

Mitch Plotkin, who was general manager of the Record Plant

when I interviewed him in 1985, makes clear that Lennon did not spend his last two weeks slaving away only for Yoko. 'He was working on the tracks for the new album as well as mixing Yoko's single,' he said. 'He was very well liked here. He was like family. He was in good spirits at that time. You'd come in after he had been working all night and see him sitting on the floor with the other guys "jiving" and playing guitars. He was a private person but after he accepted someone he was a very nice man.

'I was absolutely heart-broken when I heard he was killed. I went into a room by myself and started to cry. It was just tragic, a senseless waste of life.'

When Andy Peebles of BBC Radio One interviewed Lennon and Yoko at the Record Plant on the evening of Saturday, 6 December 1980, he too found a Lennon who was warm and friendly, bursting with ideas and vitality. Asked about his forecast for the months and years to come, Lennon replied with sadly unconscious irony: 'I think it's going to be the one period they say, "Those two will do anything for publicity, for Christ's sake get them off the front pages, oh get them off!" You know, people were bitching at us because we weren't doing anything. And I have a funny feeling that it's going to be the other way round again, because we're talking and talking and talking and all sorts of plans and ideas we have in our heads. It's just a matter of getting it done, you know.

'We already got half the next album and we'll probably go in just after Christmas and do that. We're already talking about what the idea for the third album is. It's already laid out and I can't wait . . .'

Significantly his ideas were not only musical but related also to the world outside. He was recovering his old political militancy, though tempered by experience and with the benefit of maturity. He and Yoko had not taken to the streets in political protest for over eight years, not since May 1972, in the early days of their battle against deportation, when he had spoken at a rally in midtown Manhattan demonstrating against President Nixon's mining of Haiphong Harbour and massive new bombing raids in a dramatic escalation of the Vietnam conflict.

Now, in the first week of December 1980, the tickets were bought for Yoko, Sean and himself to fly to San Francisco the following week – the week he never lived through – to attend a rally called by the Teamsters Union and to march through the streets in support of striking Japanese-American workers in the cause of wage equality. They had been on strike since 13 November protesting the wages structure of the Japan Foods Corporation (JFC) and two other Japanese-owned subsidiaries that together imported and distributed 90 per cent of all Japanese food sold in the United States.

A major question of principle was at stake: equal pay with the white employees of these three large corporations. Why should yellow-skinned men and women receive less wages for equivalent work just because of their skin-colour? Ironically, that colour was the same as that of most of the management; but money spoke louder than racial solidarity. That was why other mammoth Japanese-American corporations like Sumitomo and Mitsubishi were watching the dispute anxiously while supporting the three companies in every way they could.

The strike had led to a boycott of the three companies' products and spread to Los Angeles where a rally was to be held on the same day as in San Francisco. Lennon and Yoko sent a message of support to the Los Angeles branch of the Teamsters, which the union in turn sent to the media. It was to be Lennon's last written political pronouncement:

We are with you in spirit. Both of us are subjected to prejudice and abuse as an Oriental family in the Western world.

In this beautiful country where democracy is the very foundation of its Constitution, it is sad that we have to still fight for equal rights and equal pay for the citizens.

Boycott it must be, if it is the only way to bring justice and restore the dignity of the Constitution for the sake of all citizens of the US and their children.

Peace and love,
John Lennon and Yoko Ono
New York City
December 1980

And so Lennon was planning to march through the streets of San Francisco with his wife and five-year-old son in support of this anti-employer, anti-racist cause. Who knows what other demonstrations he might have supported or led, if Mark's .38 had

188

not belched its fatal fire? *Newsweek* included news of his intended participation in the San Francisco rally in their 'Special Report' on Lennon after his murder.

But meanwhile he was still alive and enjoying every minute of it. On Saturday afternoon, 6 December, he was having his usual *cappucino* and reading the newspapers at the Cafe La Fortuna round the block from The Dakota, when the owner Vincent Urwand jokingly asked him why he had bothered to make the comeback *Double Fantasy* album. Surely he did not need the money? Lennon laughed: 'I swore I'd look after Sean until he was five, and now he's five and I feel like going back to music. The urge is there. It's been a long time since I wrote a song but they're coming thick and fast now.'

At 6.00 p.m. that evening, he and Yoko started their long interview at the Record Plant with Andy Peebles for BBC Radio One. It was a good session and did not end until the small hours of Sunday morning at his favourite New York restaurant, Mr Chow. He was still clearly very much in love with the city and, before they went off to Mr Chow, Peebles asked him what it was like living there. As part of a long reply that was almost a hymn of praise to life in the Big Apple, Lennon said: 'When I left England I still couldn't go on the street. We couldn't walk around the block, couldn't go to a restaurant, unless you wanted to go "with the business of the star going to the restaurant" garbage. [Here] I've been walking the streets for the last seven years. . . . When we first moved here, she [Yoko] says, "You will be able to walk here;" but I would be walking around tense like, waiting for somebody to say something, or jump on me, and it took me two years to unwind.

'[But] I can go right out this door now and go in a restaurant. You want to know how great that is?'

Of course, it was great but mercifully he did not know that, after he had left home that day to go to Cafe La Fortuna and then on to the Record Plant, Mark had turned up outside The Dakota with his loaded gun.

On arriving at La Guardia Airport earlier that day, Mark had gone straight to the nearest YMCA hostel to The Dakota: the West Side Branch at 5 West 63rd Street, just nine blocks away. Despite his having been 'upset with the homosexuals', to use Allen Sullivan's term in cross-examining Dr Daniel Schwartz, at the Vanderbilt Branch during his previous visit, he seems to have experienced no great inner torment in booking himself into Room number 1041 for the next three nights for $54.50, paid in cash.

He dropped off his bag and set off at once to stalk his prey.

But there was no sign of Lennon. None of the fans hanging around outside The Dakota knew when he would be back: he had gone out, that was all they knew. Frustrated and angry, Mark persisted for a while then walked back to the 'Y'.

At about 7.15 that evening, carrying a satchel (something that has never been properly explained), Mark flagged down a cab driven by Mark Snyder, a thirty-year-old law graduate and part-time cab driver, at the corner of 8th Avenue and 55th Street, eight blocks the other side of his hostel down towards midtown Manhattan. Snyder later described him to the *New York Post*'s David Seifman as 'very agitated'. He would seem to have been delivering or collecting something, which is strange for someone who allegedly knew no one in town. For he started on a half-hour journey that took him first of all up back almost to his hostel, where he disappeared into a building on West 62nd Street for about five minutes, then across Central Park to the corner of East 65th Street and 2nd Avenue, where he disappeared for another few minutes, and then to the other side of town down in Greenwich Village where he got himself dropped off at the junction of Bleecker Street and 6th Avenue.

He offered Snyder a 'snort' of cocaine and told him that he was a recording engineer delivering cassette tapes from Lennon's recording session to various locations around the city. At least, that is the version in the *New York Post*. Huge printed posters stuck up around New York after the murder by something calling itself 'The Assassination Information Committee' quoted the cab driver as saying nothing about cocaine but claiming that Mark had told him he was Mick Jagger's engineer dropping off tapes of a Lennon-McCartney session where he had been present along with Yoko and Jagger. That would have been even more bizarre, but I have been unable to trace Snyder to ask him for myself. In June 1988, the New York Bar authorities had no current listing for him and a letter by way of the Limousine and Taxi Commission went unanswered.

So what was Mark doing, making those two stops? What did

he have in the satchel? What messages, if any, did he deliver or receive? He was not known to be a cocaine-user, so what is all this about offering Snyder a 'snort'? A doorman at an apartment block near to where Mark made his second stop says that, back in 1980, the building that he went into was a place where dealers were known to hang out – but how would an 'out of towner' like Mark have known that, even if he was interested?

In June 1988, I flagged down a cab myself at about 7.15 on a Saturday evening at the corner of 8th Avenue and 55th Street and followed the same route as Mark took. Apart from the drive across Central Park at mid-park level, which happens to be the quickest way to get from the West Side to the East Side at that point, the route has no scenic value at all. One sees none of the famous sights of New York. Both addresses outside which cab driver Snyder waited for Mark are ordinary-looking apartment blocks: unless this young stranger in town really was on some kind of pre-planned errand, there is absolutely no logical reason for his journey.

As to the corner of Bleecker Street and 6th Avenue, where he finally left the cab, it happens to be just one block from the notoriously gay cruising area of Christopher Street, which was, in those pre-AIDS days, the one thoroughfare in Greenwich Village where, with its bars, shops and crowds, there was the most 'action'.

Perhaps, after attending to business, Mark wanted to relax on that mild Saturday evening. Was that why he asked to be let out of the cab one block away, like any other married man perhaps without the courage to be dropped off at Christopher Street itself?

The next morning he checked out of the 'Y' on West 63rd Street and booked himself for seven nights into a $82 a night room – number 2730 – at the Sheraton Center Hotel on 7th Avenue at 52nd Street in midtown Manhattan. He paid with his Bank of Hawaii Visa Card, as if wanting to preserve his cash – although he still had over $2000 with him even after he had paid his airfare. (The ready availability of money on his two trips to New York, even allowing for his original sale of the Rockwell lithograph and Gloria's alleged loan of $2500, is something that no commentator has ever really been able to explain. In fact, none that I have read – including Unger, Gaines and Goldman – has even tried to. I

191

have my own cynical thoughts as to who was making up any 'short-fall' in finances.)

Why did he move further away from the area around The Dakota? It would seem to have been not only a desire for the greater comfort of a semi-luxury hotel as against the frugality of a 'Y' hostel. According to Jim Gaines, he later told an unnamed psychiatrist in prison: 'What bothered me was across the hall were these two fags talking about hairy chests and things like that, and I just God, wanted to go over and blow them all away. I said, "Don't do it." So I checked out [the next day].'

If he did not like that sort of behaviour why had he ever booked into a YMCA hostel in the first place? Especially in those days, 'Y's' were known in big cities to be favoured by gay young men. They were an obvious place for gay or 'interested' men from out of town to try out. After his 'upsetting' experience at the Vanderbilt 'Y' only a few weeks earlier, why had Mark booked in there anyway? Was he, despite himself, intrigued? Could it be Mark Chapman who, plagued with doubts about his own sexuality, booked into the 'Y' but Mark/Holden who checked out so abruptly?

His programming, based on identification with Holden Caulfield, was now fully functioning, and Holden would have reacted in exactly the same way to the posturing homosexuals in the hostel. The violence of his language is remarkably similar to that used by Mark: 'As soon as old Maurice opened the door, he'd see me with the automatic in my hand and he'd start screaming at me . . . to leave me alone. But I'd plug him anyway. Six shots right through his fat hairy belly.'

And, even more important, an aversion to physical manifestations of homosexuality runs deep in Holden's personality. This could account for Mark's reaction, on this one occasion far more aggressive and hysterical than his own usually tortured ambivalence on the subject. Holden Caulfield did not like 'perverts', as he called them: in one crucial episode in *Catcher*, where he is sleeping on a couch when spending the night innocently in a married teacher's apartment, he is awakened by the man's hand stroking his head. He wakes to see him sitting there 'admiring' him. He cannot grab his clothes and get out of the apartment fast enough, even though it is in the middle of the night. 'I know more damn perverts, at school and all, than anybody you ever met, and they're always being perverty when *I'm* around. That kind of stuff's happened to me about twenty times since I was a kid. I can't stand it.'

Mark was not sure about his attitude to gays. He was intrigued and uncertain: capable of close, intimate friendships with members of his own sex. But Holden was almost pathologically anti-gay. Mark/Holden was just unbelievably mixed up on the subject.

Once transferred from the 'Y' and checked into the Sheraton Center Hotel, Mark did a strange thing: he set up, on a bureau in his room, a display of his most treasured possessions. Sullivan tersely dismisses them as his 'props'. They were designed to show the police the 'real' Mark when, as he anticipated, they later entered the room after he had accomplished the murder. 'He laid them out in such a way that they would make a display as you came into the room,' Sullivan told me in 1985. 'He even went out of the room and came back in again, to make sure that it had the maximum impact.'

What he chose to put out provides a fascinating insight into his troubled soul, half Mark/half Holden. First was a pocket Bible inscribed 'Holden Caulfield', with 'Lennon' added to 'The Gospel According to St John' so that it read 'St John Lennon' – and carefully laid open at St Mark, Chapter 7, describing Jesus among the Pharisees, a polite biblical euphemism for 'phoneys'. His expired passport showing his different immigration stamps received in so many foreign countries during his world trip in 1978. The letter of introduction that David Moore had given him for use in that trip. An eight-track tape by his true rock idol, Todd Rundgren, whose music was so different from his so-called idol, John Lennon. A photograph of himself with Vietnamese refugee children in his 'Pied Piper of Hamelin' days at Fort Chaffee. A photograph of his old 1965 Chevrolet car from his primarily happy Columbia High School days. His intriguing Honolulu–Chicago–Honolulu return ticket in its folder with his baggage tag attached – but no ticket from Chicago to New York.

And perhaps most significant of all in Freudian terms, there was a movie still from *The Wizard of Oz* showing the young Judy Garland as Dorothy wiping away the Cowardly Lion's tears with 'To Dorothy' written on it in Mark's own handwriting. Why Dorothy? Only homosexuals venerate the character so much, hence the term for gays 'Friends of Dorothy'. If this was truly the 'real' Mark Chapman, he was certainly baring his innermost feelings: Holden Caulfield would totally have disapproved.

But the display was never seen that Sunday – in fact, not until the early hours of Tuesday morning. Mark spent a long time waiting outside The Dakota on Sunday, armed with his loaded gun and a copy of the *Double Fantasy* album that he had bought the previous day to give him an excuse for hanging around (this so-called 'fan' had not bought it before); but he never set eyes on Lennon or Yoko. Fortunately for them, they seem not to have gone out of doors that day – or, if they did, at a time when the would-be assassin was temporarily away from his post.

Disgruntled, Mark ended up having dinner on his own in the restaurant at the Sheraton Center with a visit from a call girl to his room as a somewhat unusual dessert. Perhaps that was more Holden than Mark, for not only is this the only instance where we know him to have been anything like unfaithful to his wife Gloria with another woman, but also intercourse did not take place nor was even attempted. That is exactly the same as happened with Holden in a similar incident with a prostitute in a New York hotel room in J.D. Salinger's novel.

But after the call girl left, the real-life Mark took over and, like any other guilty married man, he telephoned Gloria back home and told her how much he loved her. With that much absolution to his troubled mind, he turned out the lights and went to sleep.

15

The Day John Lennon Died

Monday, 8 December 1980 was one of the warmest December days that New Yorkers could remember for many years. By mid-day the temperature had soared to the mid-60s Fahrenheit, not much cooler than Los Angeles and way above the wintry chill that held all of Western Europe shivering in the low 30s. As Allen Sullivan, a Roman Catholic for whom it was a day of obligation, returned from Mass that morning he thought to himself what a lovely day it was.

Lennon and Yoko looked down from their seventh-floor apartment over a Central Park whose trees bore the light-brown foliage of autumn rather than the sterile, leafless branches of winter.

They had another full working day ahead of them. First, there was a photo session with Annie Leibovitz, a leading rock photographer, for the cover of *Rolling Stone*'s next issue. In fact, it appeared as the magazine's famous memorial cover, showing a naked Lennon embracing a black-clad Yoko. When Leibovitz showed Lennon the Polaroid, Goldman reports him as enthusing: 'That's great! That's really our relationship. Promise it will be on the cover.' Perhaps predictably, Goldman dismisses it as 'the image of an impassive bitch and her blindly sucking whelp'.

Then, at shortly after 1 o'clock, in Studio One on the first floor, the apartment that they had converted into their office, they started another long *Double Fantasy* interview, this time with Dave Sholin, a radio producer from San Francisco who put together special programmes for the RKO General Radio Network. 'It was the most enlightening, rewarding and thrilling interview I've ever done,' Sholin told a *San Francisco Chronicle* reporter the next day. Lennon 'jumped into the room as if to say,

"Here I am!"' He sat down on a couch, a relaxed and barefoot Yoko curled her legs over the arm of a sofa chair a few feet away, and they began to talk.

So the afternoon was spent on what was to prove to be Lennon's last interview. Excerpts now have a weird, bitter-sweet quality:

We're either going to live or we're going to die. If we're dead we're going to have to deal with that, if we're alive we're going to have to deal with being alive. So worrying about whether Wall Street or the Apocalypse is going to come in the form of the Great Beast – is not going to do us any good day to day . . .

The thing the sixties did was show us the possibility and the responsibility that we all had. It wasn't the answer, it just gave us a glimpse of the possibility – and in the seventies everybody's going 'Nah, Nah, Nah' and possibly in the eighties everyone will say, 'OK let's project the positive side of life again' . . .

I don't want to have to sell my soul again, as it were, to have a hit record. I've discovered that I can live without it, and it makes it happier for me . . .

We feel like this is just a start now, you see, *Double Fantasy* – this is our first album – I know we've worked together before, we've even made albums together before – but this is our first album, we feel. I feel like nothing has ever happened before today. . . .

You have to give thanks to God or whatever is up there to the fact that we all survived. We all survived Vietnam or Watergate, the tremendous upheaval of the whole world. It changed. We were the hit ones of the sixties.

But the world is not like the sixties, the whole world's changed. I am going into an unknown future, but I'm still all here. And still, while there's life, there's hope . . .

Even more poignant was this passage:

My life revolves around my son, Sean. Now I have more reason to stay healthy and bright. . . . And I want to be with my best friend. My best friend's me wife. If I couldn't have worked with her, I wouldn't have bothered. . . . I consider that my work won't be finished until I'm dead and buried, and I hope that's a long, long time.

Mark had awakened at about 10.30, showered and got himself ready for his grim task. He felt sure that somehow this would be the day when he achieved his destiny. He was prepared to wait all day, if necessary, outside The Dakota and, although the weekend's weather had been mild for the locals, he knew that it would be chill for his blood, used to the warm airs of Hawaii seldom out of the 80s. So he pulled on thermal underwear before dressing himself in shirt, sweater, green trousers and blue jacket. Then, after a last minute adjustment to his most intimate personal possessions 'displayed' on the bureau, he threw a green scarf round his neck, put on a dark olive-green military type overcoat, black imitation fur hat and black wool gloves and left the room. As he stood in the lift, descending the twenty-seven floors to the entrance lobby, he patted comfortingly the loaded gun snug and secure in his right-hand overcoat pocket. He came out of the lift, turned left and almost ran down the five steps to 7th Avenue.

As he walked the twenty blocks up to The Dakota on West 72nd Street, incongruous amid the lightly dressed New Yorkers with his heavy winter gear, he realized he was missing a prop. He had with him his *Double Fantasy* album – but something was missing. He halted his progress towards Lennon's selected place of execution and dived into a bookshop to emerge with a red paperback copy of *The Catcher in the Rye*. On the title page he wrote: 'To Holden Caulfield from Holden Caulfield' and below that: 'This is my statement.'

Arrived at The Dakota, he discovered from the doorman that Lennon (busy with his photo session) had not yet been seen that day. He waited around for a while then, with his usual eye for a pretty girl, he gave himself a break from duty. He invited two young girl fans hanging around The Dakota entrance to come and have lunch with him. Over a hamburger and two beers at a nearby coffee shop, he boasted about his journey around the world two years before. They were suitably impressed.

Back at his post after lunch, he got talking to Paul Goresh, a twenty-one-year-old store detective and amateur photographer who sometimes hung around The Dakota in the hope of taking photographs of its star residents and their famous visitors that afterwards he might sell. It was a busy afternoon: Lauren Bacall, Paul Simon and Mia Farrow came by and Goresh's camera flashed. Then a station wagon pulled up with five-year-old Sean and his

197

nanny. The girls knew him and screamed: 'Oooh, it's Sean!' They introduced Mark, and he shook the limp hand of the little boy whose father he had come to kill.

In between times, he opened his book and read from *The Catcher in the Rye*.

Soon after 5 o'clock, with Lennon and Yoko's RKO Radio Network interview over, Dave Sholin and his crew came out of The Dakota and began to load up their rented limousine to take them back to La Guardia Airport for their return flight to San Francisco. A few minutes later, Lennon and Yoko also emerged to take their own rented limousine down to the Record Plant for another working session on their post-*Double Fantasy* tapes – but their car was nowhere in sight. They stood aimlessly around on the pavement waiting for it to appear. A small crowd gathered. This was Lennon and Yoko standing around on the streets of New York! Sholin said in his interview the next morning: 'Lennon may have signed some autographs' – in fact, one of the people to whom he *did* give an autograph was Mark David Chapman.

Finally, after so many weeks and so many missed chances, their paths crossed. The moment of destiny arrived. Mark's heart pounded, the blood rushed to his head, he almost trembled with excitement – but he did not draw his gun. With a sheepish smile on his face, he merely handed the singer his *Double Fantasy* album and Lennon signed it, just as he had obligingly scrawled his name for several others in the small crowd that had quickly formed. Goresh snapped a quick shot of the famous star signing his album for this adoring fan. Before the night was out this would earn him an estimated $10,000 fee – but we do not know how many other photographs were taken of Lennon giving other autographs at that time.

The problem is that public attention has solely figured on Mark getting *his* autograph. Dave Sholin's *San Francisco Chronicle* interview was picked up by no other major newspaper around the world as far as I can see. The picture has been created of a solitary Lennon facing a solitary Mark – and Mark choosing not to kill him when he easily could have done. *That was not the true picture.* There were quite a lot of people standing around. 'Several people with me said they saw a guy who looked a little weird ask for an autograph,' Sholin told his interviewer. It was not a lonely one-to-one encounter.

'Did I have my hat on or off in the picture?' gushed Mark to Goresh. 'I wanted my hat off. They'll never believe this in Hawaii!' This could have been a genuine response – or play-acting.

Anyway, by then, Yoko had asked Sholin for a lift and he had gladly taken them off in his limousine, to drop them off at the Record Plant on his way to La Guardia. Why had not Mark shot Lennon when at last they had come face to face? After all, that is what he was there for! Later, he was to give the police a mumbo-jumbo explanation in his written statement about his so-called inner torment at that time: 'I have a small part in me that cannot understand the world and what goes on in it. I did not want to kill anybody. . . . I fought against the small part for a long time. I'm sure the large part of me is Holden Caulfield. The small part of me must be the Devil. I went to the building called The Dakota. I stayed there until John Lennon came out and asked him to sign my album. At that point my big part won and I wanted to go back to my hotel, but I couldn't. I waited until he came back.'

The world has accepted this view of Mark struggling with his conscience like a modern Don Quixote battling with his imaginary windmills. But there is another, much simpler explanation: he could not have shot Lennon when he first got the chance – there were too many people around, not only Dave Sholin and his crew and their driver but also the fans and curious rush-hour pedestrians passing by on their way to the subway. The gun would have been grabbed from his hand before he was even able to pull the trigger or, at the very least, someone would have shouted a warning and Lennon would have ducked. Anything could have happened. Far better to wait until later when there would be fewer people around.

But none of this has got into the public legend: it has always been projected as one more crazy episode in the course of a crazy crime. And Mark has – for whatever reason – played along with that.

His wait proved a long one – over five hours. When white-haired doorman Jose Perdomo came on duty, he asked him why he was still hanging around. Except for Goresh, all the other fans and general hangers-on had departed. Mark said he was waiting for Lennon and Yoko to come back so that he could get Yoko's autograph as well. At about 8.30, Goresh said that he too was going off and why did not Mark come with him. Mark replied ominously: 'I'd wait if I were you. You never know if you'll see him again.' But Goresh left, and the lone figure in the long overcoat remained.

At the Record Plant, all was going well. Terry Kaplan, who had worked at the studios for nine years, remembers that evening well. 'John and Yoko were fine. It was a good session,' she says. David Geffen, their producer, came round to tell them that *Double Fantasy*, which stood at twelve with a bullet in the US ratings, had just gone gold in Britain. 'The last day of his life was the happiest I'd ever seen him,' Geffen later told *Newsweek*'s Barbara Graustark. No one had any premonition of the dark tragedy that soon would strike.

'We're going over to the Stage Deli to grab a bite,' announced Lennon as they were leaving. He said they would be back tomorrow morning at 9.00 a.m.

But once they left the building on West 44th Street just off Times Square, they decided to go straight home. By this time their rented limousine was on hand and it took them up 8th Avenue to Columbus Circle then glided north along Central Park West to 72nd Street, where it turned sharp left at the lights and pulled up in front of The Dakota. It was 10.50 p.m.

Yoko got out first, with John clutching the tapes from their session in his hand and trailing a few steps behind. As he passed under the ornate archway leading to the building's interior courtyard, a voice called out from behind: 'Mr Lennon.'

He half turned to see Mark crouched in a combat stance less than twenty feet away. Five times his .38 fired at point-blank range, pumping four bullets into Lennon's back and left shoulder. One went astray as Lennon, almost killed outright by the first explosion of steel particles shattering into his body, staggered up the five steps to the entrance office – to fall flat on his face, gurgling and bringing up blood.

Yoko screamed at Jay Hastings, the front desk clerk until then quietly reading a magazine: 'John's been shot! John's been shot!' He grabbed the phone for the police.

Unlike their earlier encounter, there was hardly anyone around. But as one witness, Sean Strub, described it, Mark had 'almost a smirk on his face'. Amazingly, he made no effort to run or to escape – although there was a subway entrance almost exactly opposite on the other side of the road, into which he could have dashed and made a strike for freedom. In fact, Jose Perdomo, in deep shock, screamed at him: 'Leave! Get out of here!'

But Mark just stood there. As a hysterical Yoko cradled Lennon's head in her arms, Jose said in consternation: 'Do you know what you've done?' 'I just shot John Lennon,' he replied. Then he threw down his gun, took off his overcoat and folded it up at his feet (he wanted the police, guns drawn, on arrival, to realize at once that he was unarmed) – and calmly began to read his paperback.

Guy Louthan, a handsome young Englishman trying to make his way in the movie industry in New York (he is now, in his early thirties, a producer in Hollywood), was in bed with a girl friend in an apartment on the other side of the road facing The Dakota. He had been in the building a few months previously at a party in Leonard Bernstein's apartment. He had met Bernstein's daughter on a movie set and she had invited him. He knew 'a lot of celebrity types lived there' and now, when he heard shots coming from that direction, he jumped out of bed and he and his girl friend ran to the window.

He looked down from the tenth floor – 'and saw two people standing there, the doorman and this other guy. The first police car had not yet arrived. There were just these two men. That was all I could see: I was slightly to the right of the building and could not see up the stairs and into the entrance office where I now know Lennon was.

'All I could see was these two men on the street outside. The doorman and Chapman. For a long time afterwards, I wondered whether I had really seen Chapman. I was actually under the impression that he must have run away.

'But I realize now that it was him alright. He just stood there. It was incredible!'

Mark gave his own chilling account of the killing in Rikers Island Prison awaiting trial. It was recorded and Kevin Sim played the tape on air in his television film documentary *The Man Who Shot John Lennon* in February 1988. This is the first time it has appeared in print:

If you ever get the chance, go to The Dakota building. I just love that building . . . to think that's where it happened. There was no emotion, there was no anger, there was nothing, dead silence in the brain, dead cold quiet. He walked up, he looked at me, I tell you the man was going to be dead in less than five minutes, and he looked at me, I looked at him. He walked past me and then I heard in my head said, 'Do it, do it, do it,' over and over again, saying 'Do it, do it, do it, do it,' like that. I pulled the gun out of my pocket, I handed over to my left hand, I don't remember aiming, I must have done, but I don't remember drawing the bead or whatever you call it. And I just pulled the trigger steady five times.

What does that steady repetition of a voice saying 'Do it, do it, do it' over and over again in Mark's head sound like to you?

Answering the urgent call: 'Shots fired – 1 West 72nd Street' on his patrol car radio, twentieth precinct police driver Steve Spiro and his partner, Peter Cullen, were on the scene within minutes. By a lucky fluke, they had only been around the corner on a newly instituted larceny search looking out for car thieves.

This is Spiro's dramatic account of what followed, taken from his own undoctored notes. He intended them to be the basis of his subsequent testimony in court, but they were not needed because Mark's eventual guilty plea meant that no police officer ever gave evidence:

I cut across W72St into the oncoming lane and screech to a stop in front of the driveway of 1W72ST (i.e., The Dakota). Upon exiting the car, a male in the street, on the passenger side, is yelling pointing toward the driveway archway. He's pointing toward the left hand side saying: 'He's the one that did the shooting!'

I automatically draw my revolver, pointing it toward the man in the shadows.

I'm still thinking is this for real? (Think. . . What's going on around you – get this guy fast.)

As I point gun at Suspect, a male white starts to put his hands up toward the top of his head. 'Don't move! Put your hands on the wall!' Suspect still has hands on his head. 'Put your hands on the wall and don't move.' Suspect does what he is told. *'Please don't hurt me!'* says the Suspect. [This is Spiro's own underlining.]

Put gun to subject's back. I see two males to my left, I don't know who they are (thinking a robbery – more than one gunman?) I place my left arm around Suspect's neck moving him against me and using him as a shield to defend myself against other possible gunmen. Turning toward my right with the suspect I see the doorman, another male, and at least three bullet holes in the glass doors. My gun is now pointed toward the doorway. The doorman, who I've seen before while working, yells that the man I have is the only one involved. I put the Suspect back up against the wall. Suspect says, *'I acted alone! Don't hurt me!'* [Again, Spiro's underlining, as throughout.] 'No one is going to hurt you.'

Still thinking that there was a robbery inside the building I start asking Suspect 'What apartment were you in?' 'Who did you shoot?' No response. I hear Jose, the doorman, yell *'He shot John Lennon'*. I ask Suspect 'Did you shoot John Lennon?' – *No response*. Pete Cullen yells 'Steve put cuffs on him!' As I get cuffs on the Suspect [he] asks once again – 'Don't hurt me.'

I see police officers Palma and Frauenberger carrying John Lennon face up, shoulder height high – blood on Lennon's face – toward Rmp [radio motor patrol car].

I yell to Pete 'Let's get this guy to the precinct right now!' I ask Suspect if clothing on the ground are his, he says 'Yes. The red book is mine too.' I pick them up. I now see PO Blake carrying a gun using a newspaper in order not to disturb any prints. Placing the Suspect in the rear of Rmp 1599 [Spiro's patrol car], I put his belongings in the front seat. On way to car, he says again 'Don't let anyone hurt me.'

I yell to oncoming police officers to set up a crime scene [police barricades, etc.] – I pick up the portable radio as I see PO Moran in Rmp 2123 turn on his turret lights and siren to take Lennon in the back seat to Roosevelt Hospital. '20 Larceny car to Central, have Roosevelt Hospital standby. There's an Rmp coming in with a shooting victim, John Lennon.'

The notes continue: 'Throwing the portable into the front seat, I turn toward the suspect and ask *"Do you know what you did?" No answer* – I really wasn't looking for one.' At this point in the narrative, Albert Goldman has Mark give Spiro the 'crazy' reply: 'Listen, I'm sorry. I didn't know he was a friend of yours.' That appears nowhere in Spiro's fifteen pages of notes. Goldman adds: 'Instantly Spiro flashed, "Wacko!"' That too does not appear in the notes and, when I discussed the prosecution's case with Spiro in 1985, he told me: 'We could show he was rational, not listening to voices or anything like that: he was not a wacko!' And he said much the same to the New York press immediately after the murder. Mark seems to have got crazier with the years.

The policemen on the scene that night were more sincere fans of Lennon than ever Mark was. Steve Spiro had often seen the singer walking the streets: 'I used to say "Hi" and he'd say "Hi" back. I would have loved to have asked for his autograph but I had to be professional!' PO Tony Palma, in the second police car to arrive, had courted his ex-wife to Lennon's music. As he bent over the dying man in The Dakota's entrance office, he realized with a shock that it was his hero whose life-force was ebbing before his eyes. 'I turned him over. Red is all I saw,' he recalls. He turned to a young policeman who was on the verge of being sick: 'The guy is dying,' he snapped. 'Let's get him out of here!'

Lennon, semi-conscious and losing a great deal of blood, was carried out to a third police car where he was placed tenderly on the back seat. Palma muttered to his fellow cop James Moran that it was John Lennon he had there. Jimmy Moran could not believe it. As his blue and white patrol car took off and, with roof-lights flashing and siren wailing, raced down West 72nd Street, jumping the lights as it intersected with Broadway, he leaned back and asked incredulously: 'Are you John Lennon?' 'Yes,' was the half-moaned almost inaudible reply. It was the last word the singer was to utter.

Palma followed in his car with Yoko Ono. 'Tell me it isn't true, tell me he's alright!' she implored him again and again.

Although doctors pronounced Lennon dead on arrival at the Roosevelt Hospital, over a mile's journey away in another part of town, a team of seven surgeons laboured desperately to try and save him. But his wounds were too severe. 'It wasn't possible to resuscitate him by any means,' said Dr Stephen Lynn, the Roosevelt's Director of Emergency Services. 'He'd lost three to four quarts of blood from the gun wounds. That's about 80 per cent of his blood volume.' Gene Scott's hollow-points had done their job well.

After about half an hour, the surgeons gave up their unavailing work. Dr Lynn went to break the news to Yoko, now joined by David Geffen whom she had called at his hotel. 'Where is my husband?' she asked the doctor frantically. 'I want to be with my husband. He would want me to be with him. Where is he?'

'We have very bad news,' said Dr Lynn. 'Unfortunately, in spite of massive efforts, your husband is dead. There was no suffering at the end.' Yoko could not understand. 'Are you saying he is sleeping?' she sobbed.

Perhaps the most poignant set of press photographs flashed around the world after Lennon's murder was those showing Yoko, grief etched deep into her face, holding on to a shattered-looking Geffen, as he helped her from the Roosevelt Hospital towards Tony Palma's waiting patrol car.

By the time they had arrived back at The Dakota, a crowd of about a thousand people had already gathered outside the building. Palma and his partner Herb Frauenberger smuggled Yoko in by the back door with Geffen. And she faced the task of telling her young son the news.

Almost every adult in New York seemed already to have heard it. Radio and television programmes had been interrupted to make the announcement.

Guy Louthan remembers that scene outside The Dakota. 'It must have been an hour after the shooting. I'd just gone back to the window to take another look and it was actually an amazing sight. It raised the hackles on the back of my neck. First I heard this noise, then I looked towards the park and there were people streaming across the park and then I looked to the other side of 72nd Street, and there were from both sides these two waves of people converging on The Dakota.

'I'll never forget it. The sight of those two waves coming together and the noise of their approaching voices. You suddenly realized something really terrible had happened.

'This short time span had passed and already there were lots of people down there. They were not wearing coats. They looked like they had come out of restaurants, out of bars, out of their homes. It was as if they had all decided at the same time to go to The Dakota. They literally swept up the road and out of the park and, as the leading people neared The Dakota, people behind were catching up with them so it was this sort of surge, a vast mass of people moving forward being constantly fed into by other people running alongside, moving in amongst the cars. It was really quite something!

'And then when they all got to The Dakota, they just stood and sang or chanted. Some of them held candles. I just had to go down and find out what had happened. When someone told me John Lennon had been shot, I just could not believe it. "John Lennon? What are you saying?" I am sure there are much more questionable characters inside The Dakota who put themselves up for being shot at. John Lennon just seemed to be the last person in the world anyone would want to shoot at that point. I was completely incredulous about the whole thing.' Louthan and the whole world.

At the twentieth precinct, near-pandemonium reigned, with newsmen virtually barricading the station-house both front and back – and with a terrified Mark, almost clinging on to Steve Spiro in his fear, because he trusted this man who had promised him that he would 'not be hurt'. In the first few hours of his interrogation, he would refuse to speak to anyone, even the homicide detectives, without Spiro being by his side.

In the police car speeding to the precinct all that Spiro could think of was the repercussions that would flow from this night's activity. He determined that no one would be able to blame him for anything: he recited to Mark his 'Miranda rights'. This is a formula seared into every US policeman's memory by a landmark (and controversial) decision of the US Supreme Court in 1966 freeing a convicted Arizona rapist named Miranda because he had not been told of his rights before he confessed to his crime: 'You have the right to remain silent. You do not have to answer questions. Anything you say can be used against you. You have a right to an attorney, and if you cannot afford one, one will be provided for you.' It is standard police procedure on arrest throughout the country. Mark replied that he understood.

But neither Spiro nor Pete Cullen, both uniformed men, asked him any questions. They were going to let the detectives handle this one. As the car drove fast up the higher stretches of Broadway, past the shuttered shops and the few restaurants that still remained open, Mark, huddled on the back seat beside PO Cullen, was left to his own thoughts.

On arrival at the station-house, normal routine had to be gone through. As the arresting officers, it was Spiro and Cullen's job to take their prisoner into the detention cell and do a strip search. They were amazed to see his long-johns, top and bottom, beneath his outer clothes. Spiro asked him why. It was nearly midnight and it was still only a mild 45 outside. 'I'm from Hawaii and I don't like the cold,' Mark replied softly.

The cold, antiseptic, white-tiled atmosphere of the precinct building had got to him. It seemed to intimidate him. As with police stations around the world, such places have their own particular chill quality for people brought in for questioning, let alone murderers caught red-handed. He looked scared. 'Don't worry. There are no rubber-hoses here,' Spiro jokingly told him. He promised to protect him from the press – and anyone else who might do him harm.

Only then did Mark give his full name, age and address in Hawaii. Flipping through his wallet, Spiro found his Hawaiian driving licence, Bank of Hawaii Visa Card, the receipt for his gun from J & S Enterprises – and $2201 in cash. In his pocket was the key to his hotel room.

Word came that Assistant District Attorney Allen Sullivan, on 'homicide call' that night, and a senior detective were on their way. It was midnight. Soon, in the early hours of the next day, the interrogation would start.

At home, Justice Dennis Edwards, a black Manhattan Supreme Court Justice since 1965, heard the news of Lennon's death on the radio. He was not a particular Beatles fan but he thought to himself: 'Why would anyone do a thing like that? Why kill John Lennon?'

Unknown to him, eight months later he would have to decide the fate of the man who killed John Lennon.

PART FOUR

AFTERMATH
(December 1980 to date)

16

The World Mourns John Lennon

In his lifetime, John Lennon had not been a politician or head of state. He had not been a king or president. He had had no loyal subjects bending the knee in homage or supporters casting their vote for him to rule over them by popular acclaim.

He had not been a religious leader inspiring devotion among millions linked together in the adoration of a shared God. He had formed no great political party, led no resounding crusade.

He had been an entertainer who, almost alone of his kind at that time, had spoken out on issues that he thought were important. No more and no less. But the public outpouring of grief, instant and world-wide, at his death was without parallel since the murder seventeen years earlier of President John F. Kennedy.

Newsweek, in a cover-story geared to the Goldman biography nearly eight years later, in October 1988, said: '[Lennon's] assassination wasn't martyrdom exactly, but it elevated him from an aging rocker attempting a less-than-promising comeback to a secular saint.'

Why should the death of this 'aging rocker' have had so profound an impact, when many of the teenagers mourning him with tears in their eyes were still being breastfed when he and the other Beatles had been singing the songs of their greatest success?

Paul Gray, reviewing Goldman's book in *Time* in September 1988, has written: 'The tidal wave of grief that followed the murder of John Lennon flowed from several sources. Perhaps the most gaping of these was the shocking obliteration of a decade's worth of hope. Millions awoke one morning bleak with the promise of winter to learn that now the Beatles could never get back together, that the expansive spirit of the 1960s had definitely expired ten years past its prime.'

But this 'tidal wave' would never have swelled to such giant proportions if one of the other Beatles had been shot. Almost certainly there would have been no crowds in the street or all-night vigils for Paul McCartney, George Harrison or Ringo Starr if an assassin's gun had mowed down one of them. Why then for Lennon?

Those in his own age group among the millions around the world who mourned him so deeply and so immediately were undoubtedly partly grieving for their own lost youth and their own blighted dreams. But the kids? Why were they so upset? It surely has to be because of Lennon's message and because of what he had come to represent. You may disagree with me that there is a good case for saying that his murder was politically motivated and not 'the act of a madman', as was understandably the view expressed by nearly everyone in the days following his death. Even so there can be little doubt that there was a political undertone to the world-wide outburst of grief at his murder.

The crowds who thronged the streets of the cities of the world in deepest mourning were singing 'Imagine' and chanting 'Give peace a chance'. Paul McCartney himself was later to say: 'People would remember that John had helped speed up the American withdrawal from Vietnam and that was how he would like to be remembered – as a peace campaigner.' The world was not so much mourning a singer as a protester and a political idealist; and this gut reaction by millions should be borne in mind when seeking to assess whether his murder itself could have been a political act. If his death was even partly mourned as a political event, could not the motivation behind it also have been political? Thinking about it, does not one possibly go with the other?

Even if Yoko had eventually wanted to sleep after she got back to The Dakota from the Roosevelt Hospital, she would have found it difficult for the singing and the chanting of the crowd outside that swelled, according to one estimate, to 5000 people before it gradually dispersed at dawn only for others to take up the vigil: candles lit, holding hands, many with tears streaming down their faces.

A small group of assistants, attorneys and close friends pushed their way through the throng and up the blood-stained steps of the building to do what they could to help. Sitting numbly in her kitchen, Yoko asked Rich De Palma, office manager of the Lenono Company, to make only three calls and all to England: to Julian Lennon, John's seventeen-year-old son from his first marriage, to Aunt Mimi and to Paul McCartney. Because of the five-hour time difference, he could not contact any of them directly. Meanwhile, he fielded the dozens of telephone calls that were now coming in throughout the night.

Within two hours of the shooting Elliot Mintz was on American Airlines Flight 10 from Los Angeles to New York. Alerted by a phone call from his mother in New York who had just heard that Lennon had been shot, he had rushed direct to the airport hoping against hope that his friend might yet survive. In the plane, however, a woman had asked a stewardess why she was crying and Mintz heard the muttered answer: 'John Lennon is dead.'

Arrived in New York, he went direct to The Dakota. 'It was about six in the morning,' he later told Ray Coleman. 'The police had not disturbed the spot where it happened. The image of the broken glass and the chalk marks and John's blood on the cement will haunt me for ever.' He stood for a long time by the bedroom door listening to Yoko crying before he knocked and said, through the closed door: 'It's me. I'll be right here if you need me.' He was to stay for the next two months.

At 10.30 on the Tuesday morning, Dr Elliot Gross, New York's Chief Medical Examiner, raised his scalpel and began the autopsy. Tony Palma, the policeman who had rushed Yoko through the streets to the Roosevelt after the murder, was present. 'This was my boyhood idol,' he told me in 1985. 'I had courted my ex-wife to his music and now he lay there naked on the slab, his penis taped to his leg. I had been to many pm's before, but this was too much.

'When the guy started to cut him open, I had to leave.'

While the autopsy was still going on, Ringo Starr and his fiancée Barbara Bach arrived at The Dakota to console Yoko. He was to be the only one of the Beatles to visit her at that time. On holiday in the Bahamas, as soon as they heard the news of Lennon's death, they had boarded a plane for Manhattan. Emerging ashen-faced after two hours with Yoko, Ringo would make no comment but later he told a *People* interviewer: 'Yoko's strong but that day she cried just like a little girl.' He also said revealingly that, on first arrival, Yoko had asked only to see him by himself but, 'Look, it was you who started all this,' he told her. 'We're both coming in.'

Paul McCartney went to work as usual that Tuesday morning: he was working with ex-Beatles producer George Martin on a new album for his group Wings. As he left his secluded farm at Robertsbridge in Sussex with his wife Linda and two of their children, he told waiting reporters: 'I'm shocked, it still hasn't hit me yet. He was a great guy and the whole world will miss him.' One of the session musicians later said: 'There was a kind of unspoken sadness among Paul and the Wings lads like the kind when you lose an old soccer mate. It was subtle and there wasn't any crying or moping about. Get on with the job was the attitude.'

The news was broken to the third Beatle, George Harrison, at his Henley home outside London in a phone call at 4.45 a.m. from his sister Louise in Florida. In his turn, he told reporters: 'I'm shocked and upset like everyone else. What can you say? It's such a waste of life.' He added: 'After all we went through together, I had, and still have, great love and respect for him. I am shocked and stunned. To rob life is the ultimate robbery in life.'

One could be forgiven for thinking that, with the exception of Ringo, the ex-Beatles were less drastic in their grief than many of the ex-Beatle fans. It was left to Lennon's two closest relations in England, Aunt Mimi and young Julian Lennon, to present the true face of really deep loss. 'I was listening to the World Service News on the radio,' Mrs Mimi Smith told a reporter, 'when I heard it had happened. I really can't find the words to speak of him at the moment – I am so very, very upset.' Julian, clearly very distressed, could hardly mutter any comment at all as he hurried past reporters at London Airport before boarding a plane for New York.

Needless to say, the politicians put in their own condescending word. In Britain, Sir Harold (later Lord) Wilson who, as prime minister, had recommended the Beatles for their honour as Members of the Order of the British Empire (the decoration which Lennon later returned partly because of British support for the Vietnam War), said: 'It was a great shock to my wife and myself. He gave the kids something to think about, he kept them off the streets and did more than all the forces of law and order could have done put together.' In the United States, President Carter paid fulsome tribute to Lennon's music: 'His spirit, the spirit of the Beatles – brash and earnest, ironic and idealistic all at once – became the spirit of a whole generation.' While President-elect Reagan, by chance visiting New York that Tuesday, called Lennon's death 'a great tragedy', adding that 'we have to try to stop tragedies of this sort' – so long, of course, as it did not involve legislating for effective nationwide gun control. (His son, Ronald Jr, later told a *Rolling Stone* reporter rather more feelingly that, when he heard Lennon was dead, 'there was no real reason for me to feel remorse, but I did. I felt empty, like my past was gone.')

New York's Mayor Ed Koch expressed concern that the murder should not be laid to any mood of violence in his city: 'The person who is bent on killing you will follow you wherever you are,' he said. Hugh Carey, governor of New York State, contented himself with platitudes: 'Lennon was a man of peace, non-violence, love and kindness,' he proclaimed in a telegram to Yoko.

The one politician whose views on the tragedy would really have been interesting seems not to have been asked. In June 1988 I remedied this omission but Carmen Ballard, Richard Nixon's staff assistant, replied, in an obviously standard letter: 'Because of scheduling limitations and also the large number of requests he receives, President Nixon is unable to meet with scholars, researchers and authors or to review their written questions.

'I am sure, however, that the former president would want me to thank you for writing as you did and to send his best wishes.' One can almost hear Lennon's sardonic laugh in heaven coupled, no doubt, with his favourite expletive.

(When I wrote asking Mrs Margaret Thatcher, the British premier then and now, her reaction on hearing of the murder, her private secretary replied in similar vein that she could not make an exception to her general rule of not answering such questions, but she had the grace to add: 'If it is of any help, I can tell you that the prime minister was in Ireland on 8 December 1980.' She obviously would have had other more immediate things on her mind.)

Meanwhile, in those first twenty-four hours after Lennon's death, the first of three fans had already killed herself in grief. Yoko broke her seclusion to beg through David Geffen: 'John loved and prayed for the human race. Please do the same for him.'

Geffen also said on her behalf that there would be no funeral but that the time for a silent vigil and prayers 'at wherever you are' would be announced later.

To appreciate just what the emotional intensity was of people at that time I can do no better than quote William E. Farrell's description in the *New York Times* of the scene outside The Dakota on that first day after the murder:

The filigreed wrought-iron entry gate is a Wailing Wall completely covered with flowers, messages of love and peace, Christmas wreaths and a long tinsel streamer that was crudely framed like a Crucifix until the wind got hold of it.

An informal procession of mourners – groups of friends, tearful couples, sad-faced strangers – walks along 72nd Street from bus and subway stops to the open-air wake in front of John Lennon's apartment house. . . .

Many of them carry small bouquets of flowers that they place in crannies in the gates before the police politely urge them to get behind the barricades running alongside. The iron mouth of a roaring lion on the gate is stopped by a sticker the size of an envelope. It says, 'The Beatles'. . . .

The mourners ebb and flow. Sometimes there are more than a thousand, sometimes no more than a couple of hundred. They keep coming and going. The scene in front of The Dakota is a 1980's Breughel painting in its busyness, its congestion and its colour. Morning joggers in shorts, headbands and knee warmers, break their 'Me Generation' stride to pay homage. Some young men in three-piece business suits stop by. Platoons of men and women, carefully coiffed and wearing a dizzying array of designer jeans, stand behind the barricades with boys and girls in ratty hairdos and army surplus gear, those nostalgic fixtures of the 1960s. . . .

There are huge portable radios everywhere – cacophonous boxes blaring taped Beatles music transformed into dirges by the occasion. Frequently different songs merge incoherently in the cold air. Others are tuned into all-news radio stations that tell the spectators where they are and why they are there. . . .

Down the block from The Dakota, heading towards Columbus Avenue, a woman walks alone trying to hide her tears. . . . A few feet behind her a man with a portable radio sits on a building stoop listening to the Beatles singing 'It's Been A Hard Day's Night'.

Variants of this emotion erupted throughout the United States and around the world. In Chattanooga, Tennessee, the Rev. Jesse Jackson, who eight years later was nearly to win the Democratic nomination for president, led 3000 people in prayer. In Sacramento, California, 2000 paid tribute by candlelight. Another 2000 gathered in West Los Angeles, more than 1200 in Cincinnati and 1500 in Philadelphia. So unlikely a person as Frank Sinatra commented: 'It was a staggering moment when I heard the news. Lennon was a most talented man and, above all, a gentle soul. John and his colleagues set a high standard by which contemporary music continues to be measured.'

In Britain, a portrait of the Beatles draped with a floral tribute was placed at the entrance to the Tate Gallery. 'We usually do this when a British artist whose work is represented in the Tate dies,' said a spokesman. 'But we thought John Lennon was a special case.' In Liverpool, the lord mayor announced that a memorial service would be held at the hugely impressive, recently-completed cathedral and local teenagers placed wreaths at the car park in Mathew Street that had been the site of the basement Cavern Club where the Beatles had got their start.

Even Communist countries mourned the death of a man whom the *New York Post*, hardly a left-wing publication, called 'a universal symbol of brotherhood and peace'. 'The bitter irony of this tragedy is that a person who devoted his songs and music to the struggle against violence has himself become its victim,' said an article in *Komsomolskaya pravda* in Moscow. The Hungarian government newspaper *Esti Hirlap* praised Lennon for his music and his 'commitment to the cause of world peace'. Yugoslavia's most influential newspaper, *Politika*, said the Beatles were 'youth's breakthrough into all pores of life . . . the sound rebellion against established visions'.

So far as the Western world was concerned, there was also a financial side to all this. '(Just Like) Starting Over' and *Double Fantasy* that until now had only enjoyed moderate commercial success immediately began to soar in the charts both in Britain and the United States. The album was eventually to sell more than six million copies and the single, which had already dropped from number 8 in the British charts soared at once to number 1 in the week after his murder. Workers at the EMI factory at Hayes, Middlesex, were put on overtime to press, package and distribute extra supplies of all his available records.

David Geffen said: 'John was very anxious to have a number 1 hit in England. That would have been a real kick for him and it had nothing to do with money . . . he wanted this record to be a hit in England for Yoko – and himself.' Sadly, he had to die to achieve it.

In Holland, on the Tuesday night, the management of the Amsterdam Hilton, in whose Suite 902 Lennon and Yoko had held their first bed-in in March 1969 on their honeymoon, turned out all the lights in the building as a mark of respect – except for Suite 902. Its lights shone out, from the seventh floor, like a beacon.

Wednesday, 10 December, was an eventful day. Shortly after noon, Lennon's body, wrapped incongruously in a black bag on a stretcher like a dead US Vietnam soldier, was taken from the chief medical examiner's city mortuary at 1st Avenue and 30th Street and driven uptown to the Frank E. Campbell funeral home at 1076 Madison Avenue near the junction with 80th Street. Dubbed 'The City's Undertaker to the Stars', this venerable organization, founded in 1898, had been the last resting-place-but-one for a whole host of celebrities from Enrico Caruso to Rudolph Valentino and from Robert Kennedy to Judy Garland. They knew how to handle the situation with discreet efficiency.

Shortly afterwards a hearse drove slowly out laden with flowers all but masking the coffin beneath. The posse of waiting reporters jumped into their cars and taxis and drove off after it. Five minutes later another hearse drove slowly out, also decked inside with flowers but this time the coffin was not empty but bore the mortal remains of John Winston Ono Lennon.

Within the hour, at the Ferncliff Mortuary in the New York suburb of Hartsfield, he had been swiftly and privately cremated – but not before a city mortuary attendant had made himself a cynical $10,000 by sneaking a photograph of him on the mortuary slab, and selling it to the world's newspapers including the *New York Post*, the London *Daily Mail* and, in colour, the *National Enquirer*.

Already the smell of money was in the air as well as grief. That afternoon, David Warmflash, Lennon's attorney, applied to the Manhattan Surrogate's Court for probate of a four-paged will that Lennon had made just over a year before, on 12 November 1979. It gave half his estate to 'my beloved wife Yoko' and the other half was put into a trust, whose provisions did not have to be publicly declared but were generally considered to provide for his children and perhaps even for Kyoko, Yoko's estranged daughter. A value of $30 million (£12.5 million) was put upon the estate for probate purposes but its true value has generally been agreed to be in the region of $150 million (over £100 million).

Yet not all the wealth in the world could bring him back to life. Yoko now issued this typed statement on her official Dakota stationary:

> I told Sean what happened. I showed him the picture of his father on the cover of the paper and explained the situation. I took Sean to the spot where John lay after he was shot. Sean wanted to know why the person shot John if he liked John. I explained that he was probably a confused person. Sean said we should find out if he was confused or if he really had meant to kill John. I said that was up to the court. He asked what court – a tennis court or a basketball court? That's how Sean used to talk with his father. They were buddies. John would have been proud of Sean if he had heard this. Sean cried later. He also said, 'Now Daddy is part of God. I guess when you die you become much more bigger because you're part of everything.'
>
> I don't have much more to add to Sean's statement. The silent vigil will take place December 14th at 2 p.m. for ten minutes.
>
> Our thoughts will be with you.
> Love, Yoko and Sean

Later that evening, she granted her first interview since the assassination. Appropriately it was to an old friend, Robert Hilburn, the pop music critic of the *Los Angeles Times*. He told his readers the following day (and his words were repeated in other newspapers around the world) that he found a Yoko who was occasionally tearful but remarkably resilient as she rested in bed in her semi-darkened bedroom seven floors above the several hundred people still gathered outside the building to pay respects to her slain husband. 'Their words were not distinguishable, making their singing sound like tribal chanting.'

'It was so sudden . . . so sudden,' said Yoko, recalling the horror of Monday night. 'We were walking to the entrance of the building when I heard the shot. I didn't realize at first that John had been hit. He kept walking. Then he fell and I saw the blood.'

She said that it was not a time for hate or disillusionment. 'The future is still ours to make,' she told Hilburn. 'The '80s will blossom if only people accept peace and love in their hearts. It would just add to the tragedy if people turned away from the message in John's music.'

She hoped that people would not blame New York City for the murder. 'People say that there is something wrong with New York, that it's sick; but John loved New York,' she said, lighting one of the many cigarettes that she smoked during the interview. 'He'd be the first to say it wasn't New York's fault. There can be one crank anywhere.'

The interview ended on an upbeat note: 'We had planned on so much together. We had talked about living until we were eighty. We even drew up lists of all the things we could do together for all those years. Then it was all over. But that doesn't mean the message should be over. The music will live on.' The music, yes: but not the capacity for continuing political protest, so conveniently removed by that so-called 'one crank'.

On Sunday, 14 December 1980, a ten-minute vigil was held around the globe in answer to Yoko's call. It took place at 2.00 p.m. New York time and 7.00 p.m. English time. In New York an estimated crowd of 100,000 people, including Mayor Ed Koch and actress Jane Fonda and her politician husband Tom Hayden, assembled in Central Park. As normal radio and television programmes in the United States were suspended, millions of viewers watched the tearful mourners lift two-finger 'peace signs' into the air as 'Give Peace a Chance' boomed out over the public-address system. Then, as the dying sounds echoed across the trees, the crowd was asked to turn off their radios, the vendors – who were doing a roaring trade – were asked to stop selling popcorn and hamburgers, and through the loudspeaker system a solitary voice said: 'John Lennon is with us today.'

For the next ten minutes the only sound was that of sobs and the throb of TV and police helicopters hovering in the chill air above. Then scores of white balloons were released to float upwards towards the overcast sky.

All over the United States, similar scenes were enacted. Over 1000 people stood silent at the statehouse in Columbia, South Carolina; 1200 at the statehouse in Columbus, Ohio; 3000 at the site of the 1962 World Fair in Seattle; 1000 on Cricket Hill along Chicago's lake-front; 600 at Louisiana State University in Baton Rouge; 600 at Miami's Bicentennial Park and 800 at Salt Lake City's Memorial Grove Park. In San Francisco, where Lennon and his family were due to have taken part in the Teamsters' strike rally that weekend, 200 mourners, many of them breaking into tears, gathered at the local state university's Merced Hall and at least six Bay Area radio stations went off the air during the ten-minute observance.

In Liverpool, an estimated 20,000 people had gathered earlier in the day in St George's Square to hear tributes and five long hours of Lennon's music, both recordings and played by local groups. Then, at 7.00 p.m. local time, with candles held high in hands cupped against the wind, the crowd fell silent for those ten precious minutes. The Liverpool-born Dr Robert Runcie, the Archbishop of Canterbury, held a solitary 'one-man vigil' of prayer.

In London and Brussels, Paris and Hamburg, Toronto and Madrid, tens of thousands of people similarly mourned. Across the Pacific Ocean, in Australia, although it was 6 o'clock in the morning local time, several thousands poured into Melbourne's city square to pay homage.

In Atlanta, Mark Chapman's former home town, nearly 1000 mourners spontaneously joined hands to form a human fence around a grassy field in Piedmont Park where free symphony concerts were normally held in warmer weather. They had no leader. No one gave any command. With many weeping openly, they silently stepped back into an ever widening circle that finally embraced an area big enough for eight regulation softball fields. No one had ever seen anything like it before.

Barbara Walters, the famous American television interviewer, wrote to me in July 1988 that she 'was saddened by his death'. Even though the veteran British-born commentator on American affairs, Alistair Cooke, expressed himself to me in June 1988 more in line with his older generation: 'Am sorry to say Lennon's death meant nothing to me.' He added: 'I was only astounded at the world memorial on that Sunday via TV. I suppose no human being has ever been mourned by so many people in so many countries at the same time.' As the father of young Susan Christian, later to be a columnist on the *Santa Monica Outlook*, told her: 'To us, John Lennon was just a hippie who fanned the drug culture.' But for the world's younger people a light had gone out, and a light that made of rock music something more than a pastime, something more than mere 'entertainment'.

A surprisingly poignant tribute remained to be paid nearly eight years later. In July 1988, Tim Rice, the rock composer and musician, wrote to me: 'After five years' retirement Lennon's final album, released shortly before his death, contained several songs that ranked with his finest efforts over the years. Half of the album was devoted to the less than memorable offerings of Yoko Ono but Lennon's contributions, notably 'Woman', 'Watching The Wheels' and 'Starting Over', would not have been disgraced had they appeared alongside some of his earlier masterpieces such as the songs of the *Imagine*, *Rubber Soul* and *Revolver* albums. I did not know Lennon personally but, like many of my generation, felt that I did. I shall always wonder what future masterpieces we lost on 8 December 1980. The great man himself, in his cynical youth, laughed at the idea of any pop star reaching thirty, let alone forty. He proved his assessment wrong by his own continuing abilities and it is a tragedy he will not be around to be part of rock's first old-age generation.'

17

Recovering from the Shock

The last thing that the detectives of the twentieth precinct wanted in early December 1980, with Christmas looming comfortably ahead, was a major murder investigation, let alone one with such world-wide implications as the Lennon assassination.

As we have seen from the start, back in Chapter 1, the beleaguered staff of twenty men and women serving a district of one million inhabitants under Lieutenant Arthur O'Connor had finally got the Metropolitan Opera House murder off their hands with the release of Craig Crimmins on bail, when now they suddenly had the Lennon assassination to contend with.

As O'Connor said in June 1988, 'We had just settled back. The office had just got back to normalcy, or as much as you could expect – and John Lennon goes and gets shot! That was the last thing we needed!'

But fortunately for them, the case was, in their view, 'grounded from the start': as O'Connor explains, 'solved with the arrest of Mark Chapman'.

This view of the matter was, as we already know, to colour the police investigation of any possible conspiracy so that there was, in effect, *no* police investigation into a possible conspiracy. But that did not mean that all was quietness and calm at the twentieth precinct station-house on the night of 8 December. In fact, near-pandemonium reigned. 'I had never seen anything like it,' says O'Connor, 'not even in the "Met" case, and that was big enough. I never saw the amount of international interest in a case that I saw then. Within two hours of the murder, there were literally 150 press reporters at the station-house. It was like we were under siege.'

Perhaps that is the explanation for a strange story later told by Paul Goresh, whose photograph of Lennon autographing Mark's copy of the *Double Fantasy* album only hours before the murder was on the front page of the *New York Daily News* and many other newspapers around the world within hours. Goresh claimed that his first thought had been to show it to the police. He said that he had twice called them that night to say he thought he had a picture of the man who probably killed Lennon but on both occasions they hung up on him. Only then, 'upset and frustrated', did he pick up the phone to the *Daily News* and an estimated $10,000. Not the most efficient way for the police to start a major investigation into a murder, one would have thought.

What was O'Connor's impression of Mark that night amid all the activity and chaos? 'I saw him within half an hour of his arrest. I was the first one to interrogate him. He was in a daze. He was composed yet not there. He gave me the impression he had done something: it was something he had to do and he'd done it.'

But he was very uncommunicative. 'He wouldn't speak, talk. I had to use different things to get to him. Finally, I got to the family and that worked! Until then he would not vocalize, he would not speak – at least, not to me. But I said: "Are you married?" I got an acknowledgement. So I said: "You know, your wife's going to be pretty upset about this." As soon as I hit that point, I got emotional response. He said: "Will she know about this?" I said: "Of course, she will! Can you tell me why you did this?" And his answer was: "I had to." That was about the only statement: "I had to do it."'

Eight years later O'Connor would admit to me: 'It's possible Mark could have been used by somebody. I saw him the night of the murder. I studied him intensely. He looked as if he could have been programmed – and I know what use you are going to make of that word! That was the way he looked and that was the way he talked. It could have been drugs – and no, we did not test for drugs! It was not standard procedure. But looking back, he could have been either drugged or programmed – or a combination of both.'

Suddenly at that early stage of Mark's interrogation in the early hours of Tuesday morning, 9 December, the phone rang in the station-house with a call from Honolulu. It was the detained man's wife on the line. 'At first, I thought: "Hey, what's all this about?

How did she know he was here – and at this time of the night?"' Allen Sullivan, by then at the station, told me in 1981. 'I thought – for the only time – it might be a conspiracy.' But he soon put the idea out of his head: the time in Honolulu is eight hours behind that in New York and Gloria had been besieged in her apartment in Kukui Plaza by local reporters – literally shouting at her through the door with news of what her husband had done, and where he was.

Steve Spiro was with Mark when the call came through. This is his note of the conversation:

I pick up the phone and introduce myself to Mrs Chapman as Police Officer Spiro 20 pct New York City PD and that it was the officer who arrested her husband. I tell her that Mark is OK and I assure her no one will hurt him. She thanks me and then I give Mark the phone.

Chapman's calm rational thinking amazes me under the circumstances (Spiro's own underlining throughout). Chapman asked wife if she's OK. – *Tells her not to talk to the press, 'Don't open the door. Call the police to protect you.'* Wife says something about Mark's mother. *Mark tells wife to call a doctor for her. Mark tells wife maybe she should call a lawyer, that they had once used before, for guidance.*

Can't tell what's being said at points. *Toward end of conversation Mark gets teary eyed, fights them back. Wife apparently tells him she still loves him – he says he still loves her.* Phone call ends. *Go back into interview room Silence. . . . He says he was praying.*

During the night Mark made and signed a written statement. Parts of it were leaked to the press soon afterwards but it has never been printed in full. I shall let it speak for itself. One does not have to be a trained psychiatrist to make one's own assessment of whether this is a criminally insane person speaking (which, it must be remembered, is not the view of the law; Mark is incarcerated in a prison for the sane). Or a troubled, deeply disturbed individual whom someone has got hold of and manipulated into killing someone whom, as he says, he has 'nothing against' – he does not even call Lennon a 'phoney':

I never wanted to hurt anybody my friends will tell you that. I have two parts in me the big part is very kind the children I

225

worked with will tell you that. I have a small part in me that cannot understand the big world and what goes on in it. I did not want to kill anybody and I really don't know why I did it. I fought against the small part for a long time. But for a few seconds the small part won. I asked God to help me but we are responsible for our own actions. I have nothing against John Lennon or anything he has done in the way of music or personal beliefs. I came to New York about five weeks ago from Hawaii and the big part of me did not want me to shoot John. I went back to Hawaii and tried to get rid of my small part but I couldn't. I then returned to New York on Friday December 5, 1980 I checked into the YMCA on 62 Street I stayed one night. Then I went to the Sheraton Center 7th Ave. Then this morning I went to the book store and bought *The Catcher in the Rye*. I'm sure the large part of me is Holden Caulfield who is the main person in the book. The small part of me must be the Devil. I went to the building its called the Dakota. I stayed there until he came out and asked him to sign my album. At that point my big part won and I wanted to go back to my hotel, but I couldn't. I waited until he came back. He came in a car. Yoko past first and I said hello, I didn't want to hurt her. Then John came, looked at me and past me. I took the gun from my coat pocket and fired at him. I can't believe I could do that. I just stood there clutching the book. I didn't want to run away. I don't know what happened to the gun, I just remember Jose kicking it away. Jose was crying and telling me to please leave. I felt so sorry for Jose. Then the police came and told me to put my hands on the wall and cuffed me.

The talking and the explaining, such as it was, were now over. Lieutenant O'Connor had to get his man out of the station-house and into the holding overnight gaol at downtown Center Street for Mark's arraignment (i.e. formal charging with the murder) at Manhattan Supreme Court later that day. It was 3.00 or 4.00 a.m. but the station-house was still ringed by reporters. Nor was that O'Connor's only worry: 'There was a lot of fanaticism about,' he recalls. 'This was the man who shot John Lennon I had there. I was worried about the Oswald thing.' He did not want any Jack Ruby getting in and killing his prisoner in *his* station-house. 'I put a bullet-proof vest on him!'

Yet the press of reporters around the building was still so great that they could not just take him out and drive off downtown. So they hit on a ruse – which ended in farce. Steve Spiro's notes explain: 'They believed that by putting a coat over Chapman's head and marching him past the reporters and into the downstairs cell block in the station-house itself and by telling the media beforehand that there is a back-door that Chapman will exit through, to be taken to court, this would persuade the media to leave the building.'

So they did that, and next day appeared in many of the world's newspapers dramatic photographs of Mark 'being taken off to court' with his coat over his head surrounded by grim-faced police escorts.

Everything seemed to go well – except about ten reporters and photographers did not leave. They did not buy the 'back-door exit to the holding gaol' story, they hung around. And they were right to do so, for there was no back-door! Mark and his party were waiting in the downstairs cell block to come out again by the front door and go off to Center Street.

So what happened? The small convoy of pressmen did not budge, the lights had been put out in the downstairs cell block to make it look as if Mark had indeed gone off to the holding gaol – and Mark was left sitting in pitch-black darkness in cell number 1 in the downstairs block with Steve Spiro, two detectives and Lieutenant O'Connor. It was pure Keystone Cops. Spiro's notes continue: 'There's a reporter pulling at the locked door of the cell block and asking through the door, "Hey, Mark Chapman, are you there?" At first, we thought it was quite funny but after twenty minutes I was getting pissed off. It was cold and I was tired. Chapman was tired and afraid of the press and wanted to know what was happening. I explained it was all being done for his protection.'

After over an hour sitting in the dark with Lennon's killer and the three other policemen, Lieutenant O'Connor had had enough. He gave his orders: without warning, the cell block door was opened and all five men rushed out into the courtyard where an unmarked police car was waiting. A lieutenant from the nearby twenty-third precinct was at the wheel; Mark was bundled in, Spiro and the two detectives also jumped in and the car zoomed out of the precinct block past the small waiting group of pressmen taken entirely by surprise. It braked hard to turn left at Columbus Avenue then sped through the night at sixty miles an hour, running every red light on the way, to arrive at the Police Academy garage on East 20th Street between 2nd and 3rd Avenue in downtown Manhattan in what must have been an all-time record, according to Spiro, of under ten minutes.

Mark was then hurriedly fingerprinted and a 'mug shot' taken in a squad room of the thirteenth precinct, which shares the building with the Police Academy, and he was whisked off to the overnight holding cells at Center Street even further downtown. The weary Spiro was left to end his long working day with the dull routine of 'doing the paperwork' that makes tedious every modern policeman's professional life.

At about 9.00 a.m., Herbert Adlerberg, a part-time jazz player as well as a veteran criminal practitioner (and now himself a Manhattan Supreme Court Judge), heard the news of Lennon's death on his car radio as he was driving to his first stop of the day – at the Federal gaol – to interview a client. He did not think all that much of it. Rock was not his kind of music. As he told me only two months later, in February 1981: 'If this had been 1939 and I was a practising lawyer and somebody knocked off Louis Armstrong, I might have wanted to prosecute the son of a bitch. But Lennon was no big deal.'

Yet it was to be *his* 'big deal' – for a short while. His name was next on the homicide list of the indigent defendants' panel, a sort of New York version of British legal aid for major crimes, and, when he called his office after leaving the Federal gaol at about 10.45, his secretary told him to call the panel people immediately – 'They want to put you in the Lennon case,' she told him. Adlerberg did not jump for joy. 'Oh shit!' he said.

Before he put through the call, Adlerberg, fifty years old, married and with two children, had a cup of coffee and thought that maybe he should not get involved: 'This could be a pain in the neck. Not from the point of view of any threats to me personally,' he later told me, 'but because it would probably be very time-consuming. I toyed with the idea of not taking it for the simple reason that I didn't want to become a one-case lawyer for the next seven months. *One*, I can't afford it and, *two*, I don't want to do it anyway. But in the end I said: "All right. I'll take it. What the hell!"'

And so this remarkably reluctant champion of the oppressed spent twenty-five hurried minutes with his client before it was time to go into court in front of Judge Martin Rettinger and speak for Mark on his arraignment for second-degree murder. (Since New York State abolished capital punishment in 1965, all cases of murder, however severe, are 'second-degree murder' with a maximum possible sentence of 'twenty-five years to life imprisonment': i.e., you cannot even be considered for parole until you have served twenty-five years in prison.)

In February 1981, Adlerberg described his interview with his new client in those highly charged twenty-five minutes: 'It was under very bad conditions. I was in the detention panel, what they call the bull panel, just behind the courtroom. The judge was getting nervous because the court was packed with reporters. This was just an ordinary crummy arraignment court, with prostitutes and gamblers and all that kind of thing, and this was a very big case. The judge wanted us to get the hell out of there and, to make things worse, it was getting late in the afternoon.

'But I wanted to get a crack at this guy. The court officers kept coming in and saying: "Can you move it along? Let's go! Let's go! The judge wants it called," and I kept saying I wanted to talk to him for a few more minutes.

'I was looking for one particular thing. A motive. But I couldn't come up with anything. Obviously the crime doesn't make sense as you and I would make sense of something. I was gearing my questions mainly as to his psychological background.'

Adlerberg could not get anywhere with his client. 'He speaks very well. He's apparently very well read or well educated or both. He detailedly told me what I was asking. However when it came down to questions relating to the incident, he seemed all over the place. Now he could have been malingering – I've had that before with defendants – but I honestly cannot tell you what his motivation was. He had *The Catcher in the Rye* with him when he killed Lennon and they found those weird belongings in his hotel room, but in the short time I was in the case I have to tell you that I thought the guy was a nut. He was crazy!'

In fact, Adlerberg's 'short time in the case' was only two days. The threats on his life from true-life 'devoted fans' of Lennon began to come in from the moment the New York newspapers carried the news, on Wednesday, 10 December, that Adlerberg had taken on the defence. Adlerberg has his own individual style of speaking that you would not find in your average British barrister: 'I'd been threatened before. Every lawyer worth his salt has been threatened. But this was different. Usually you know where the threats come from. In this particular instance, I didn't know who was calling me up – and another thing, I was watching TV and I was watching this alleged vigil outside his house. Round the clock. "Who the hell are these people?" I thought to myself. "Don't they work for a living? Are they such lonely people that they have nothing on their mind except stay on vigil for a deceased rock star?" That bugged me. Then I thought: "If that's the amount of people that are out there, I'm going to be singled out."'

But he still did not take himself off the case at once. 'There was only one real threat. The rest were all crap. I mean, people called me up without identifying themselves and calling me "creep" and things like that. There was even one woman who said: "You'll be associating with evil. You will be representing the Anti-Christ!" But it was a real cool call from one son of a bitch that did the trick. He said: "Are you the guy that's representing Chapman?" and I said "Yes." He didn't identify himself but he went on: "If you get this guy off, you're going to meet John Lennon." Just like that! Very cold and deliberate. Usually when a guy shouts at you, that's how he gets his rocks off but this guy was very quiet: deliberate, well educated, well spoken. So I said to myself, "To hell with this! I don't need this!"'

He called Allen Sullivan and told him that he was going to court the next day (Thursday, 11 December) to get the judge's permission to withdraw from the case.

He told Sullivan about the 'real cool' threat and the assistant district attorney had him put under immediate police protection.

Next day, Adlerberg appeared in court before Judge Rena K. Uviller and had himself formally withdrawn from the record. That in itself was scary: 'The scene was unbelievable. I've never seen anything like it and I've been in hairy cases before. Chapman is standing next to me and he has a bullet-proof vest. There were four court officers in a ring around him, not facing the judge as is usual, but facing the audience. Everybody coming into the courtroom had to be frisked. The courtroom was wall-to-wall with people. Solid. But nobody is covering me! I am standing right next to this guy and I have no bulletproof vest, nothing. My back is to the audience. It was a hairy experience!'

But, although he had only that one twenty-five-minute consultation with Mark on the afternoon after the murder before his brief courtroom appearance on arraignment, Adlerberg had already done a smooth professional job for his client.

He had persuaded the arraignment judge, Judge Martin Rettinger, to remand Mark for thirty days' examination by two court-appointed psychiatrists to see if he was 'fit to stand trial': i.e., that he could understand the nature of a criminal trial and what was going on. And, because of Mark's two previous suicide attempts, however half-hearted, he got the judge to order a 'suicide watch' on the defendant. On the very next day he had also signed up for the defence a senior psychiatrist, with a good courtroom reputation, who normally appeared only for the prosecution.

In fact, Adlerberg thought he had a good chance of getting his client off. He had already formulated a two-level strategy: at Mark's trial – which he thought would take 'at least three months' – he reckoned he stood a good chance of getting an acquittal because 'the DA would have a hard job convincing twelve jurors that this guy was in his right mind'. And, if Mark *was* convicted, he thought he would have 'a very good chance' on appeal of getting the conviction quashed 'by reason of saying that he didn't get a fair trial because he didn't get an impartial jury. The only way of getting a fair jury would have been to get everybody over the age of sixty – which would have been an impossibility!'

This able but reluctant defender has one other thing of interest to say. He was, of course, present when, on Mark's courtroom arraignment, the prosecution made their embarrassing mistake of saying that Mark had 'convictions dating back to 1972 and an arrest this year for armed robbery and abduction for which there is a warrant outstanding'. Normally, if this was not true, Adlerberg would have jumped up at once to object in the best movie-lawyer tradition. *But at the time Adlerberg believed it to be true.* His reason is fascinating: 'As the DA was rattling off all these charges my client was supposed to be involved with, Chapman was standing like this . . .' (He jumps up in the downtown Manhattan bar where we are having a drink before he goes off to play in his jazz group, and stands straight in front of me: motionless, expressionless, looking straight ahead.) 'He doesn't turn to me to ask what the hell he was talking about! He just stood there. So I believed the charges to be true, because my client wasn't denying it – even though within the hour the DA had to apologize and say they had run their name check too hastily and got the wrong guy.'

If Mark, in his state of post-murder shock, could accept blindly that he had a criminal record going back eight years which was a total nonsense, could he not also have accepted equally blindly – and inaccurately – his own lawyer's assumption in their rushed twenty-five minutes together that he was 'a devout fan of John Lennon'?

Adlerberg was succeeded at once by Jonathan Marks, the next attorney on the court's homicide panel for indigent defendants. Thirty-seven years old, Harvard-educated, he was a very different sort of man. Only two years in private practice, having previously served for four years in the US attorney's office in Brooklyn, he was ambitious, able and only too anxious to make his name as the man who defended John Lennon's killer. It was irrelevant that he had been 'a mild fan' of Lennon. The death threats that now began to be directed at him never troubled nor deterred him, although over the ensuing months he had sometimes to be given police protection.

After his first session with his client, for an hour on Friday, 12 December, he told the press: 'Mark Chapman desperately needs a friend. This man is very much alone. The whole world is against him.' He also said that he found him 'cooperative' and that he would enter a plea of not guilty by reason of insanity – which only served to emphasize to Allen Sullivan and the overworked New York police that the only thing they had to worry about was the defendant's mental condition and not whether he had actually committed the crime – alone or with others.

As for Mark himself, he seems to have been in a state of numbed shock – 'daze' is the word often used – for days after the murder. Psychiatrists, consulted by the US press, vied with each other in suggesting possible motives for his apparently motiveless killing: the *Los Angeles Times*, for instance, cited no less than five distinguished experts of that somewhat suspect school of medicine boldly stating their opinions as to why Mark might have committed his crime, regardless of the fact that they only had quickly put together newspaper versions of the facts to go on. A Honolulu psychiatrist, who had never seen Mark nor treated him, even felt free to surmise to a *Honolulu Advertiser* reporter that the arrested man 'might have come to see himself as the real John Lennon. He might find his rightful place as John Lennon, if he got rid of the imposter.' Even *Time* quoted instant-wisdom from a Manhattan psychiatrist: 'Chapman had a super-identification with Lennon, but he was also in competition with him. His murder of Lennon was a substitution for his own suicide.' A lot of pretentious hot air was spoken to reporters and repeated by them to their readers, anxious to try and understand at all costs what on earth had gone on.

Meanwhile, as ordered by Judge Rettinger, Mark was detained in circumstances of maximum security at Bellevue Hospital while two court-appointed psychiatrists began their examination of his mental condition. He was confined in a second-floor room in a prison ward at the hospital, into which daylight barely filtered from a barred window 'fogged over' with opaque paint. The volume on the television set in a nearby day room was kept permanently turned down so that he could not hear news reports dealing with Lennon's death. 'We're being really careful because of the nature of this,' a hospital spokeswoman said. 'He's not a screaming crazy. Everything is really normal.' That depends on what you mean by normal. Dr Marvin Stone, a ward doctor and one of the two court-appointed psychiatrists, told a reporter that Mark seemed 'a little depressed and was a little off his food'. Hardly surprising in the circumstances in which he now found himself: every fifteen minutes one of the four prison guards on Mark's 'suicide watch' looked in on him and, when he was not being interviewed by Dr Stone and his colleague Dr Naomi Goldstein, he spent all his time alone in his room, wearing hospital pyjamas, a robe and foam slippers. 'He spends most of the day sleeping,' the *New York Post* quoted a hospital source as saying. 'He doesn't watch television or read newspapers or magazines, though he could if he wanted to. He just doesn't seem to be interested.'

After nearly four days of this purgatory-like existence, he was hurriedly transferred, under armed guard and again wearing a bullet-proof vest, to Rikers Island, a remote gaol on the outskirts of New York, to which access can only be gained by a bridge that is kept under constant surveillance. The forty-minute journey must have been a terrifying experience: with hands manacled over his head and a coat pulled over his face, he was hustled down to a green prison bus at 4.45 in the afternoon and, protected by six police cars with sirens wailing, driven at speed, zig-zagging through the early rush-hour traffic.

The reason always given for the tight security that constantly surrounded Mark's movements and his appearances in court was that a distraught Lennon fan might strike him down: he was the object of unbelievable hatred from many of those who loved the dead singer. But he was perhaps doubly lucky to get this protection: there is also the possibility that he could have been at risk from totally different killers, worried that he might talk too much. There are many people today who still believe that was the reason why Jack Ruby gunned down Lee Harvey Oswald.

At Rikers Island, he was promptly isolated in a half-floor section of the medical and psychiatric building that (as I have seen for myself) stands in the middle of the island's prison complex. The section normally held about twenty prisoners. Everyone else was cleared out and he was put there on his own, like a pyjama-clad, modern Man in the Iron Mask.

At dinner that night, scared out of his wits, he promptly went on hunger strike. Before being relocated elsewhere in the building, one inmate had scrawled a death threat on the wall by way of greeting. For two days he refused all food, terrified that inmates in the prison kitchens who cooked or handled his food might poison him. Only after Jonathan Marks arranged with the authorities that his food should be passed straight to prison staff by a civilian cook, did he relent and, at 4.30 p.m. on the Sunday, break his fast.

Granted that he was a killer, he was most certainly not having an easy time.

Yet the amazing thing, at least to a British lawyer like myself, is that throughout this period – and for all the time that he has been in prison thereafter – he was still allowed to be in open contact with the outside world. In accordance with American penal thinking, he was at all times – even when on 'suicide watch' and supposedly under strict testing by two court-appointed psychiatrists – allowed to make outgoing telephone calls so long as the other person was prepared to pay for them: 'reverse charge calls' as they are dubbed in Britain, 'collect calls' as they are styled in the USA.

Alcoholics, going into a clinic to be dried out, are put under more stringent isolation: not allowed to make or receive calls or entertain visitors for at least the first week. But the Rev. Charles McGowan, his ex-pastor who had not even seen or talked to him for about six years, interviewed by me over the telephone in October 1985, says that he telephoned Mark *on the very day after his arrest* and the prison authorities allowed Mark to make a collect call in reply. This only confirmed what Sam Hopkins, an *Atlanta Constitution* staff writer, reported as far back as January 1981. Dr Lee Salk, a psychiatrist/writer working on his forthcoming book *My Father, My Son: Intimate Relationships*, was also later allowed into Rikers Island to talk to Mark about his relationship with his father. It was practically open house.

We simply do not do things like that in Britain. No one, however much a friend or distinguished in his own field, can just call up a prison, before or after trial, and be able to speak to a prisoner or visit him for a cosy chat. A prison is not a hotel and prisoners, especially those awaiting trial, should surely, apart from normal humanitarian visits by their nearest and dearest, be kept isolated from the outside world so that they cannot be 'got at' in any way.

I am not criticizing Dr Lee Salk or suggesting for one moment that the Rev. Charles McGowan said anything improper to Mark over the telephone in prison – or when he later saw him, by a judge's special dispensation, alone in a room at Rikers Island with no one else present. But if McGowan got through to Mark in those vital early days after the murder, who else did? Who else, in coded language or otherwise, might have told him what to say or what to do or given him fresh instructions? The possibility cannot be ruled out. The means of access were there.

18

Preparing for the Trial
of the Decade

As the old year of 1980 was ending, the crowds had disappeared from outside The Dakota. Yoko was left alone with her grief inside the suddenly empty-seeming apartment on the seventh floor. She cut her hair short as a mark of respect for her dead husband's memory. She closed off the bedroom they had shared. And with her tears and her love for her young son came a kind of peace.

But she was a tough lady. As she later told Phoebe Hoban for *Premiere* magazine, 'Nothing could be worse than what I experienced that December night. It sort of humbled me. So the thing is, you take it from there.'

Some hard decisions were soon made. She and Sean were going to continue living in The Dakota, although that did mean walking past each day the spot where Lennon had been gunned down. She was not going to abandon her work: early in the New Year, the single 'Walking on Thin Ice', whose spool was one of those which fell from Lennon's hands as Mark's bullets tore into him, came out and soared to the top of the charts ending up being nominated for a Grammy Award. In March, it was followed by another single, with Lennon's track 'Watching The Wheels' from *Double Fantasy* on one side and Yoko's 'I'm Your Angel' from the same album on the other: the photograph for the sleeve came from, of all people, Paul Goresh who had snapped the final shot of Lennon autographing Mark's copy of the album. This young store detective and amateur photographer had given up his plans of becoming a police officer and was beginning to make a full-time career for himself as a photographer. As he later told a reporter on the first anniversary of Lennon's death: 'I was forced into it. People like the Beach Boys just started calling me to do assignments!' – although he added: 'I honestly would give all of this back to have John here . . .'

There had to be a fundamental change in Yoko's way of life. No more walking with her husband or son unescorted through Central Park or out into the streets of New York's Upper West Side. Never again would she feel safe, either for herself or her son's sake, in being unprotected from attack. On the very night that her husband died, a call had come through to the receptionist at The Dakota's front desk from a man in Los Angeles to swear that he was leaving for New York to 'finish the job Chapman started'. Every major crime sparks its inevitable sequel of copycat gestures by the lonely and unhappy. The man was arrested at Los Angeles Airport before he could get on the plane but the message was clear: thenceforth something must be done about personal security.

In September, Lennon had rejected Yoko's suggestion that they employ an armed bodyguard (as she was to say later in the film *Imagine: John Lennon*, for several weeks before the murder she had had a disturbing premonition about his safety); but now she felt that she owed it to her son that at all times they should be protected. From then on, they were never to be seen out in public without personal bodyguards. Says ex-lieutenant of detectives Arthur O'Connor: 'She became genuinely worried. I understand she was spending up to $5000 a day for security protection. Lots of detectives from the twentieth precinct were moonlighting for her, and I think it has gone on to this day.' *Playboy* estimated in January 1984 that, at every level, she spent more than $1,000,000 on personal protection in the year following Lennon's death.

But not even a million dollar's worth of 'minders' can guarantee peace of mind. Once, after learning of another wild threat against his mother's life, Sean, who for years was unable to sleep alone after his father's death, told Yoko: 'If you go, Mommy, I'm going too. Because I know Daddy is up there waiting for us.'

New York in those last days of 1980 was a city of hate directed at one man: Mark David Chapman. 'There was like a sort of lynch feeling around,' the Rev. Charles McGowan recalled five years later. 'I made my trip to see Mark in strict secrecy for fear of my life. When my wife called a nephew to tell him I was coming, he said he was sorry I was going to be there. "He may be killed. The city hates Mark David Chapman." I actually crept around the city with a degree of anonymity for fear of my life. If anybody knew I was befriending Mark Chapman, I think I would have been accosted. I believe there was a threat, I felt that threat. There was an air around the city like that.'

Why, in fact, did McGowan make that expensive journey from Alabama and spend at least two days in New York, ensconced with Mark for about two and a half hours at Rikers Island on 18 December and on the following day at Bellevue Hospital where he was undergoing his 'fitness to plead' psychiatric tests? After all, he was not Mark's present pastor – that was the Rev. Pete Anderson over in Hawaii – but his ex-pastor who had not seen him for about six years.

Five years later, he told me that he had decided to contact Mark because he was worried if 'anybody was caring for him and I really had a love for him'. But how did he get the money to make the trip? 'One of the members of the church I pastored when I was in Atlanta [Chapel Woods Presbyterian Church in South De Kalb County] called me and he said: "Are you in contact with Mark?" And I said, "Yes, I am." He says: "Well, I know you can't afford it financially but if you feel like you need to go and be with him, I will pay for your plane fare."'

McGowan gratefully accepted this kind offer – and why not? But, thinking back now, does it not all seem a bit odd? Who was this strange anonymous benefactor so anxious for Mark's well-being at a time when most people in the country would probably gladly have wished him dead? Furthermore, McGowan has told me that another reason for his wanting to visit Mark 'was to introduce him to a friend of mine who's a pastor in New York who could continue a relationship with him because it was just impossible for me to do so, being as far from him as I was'.

All very laudable, of course, and I make no accusations what-soever against the worthy pastor from Alabama; but could he not have been unwittingly used by those who wanted to get in touch with Mark face to face? McGowan says that the New York pastor *did* see Mark in gaol 'for a few weeks'. And, be it noted, apart from the fact of McGowan's own two visits (which he made public to an *Atlanta Constitution* staff writer at the end of January 1981), all this has been kept back from public gaze until now. On 7 January

1981 the *New York Times* quoted defence attorney Jonathan Marks as saying that his client had had no visitors during his detention – and this was two and a half weeks after McGowan's two visits and at a time when presumably the New York pastor was already seeing him. The myth, for one reason or another, was created from the very start of Mark as a lonely man cut off and hated by the rest of the world. He *was* hated – 'I'm gonna be shot and killed before I ever go to trial!' he told McGowan – and I can understand a diligent defence counsel waiting to paint a pathetic picture for the general public of his isolated, friendless client – Mark needed whatever faint sympathy could be rustled up for him – but the fact remains that he was not shut off from the outside world like a monk in a monastery.

From the very start, he could and did receive visitors. From the very start, he could and did make phone calls – and even receive some, as we have seen within hours of the murder when Gloria was put right through to him from Hawaii (unthinkable in Britain even under the new, relaxed guidelines of the 1984 Police and Criminal Procedure Act). The strictly preserved confidentiality of all such contacts by a prison inmate means that we will never know exactly whom Mark saw in the weeks and months following the murder – or whatever calls, or instructions, he may have received over the telephone.

What I *do* know is that, when the Rev. Charles McGowan saw him, he had a number of things that he wanted done for him – and one was 'to communicate with Gene Scott and tell him he was alright'. 'I had a hard time getting to talk to him on the phone,' the pastor told me. 'And when I finally reached him, he did not want to talk to me – it was almost as if he was afraid he'd be implied, implicated in some way, in the shooting.' (If this strikes you as familiar, it is the same reaction as Georgia Bureau of Investigation special agent Wesley Nunn noted when he spoke to Gene.)

Meanwhile, apart from the two court-appointed 'fitness to plead' psychiatrists, Mark had already been examined by the first of nine psychiatrists or psychologists, six for the defence and three for the prosecution, who were to assess his sanity over the next eight months. Technically, at that early stage, Dr Dorothy Lewis, a research professor of psychiatry at New York University School of Medicine and a clinical professor of psychiatry at Yale University's Child Study Centre, was not yet an expert witness for the defence, as she was later to become. She was associated with a research programme at Bellevue Hospital on violent young adults, and it was in that capacity that she had obtained Jonathan Marks' permission to interview his client on condition that she provide him with a copy of her report.

As early as 16 December, after seeing Mark, she prepared a five-page 'Psychiatric Impression'. Its contents, like all other experts' reports submitted on the defendant's mental condition, have never been made public except for selected extracts specifically approved in the press by Mark or his attorney (who have never authorized release of any report prepared by a prosecution expert); but the briefs prepared by both sides for Mark's subsequent appeal and made available to me by Allen Sullivan contain full and highly useful summaries of all these crucially significant documents. In this very first report, Dr Lewis, although stating her view that Mark 'harbored ideas that could be classified psychotic' and, therefore, in ordinary language 'mad', added the vital phrase that she thought he might have been acting in response to a 'command hallucination' on the day of the shooting. Could any term be more appropriate for a disturbed man operating under hypnotic programming?

Indeed, in those last few days of December 1980, the first rumours of a conspiracy to kill Lennon began to surface. As so often with other apparently wild theories linked to earlier assassinations in the United States, they all too easily could be dismissed as emanating from weirdos and cranks. 'JOHN LENNON'S MURDER WAS A POLITICAL ASSASSINATION!' screamed a poster, eighteen inches by twenty-seven inches, that suddenly appeared on lamp-posts and walls all over Manhattan. Put out by 'The Assassination Information Committee' with an address on East 16th Street, it contained a mass of small-printed detail supporting its basic premise: 'It was by no accident or whim that John Lennon's assassination came at precisely the point when Lennon re-emerged into public and political life after five years of seclusion following the attempt to deport him!' Some of its stated facts were garbage – it is difficult to put too much credence in quotes from a gentleman named as a 'Chapman family friend and psychological counsellor with offices in Honolulu' and taken from the *National Enquirer*; but the committee's own representative's interview with Mark Snyder, the cab driver who had driven Mark around Manhattan on the Saturday evening before the murder, usefully filled out gaps left in his account by both the *New York Times* and the *New York Post*, and it had many other interesting things to say.

There is no single conduit for truth. It has to be amassed like a vast, intricate jigsaw puzzle from which, even at the end, vital pieces may be missing. This poster is not to be discarded out of hand. One cannot simply close one's eyes to its primary message: 'Even though Lennon was not a genuine Communist and opportunistically gave money to the cop bullet-proof vest fund, the US government and CIA could not tolerate even just an outspoken pro-Socialist, anti-religious moderate in the present complete vacuum of credible political protesters!' I can do without the poster-writer's love of exclamation marks but the document, as a whole, may have some validity.

Similarly, at about the same time, an organization calling itself the Alternative Information Service put out a three-page communique carrying no issuing address or phone number but baldly claiming that Mark worked for a 'top secret intelligence unit which has a department in Hawaii associated with the Pearl Harbor naval complex'. These people were really into fanciful theories. They maintained that the motive behind Lennon's death was to protect the Cruise and Trident nuclear missile programmes in Europe and the underground MX system planned for the American South West 'worth an estimated $1000 billion in defence contracts'.

US service chiefs had allegedly been 'watching closely Lennon's return to recording' and had been 'worried he would use his powerful influence in the cause of peace', thus wrecking youthful confidence in the nuclear arms programme.

Crazy? Almost certainly – but, in this benighted world in which we live, who can rule anything out definitively?

At the ungodly hour of 5.00 a.m. on Tuesday, 6 January 1981, Mark, wearing green trousers and his rumpled olive-green military-style overcoat, was taken, in a windowless van (to avoid a sniper's bullet), and under armed escort, from Bellevue Hospital where he had passed the night to a special holding pen at the Manhattan Supreme Court building down at 100 Center Street. There, according to an official spokesman, 'he was kept segregated, isolated and well insulated from the rest of the court population'.

At 9.00 a.m., he was brought into Justice Herbert Altman's court on the eleventh floor to plead to Indictment number 5935-80 in the case of *The People of the State of New York vs. Mark David Chapman.* Tight security prevailed: everyone entering the courtroom had been searched twice – once by metal detector, once by frisking. The atmosphere was tense but the courtroom was only half full: any possible fan of Lennon had been excluded and the only people allowed in were journalists and those on regular court business.

Mark stood expressionless and silent as the charges of second-degree murder were read to him. 'Do you understand the charges made against you?' asked the bespectacled judge. 'Yes,' Mark replied softly. 'How do you plead?' asked Altman. In a voice so low that court personnel had to strain forward to catch his words, Mark whispered: 'Not guilty' – 'By reason of insanity,' added Jonathan Marks standing beside him.

Now everybody knew clearly what the issue was to be: not who did it, but why did Mark David Chapman do it?

The two court-appointed psychiatrists had not yet filed full reports on the defendant's fitness to plead, but both prosecution and defence had been told their conclusion would be yes. So now Marks told the judge that he waived any formal ruling on the question of 'competency' – i.e., fitness to plead – but, since his client's mental condition would obviously be crucial at the trial, he requested, and got, Altman's approval to hire three expert witnesses. They were Dr Daniel Schwartz, the head of forensic psychiatry at King's County Medical Center in Brooklyn who had examined David Berkowitz, the New York serial sex killer better known as 'Son of Sam', Dr Bernard Diamond, the highly regarded Californian psychiatrist who had examined Robert Kennedy's convicted assassin Sirhan Sirhan, and Dr Milton Kline, a noted New York-based clinical psychologist who specialized in hypnosis – and whose views on the feasibility of hypnotically induced mind control are quoted on page 44.

Marks had used Kline's hypnotic skills very effectively a few months earlier to help secure the acquittal of Allen Curtis Lewis, an earlier client, who had allegedly inflicted severe injuries on a young girl music student by pushing her in front of a subway train. The attorney now told reporters that he had not yet made up his mind whether Kline would try to hypnotize Mark. In fact, Kline retired early from the case because of a dispute with the prosecution over his precise medical qualifications and later served four months in a prison in Florida on a related perjury charge. In the result, there seems to have been no hypnotic examination of the defendant and Kline, although he had one consultation, did not even submit a written report. No substitute psychologist employing hypnosis was engaged and Marks, although personally helpful in the research for this book so far as he could, has always refused to discuss the details of his client's defence.

So started the long process of preparing for what was expected to be the 'Trial of the Decade'.

Here are the eight other forensic experts' assessments of Mark's mental state, culled from their reports summarized in the subsequent appeal briefs. They are based on over 150 hours of taped interviews beginning on 7 January 1980 (Dr Bernard Diamond) and ending on 17 June 1980 (Dr Daniel Schwartz):

For the Prosecution

Dr A. Louis McGarry (psychiatrist)	A narcissistic personality disorder . . . not mentally ill.
Dr Emanuel F. Hammer (psychologist):	A narcissistic and immature personality.
Dr Martin L. Lubin (psychiatrist):	. . . suffered from a borderline personality disorder . . . without being psychotic.

For the Defence

Dr Daniel Schwartz (psychiatrist):	. . . a paranoid schizophrenic with a narcissistic personality disorder.
Dr Bernard Diamond (psychiatrist):	. . . chronic paranoid schizophrenia and a borderline personality disorder.
Dr Richard Bloom (psychologist):	. . . primarily paranoid schizophrenic.
Dr Joseph Gabriel (psychologist):	. . . paranoid schizophrenia.

243

Dr Dorothy Lewis (psychiatrist):	. . . psychotic – meaning having a lack of contact with reality – [but he] also suffers from a kind of seizure disorder [that is] often indistinguishable from the psychosis of schizophrenia.

Basically, it will be seen that all three prosecution experts were agreeing that Mark was not mad – i.e., psychotic – but had, like so many of us, a large personality problem. What does that twice-repeated use of the word 'narcissistic' mean, obviously derived from Narcissus, the name of the handsome youth in Greek mythology who died from hopeless love of his own beautiful reflection in a pond and was transformed into a narcissus? Dr Paul H. Wender and Dr Donald F. Klein, both psychiatrists, give the answer in their book *Mind, Mood and Medicine*: 'Persons with narcissistic personality disorders seem to have particular difficulty with the regulation of self-esteem. . . . Some behave in a relatively inflexible, self-seeking way but on the whole attain what they want from life and are not themselves in any pain. They are often a source of distress to those who share their lives, but not to such a degree that they are recognizable as ill . . .

'Their behaviour varies between mild callousness and outright exploitation. The inflated sense of self-worth also enables them to justify failures by facile rationalizations, blaming others and even outright lying. The more self-admiring among this mixed group also seem akin to hypomanic people in that they generally appear youthful, vigorous and cheerful. They may also spend hours primping, which is often a prelude to exhibitionistic behavior.'

None of Mark's nine mental health experts, whether for the prosecution or for the defence, was ever asked to consider the question whether he might have been programmed or otherwise subjected to mind control to commit his crime. But would not someone with a super-grade 'narcissistic personality disorder', as explained in Wender and Klein's book, be exactly the sort of massively ego-centred person you would choose if you wanted to programme someone into being a sort of armed Superman gunning for a notorious enemy of established society? In one of his taped interviews in gaol played over the air in Kevin Sim's television documentary, Mark boasted: 'I murdered a man. I took a lot more with me than just myself. A whole era ended. It was the last nail in the coffin of the '60s.' He was no blushing violet.

As against that, the diagnosis of schizophrenia which virtually all six defence experts agreed upon undoubtedly means that they thought Mark was insane. Dr Solomon H. Snyder, a professor of psychiatry, says in his book *The Troubled Mind*: 'When one thinks of madness, insanity, psychosis or craziness, the disease one usually has in mind is schizophrenia. It is the most disabling of all mental disturbances. Even though the schizophrenic may have a perfectly intact intelligence and the ability to see, hear and feel, his reasoning processes do not conform to reality. . . . He or she will speak in a bizarre, rambling, tangential, often totally incoherent fashion. Having "lost contact with reality", it is not surprising that schizophrenics begin to hear their voices which are not real and to elaborate complex delusions, systems or ideas which are totally at odds with the real world. Thinking that they were angels and could fly, schizophrenics have plunged to their deaths from high buildings. Psychiatric wards contain many patients who believe themselves to be Jesus Christ, the Virgin Mary or Napoleon Bonaparte.' I would not have thought that there were many who believed they were Holden Caulfield – but would it not be a magnificent cover for a murder plot if that was what a panel of distinguished defence experts could be made to believe?

On Tuesday, 27 January 1981 – again, with an ease of access any British prisoner awaiting trial would envy – Mark telephoned Jonathan Marks and announced: 'I am the "Catcher in the Rye" of the present generation!' That was perhaps not so surprising. After all, he had written in his copy of the book that he took with him to the scene of his crime: 'To Holden Caulfield from Holden Caulfield' and below that: 'This is my statement.' But he also added that now he knew why Lennon was killed – to promote the reading of the book.

How had he come to this second rather startling conclusion? It all depends on your source. Jim Gaines, in *People* in March 1987, has him lying the previous day in his cell on Rikers Island, after turning off a TV movie called *The Bunker* about Hitler's last stand in Berlin, 'thinking over why on earth would I kill anyone? And then it hit me, like a joyful thing, that I was called out for a special purpose, to promote the reading of the book.' Dr A.

Louis McGarry, a prosecution psychiatrist, has the more prosaic explanation – also derived from Mark – that, on the same day, he re-read the book and decided that the 'primary significance' of his act was the promotion of the book and its message.

My own view, of course, is that it could well have been the device used by his controller to trigger him on his mission.

Whatever the true explanation, on Sunday, 1 February, Mark sat down and wrote to the *New York Times* in ballpoint capitals a 'statement' which the newspaper printed eight days later. Seldom could a book that first appeared in paperback seventeen years earlier have had such a glowing sales boost:

> It is my sincere belief that presenting this written statement will not only stimulate the reading of J. D. Salinger's *The Catcher in the Rye* but will also help many to understand what has happened.
>
> If you were able to view the actual copy of *The Catcher in the Rye* that was taken from me on the night of December 8, you could find in it the handwritten words 'This is my statement.'
>
> Unfortunately I was unable to continue this stance and have since spoken openly with the police, doctors and others involved in this case. I now fully realize that this should not have been done for it removed the emphasis that I wanted to place on the book.
>
> My wish is for all of you to some day read *The Catcher in the Rye*. All of my efforts will now be devoted toward this goal, for this extraordinary book holds many answers. My true hope is that in wanting to find these answers you will read *The Catcher in the Rye*. Thank you.
>
> Mark David Chapman
> The Catcher in the Rye

For the first time, Mark now carried a copy of the book with him when he next appeared in court. The date was Thursday, 26 February and I was there myself in Justice Altman's court when he walked quickly in, looking neither to left nor to right, to sit beside Jonathan Marks, with the now customary escort of armed guards. This time, the court was packed and there was the muted crackle in the air that you only have when a major crime is involved. He looked neat but tubby in a tan sweater drawn tightly over a bulky bullet-proof vest. To me, the book in his hand looked like a prop, a piece of theatrical dressing. He had it with him throughout the brief twelve-minute formal hearing but never opened it nor even pretended to read it. It seemed a pointless or ill-defined gesture.

But then quite honestly he looked to me, and I kept my eyes on him throughout, as if he was in a world of his own anyway. He did not even look around when, as he was being led away, a dark-haired young man in a black T-shirt with the Beatles pictured on it, sitting two rows behind me, jumped up and shouted: 'You're a creep!'

At least, that angry fan, quickly hustled out by three burly policemen, was weaponless. 'The last time Chapman came to court we received over ten death threats from vengeful Beatles fans,' a court officer told the *New York Post*.

And so the pace heated up. Outside the courtroom, faced by the usual barrage of reporters, television lights and cameramen, Jonathan Marks made a desperate public appeal for help.

'People do not want to come forward and talk to me,' he said into the phalanx of tape recorders held inches from his mouth. 'There are many witnesses I would like very much to talk to, to find out what Chapman's state of mind was in the days before the shooting. Those witnesses are afraid to come forward because of threats that have been made on Chapman's life and on mine. I don't think those threats are very serious by the way.

'Or they are just angry and they don't want to have anything to do with the defence. I can understand that. On the other hand, I hope these people will reconsider because what I am really interested in is the truth.'

But did he ever discover it? We will never know because there was never a trial. All he could do was concentrate on the witnesses he had primarily to hand: i.e., the expert witnesses now augmented from the original three approved by Justice Altman.

Over the following four months and into early June, Dr Daniel Schwartz, who was to emerge as Mark's principal defence psychiatrist, visited Mark no less than six times. He seems to have won the accused man's particular confidence or was, with all respect to Dr Schwartz, perhaps the most gullible. For Mark spun him complex tales of his fantasies of ruling over a government of 'little people' from the days of his childhood. They lived in the walls of his living-room and he said he addressed them over television. He also told Dr Dorothy Lewis about them but to nothing like the same extent that he held forth to Dr Schwartz.

'I had control over their lives,' he told Dr Schwartz. 'They'd worship me like a king.' Gradually, as he grew older, he developed from despotism to constitutional monarchy and appointed a cabinet to help him rule over his thousands of loyal subjects.

But, when he put to his cabinet ministers his plans to murder Lennon, 'they didn't want any part of it. They were shocked.' So he dissolved the government. But after his arrest, some 'particularly loyal' ministers had approached him and asked him to reconstitute the administration. He was reluctant to do so because he was 'fearful that he might become attached to them and then be abandoned by them once he was in prison.'

No wonder the good doctor thought the man was insane. But why had Mark not said anything like this before to any of his intimate friends or associates? If true, is it conceivable that he could have kept this secret kingdom bottled up inside him and not told a soul until finally he kills Lennon, and only then spills it out to a defence psychiatrist in gaol? It is surely significant that he was not so foolhardy as to talk about it to any of the three prosecution experts who might have been more minded to take a cynical view of all this nonsense.

And anyway what has it got to do with killing Lennon? It is not as if he was saying that the 'little people' had told him to commit the murder. He did it against their cabinet ministers' better judgement.

It was, however, at that time in his own best interests – and that of his controller, if he had one – to be perceived as mad. Was there not, in Shakespeare's classic phrase, 'method in his madness'? Was it not all a marvellous confidence trick on his number 1 witness?

On 29 April 1981 science was brought in to aid the human factor in assessing Mark's mental condition. It showed that there was nothing organically wrong with him.

The living brain generates very small amounts of electrical voltage, roughly 10 to 150 millionths of a volt, which can be recorded by an electroencephalograph (EEG). At Bellevue Hospital an EEG was performed on Mark and the reading was 'minimally abnormal' indicating, in the jargon beloved of every profession, a 'cerebral dysfunction on the left posterior', but it was 'non-specific and of questionable significance'. A CAT scan and skull X-rays were also taken, and they were completely normal.

Time was running out. On Wednesday, 13 May 1981 Justice Herbert Altman ruled that all the pre-trial legal procedures had been completed and transferred the case to the Supreme Court's trial division. The trial was set down for 22 June. Justice Dennis Edwards was assigned to the case. So eager was he to hear it that he even put off his vacation.

On 2 June, Jonathan Marks told reporters (and on the following day it got into the *Daily Telegraph* on the other side of the Atlantic) that he was seriously worried that it was going to be very difficult to find an unbiased jury. He said that he had randomly telephoned 192 people in the Manhattan telephone directory and found that 63 per cent believed that Mark was 'definitely or probably guilty'. They either did not accept that he was insane or, if he was, thought that made no difference to his guilt.

'This constitutes a serious problem,' said Marks. He declared that he was going to ask Justice Edwards to rule that the press and public be excluded while, in accordance with the usual American practice (but not allowed in Britain), the prospective jurors were questioned in court as to their views on the case. Only if the court were cleared, said Marks, could the would-be jurors be 'comfortable in revealing their prejudices'. Certainly no one could fault the defence attorney on his thoroughness or sense of dedication to his client.

Then came the bombshell.

Six days later, on Monday 8 June, Mark telephoned Jonathan Marks to say that God had visited him in his cell and told him to plead guilty. He said that he had been lying down in his cell when he had 'heard a small voice in my heart'. It was a 'very small male voice. I could not hear it but I could feel it. It was the voice of God. He said I was to give up this trial for Him. It would be a circus!' Taken by surprise, Marks tried to talk him out of it but God had spoken and the competition was too much.

Shortly afterwards, Mark phoned back. This time he was more vehement: 'I'm not going to talk to any more phoney doctors. You're all fakes! You're a bunch of phoneys!' And he hung up.

Dr Daniel Schwartz and Dr Dorothy Lewis, for the defence,

and Dr A. Louis McGarry and Dr Emanuel F. Hammer, for the prosecution, were later to question Mark about this amazing incident of God speaking to him in his cell. Perhaps predictably, the two defence doctors said it was a hallucination which only served to confirm their diagnosis of paranoid schizophrenia while the two prosecution doctors said they took it as no more than a fanciful representation of Mark struggling with his conscience. As Dr McGarry put it in his final report: it was merely 'an internal dialogue between Mr Chapman and his religious conscience and lacked the characteristics of a genuine hallucination'.

This only goes to confirm what I have always thought about psychiatrists or psychologists when they are engaged for either the prosecution or defence in a criminal trial: in perfect good faith, they tend to see or hear only what they want to see or hear.

Of course, no one asked either the prosecution's or the defence's expert witnesses to evaluate whether Mark had, indeed, heard the voice of God speaking 'in a very small male voice' on 8 June 1981 or whether it could have been the result of a *real* male voice, that of his controller, on a collect-call telephone conversation. The possibility was never even considered that it might have been a marvellous way of ensuring that, as with Lee Harvey Oswald and James Earl Ray, there was to be no trial and no probing questions in front of some of the world's leading reporters in Justice Edwards' crowded courtroom.

And remember what Mark said to the Rev. Charles McGowan within two weeks of the murder: 'I'm gonna be shot and killed even before I go to trial.' Is it too fanciful to suggest that perhaps even from the start he had been threatened with death if he did not plead guilty and so avoid a trial? The fact remains that we do not know who was visiting him or to whom he was talking over the telephone during his six months in gaol.

But whether it was God, hallucination or a controller that directed Mark to change his plea, it really made no difference to Jonathan Marks. He must have been appallingly disappointed. What a let-down after six long months of dedicated hard work – and at the less than generous rates paid in 'indigent' public defences.

Besides he genuinely believed his client was insane and that he stood a good chance of obtaining an acquittal on that basis. That would have been a triumph for the ambitious attorney and, in truth, a tremendous victory, for it would have meant that, instead of going to prison, Mark would be sent, as later happened to President Reagan's attempted assassin John Hinckley, to the much softer regime of a secure wing of a mental hospital where his condition would be periodically reviewed and he even stood a chance that after some years he could be classified as 'cured' and let out to freedom.

Insanity acquittals under American law are not so rare as one might think: in 1978, there were 1625 in the United States. (In the United Kingdom, it is different. If charged with murder, you get convicted of the lesser offence of manslaughter on the ground of diminished mental responsibility but you still end up in a mental hospital for an indeterminate period.)

If Mark's plea of guilty to murder were accepted, however, there was only one course open to Justice Edwards: gaol for life without even the chance of parole for a fixed minimum number of years.

Would the judge accept the change of plea? Could Marks persuade him that his client's mental condition was so unbalanced that it should be ignored and the trial still take place?

19

Where to Now?

There was only one thing Jonathan Marks could do: ask Justice Edwards to order a new examination as to his client's fitness to plead. The two psychiatrists appointed by Justice Altman on the day after the murder had then both agreed that Mark was fit to plead and could understand what a trial was all about. Indeed, at the court hearing on 6 January, Marks himself had specifically told Altman that he did not dispute the issue. But that was before his client had talked about hearing 'the voice of God' in his prison cell. Surely that made a difference?

On the morning of 11 June, Marks filed a formal motion before Justice Edwards for a new competency examination of his client: i.e., that the question of his mental fitness to plead should be re-opened. He supported it with a written affirmation setting out his two telephone conversations with Mark of three days earlier, and stated flatly: 'In my opinion, there is a serious question as to the defendant's present competence to stand trial or change his plea.'

The motion could technically not be heard until 22 June, the date appointed for the trial to start (apart from anything else, the prosecution had to be given time to formulate their reply); but it so happened that on that very afternoon Marks and Sullivan were before Justice Edwards in court anyway to discuss Marks' suggestion that press and public should be excluded during jury selection.

Marks was so anxious that he was not prepared to wait for protocol. He immediately told Edwards: 'Your Honour, today I filed a motion with the court. Would the court consider entertaining that motion before 22 June?' Edwards had not even read the motion yet. He did not know what it was all about. He replied brusquely: 'I don't know what the motion is. I will deny that application.' In other words, 'You'll have to wait until 22 June.'

But he also said: 'It is my understanding, sir, that such matters were afforded a full opportunity to be explored prior to the matter being sent into this trial part [American legal jargon for "courtroom"]. As I suggest to you, you are here for the single purpose of a trial. That is my intention – to give you one!' He had not put off his vacation for nothing.

Marks persisted: 'As your Honour will see from my affirmation, there are changed circumstances.'

But Edwards was determined: 'As of this moment, I will not consider it. When we do arrive on Monday, [22 June], and commence the examination – I assume in the interim the prosecution will have an opportunity to respond – if I then determine there is merit to the application, I will hasten of course to honour it.' Yet he did not sound too encouraging: 'I only suggest that we are here for the purpose of a trial. . . . I am mindful of the significant need in my judgement not to delay the matter any further.'

That was that. For the moment, Marks could do no more. And seven days later, Allen Sullivan replied to his formal motion with an affirmation of his own opposing any new examination as to the defendant's fitness to plead and saying that there was no reason why Mark should not be allowed to change his plea to 'guilty' if he wanted to.

And so the matter was left in abeyance. The 'Trial of the Decade' entered its final days of pre-trial preparation in an atmosphere of shadow-boxing. None of the four main participants: judge, prosecution and defence attorneys or defendant, knew whether it would take place or not – but everyone had to carry on as if it might. Some of this leaked out to the press but surprisingly not all that much. Two days before the trial date, on 20 June, the *Guardian* in London ran an 'atmospheric piece' by its writer W. J. Weatherby under the come-on banner headline: 'Long summer trial follows New York's cold winter crime' which, amid all the normal scene-setting, conceded: 'A surprise is possible. Chapman has recently considered changing his plea to guilty.' And on Monday, 22 June itself, the *New York Daily News* ran a whole page on the case saying jury selection would probably take up to two weeks after which Sullivan was expected to call Yoko Ono herself and up to about forty other witnesses – but added cryptically: 'Barring a decision by [Chapman] to jettison his insanity defence and plead guilty to the charge of intentional murder.'

In fact, on the previous Thursday, there had been a secret meeting between Justice Edwards and the two attorneys. I will let Justice Edwards describe it in his own words, when speaking to me in his private room in October 1985:

The two attorneys called me in the morning and said they wanted to come in to lay down the ground-rules for the trial. They came in at 2.30 that afternoon and we sat down and chatted. The defence attorney said that he thought his client might be interested in pleading guilty and that one reason was that his client had expressed the opinion that I, the judge, had appeared to be a very fair-minded person. [Like any good lawyer, Marks would seem to have known how to 'butter up' a sometimes difficult judge.]

The District Attorney said he had to plead to the charge [i.e., he would not accept a plea to a lesser charge, for instance, manslaughter]. I said, 'Is he interested in pleading to the charge?' The defence attorney wanted to know what the sentence might be. I said: 'Well, it can be anything from fifteen to twenty-five years to life [i.e., the minimum time served before parole could be considered could be anything from fifteen to twenty-five years]. We would have had to spend probably months on the trial and we might have had to sequester the jury [put them up in separate accommodation during all that time and not allow them home at the end of the day]. That would all have cost a lot of time and public money. If I was to get a favourable probation report, I would certainly be inclined to give him some allowance for that saving. I didn't think I would go beyond 'twenty to life'.

The atmosphere was amiable. The defence attorney went to talk to his client, then came back and we agreed it would be reasonable for him to take the weekend to think about it. It was a nice sunny day. I didn't know what was going to happen.

If the judge himself did not know what was going to happen when Mark walked into his heavily guarded courtroom, 'Part 49', on the thirteenth floor of 100 Center Street, on the morning of Monday, 22 June 1981, then certainly no one else did. Such a secret conversation between counsel and judge would never have been allowed in a British criminal trial: some British courts tinkered with such 'plea-bargaining' gambits in the early 1970s but Lord Parker, then Lord Chief Justice, quickly ruled them out of order. According to British notions, all meaningful dialogue between judge and counsel in a criminal case must take place in open court and not in the judge's private room or anywhere else. As Lord Hewart, another bygone Lord Chief Justice, said in the early 1930s: 'Justice must not only be done but manifestly seen to be done.'

With all proper respect to everyone, it does seem a strangely casual way to handle the major issue in a trial upon which all eyes in the world were turned. But then, as a British lawyer, few things will ever surprise me about American law. Just before the trial was due to start, the magazines *New York* and *People* came out, each with a major article – one by Craig Unger and the other by Jim Gaines – that, in England, would have landed both writers and their editors in gaol for serious contempt of court. Unger unhesitatingly called Mark a 'killer nurd' and Gaines' article was actually entitled: 'Descent Into Madness', although the question of Mark's insanity was the one real issue which the jury would have to decide. In British legal terms, both articles, quoting at length from friends and acquaintances and full of uninhibited comment by the writers themselves, were highly prejudicial to a fair trial. 'Mark David Chapman . . . had long since surrendered to the welcome peace of derangement,' ended Gaines' article. A British prosecutor reading such a piece on the eve of a trial where he was seeking to persuade a jury that the defendant was sane would have had apoplexy – and at once set in train the legal machinery to have brought before the judge, in each case, both writer and editor to explain why they should not be sent to prison for seeking improperly to influence the minds of potential jurors.

Ironically, both articles, so strongly taking the line that Mark was insane, bore a weekly dateline – Monday, 22 June – the very day when the law, in the person of Justice Edwards, was to rule that he was sane.

The day of 22 June 1981 was as hot (in the 80s), humid and uncomfortable as only New York can be in mid-summer. It was a relief for the prospective jurors, reporters and members of the public turning up for the Chapman trial to get into the cool, stone courthouse building in downtown Manhattan.

But they found the doors of Justice Edwards' courtroom closed to them. No one was allowed in. For the judge had decided, in fairness to both parties as he saw it (although he was later to be strongly criticized in an editorial in the *New York Times*), to thrash out the question of Mark's fitness to plead and his change of plea in private, with no one but the defendant, the attorneys and court officials in the room.

What then took place has never fully been disclosed but the official transcript makes fascinating reading.

Basically, Justice Edwards took upon himself the task that Jonathan Marks wanted him to appoint two psychiatrists to do. He questioned Mark himself as to his fitness to plead and why he wanted to change his plea.

And so the questioning began:

EDWARDS: Mr Mark Chapman, would you please stand up, sir. We are now going to ask you a series of questions.

If at any time you do not understand any of the questions, please inform the court. In addition, it is your right and I suggest that you exercise it, that as to any question or comment made by the court or anyone else during the proceeding, if you have any doubts as to the importance of it or if you do not understand or you seek clarification or you merely wish to speak with your attorney who is standing next to you, Mark, then feel free to do so. What we are trying to do now is to ascertain, to decide and to determine that you do in fact wish to withdraw your prior 'not guilty' plea and to plead 'guilty'. So that we will understand what you are offering to plead guilty to I will read the indictment to you and then I will ask you if you understand the indictment.

Then I will ask you whether you wish to plead guilty to this indictment. All right?

MARK: Yes, sir, your Honour.

EDWARDS: The People of the State of New York against Mark David Chapman, defendant. The grand jury of the County of New York by this indictment accuse the defendant of the crime of murder in the second degree committed as follows: The defendant, that is Mark David Chapman, in the County of

New York on or about 8 December 1980 with intent to cause the death of John Winston Ono Lennon, caused the death of John Winston Ono Lennon, by shooting him about the chest and body with a pistol.

Do you understand the indictment, sir?

MARK: Yes, your Honour.

EDWARDS: And do you now request the court that you be given the opportunity to withdraw your not guilty plea and to plead guilty to this indictment, the sole count, murder in the second degree?

MARK: Yes, your Honour.

EDWARDS: First, do you understand that by pleading guilty today to this indictment it is the same as if you had been found guilty after a trial whether it is a trial by a judge or a trial by jury?

MARK: Yes, your Honour.

EDWARDS: Then do you further understand that having entered your guilty plea today that what remains after today is the procedure for an adjournment to have an investigation and a sentence imposed by the court?

MARK: Yes, your Honour.

EDWARDS: It is your right of course to change your plea and the importance of the changing of the plea is that it is being done knowingly, intelligently, informed and voluntarily. Do you say to the court then that you knowingly, intelligently, informed and voluntarily change your not guilty plea and now plead guilty to murder in the second degree?

MARK: Yes, your Honour.

EDWARDS: By waiving and giving up your right to a trial you do in fact give up the right that you have to have a trial either by a judge or a trial by a judge and jury. You give up your right through yourself or through your attorney at such a trial to either question the witnesses produced by the prosecution and to produce witnesses in your own behalf by the defence.

Do you understand?

MARK: Yes, your Honour.

Then the judge took Mark carefully through the essential facts of his alleged crime. No one else spoke. The courtroom was silent except for the two voices of the fifty-eight-year-old black man on the bench and the young man with the Southern twang standing in front of him:

EDWARDS: Now, the events in question took place on 8 December 1980. Where did the events take place, in what part of the City?

MARK: On Central Park West and 72nd Street at The Dakota apartment building.

EDWARDS: And about what time on 8 December 1980 did they take place?

MARK: Around 11 o'clock in – that evening.

EDWARDS: Now, take a moment and again if you wish to speak with your attorney, tell the court in your own words, what it is you did on 8 December 1980 in the County of New York in the area of The Dakota, 72nd and Central Park West at or about 11.00 p.m.

MARK: I intended to kill John Lennon and that night I drew a pistol from my pocket, proceeded to shoot him with intent to kill him.

EDWARDS: All right. Do you recall now how many shots you fired from the pistol?

MARK: Five shots.

EDWARDS: And do you now know or did you know at that time of the five shots, how many actually struck John Winston Ono Lennon?

MARK: No, your Honour, I don't.

EDWARDS: Do you now know how many shots struck the victim?

MARK: Yes, your Honour, I do.

EDWARDS: How many were there?

MARK: Four.

EDWARDS: Four?

MARK: Yes.

EDWARDS: Would you tell us approximately how far away you were standing from the victim Mr Lennon, when you started to fire the shots?

MARK: I am not quite sure but I think it is around twenty feet.

EDWARDS: And at any time during the firing of the shots did the distance between you and Mr Lennon change or did you remain?

MARK: I don't believe so, no.

EDWARDS: You remained approximately in the same area?

MARK: Yes, your Honour.

EDWARDS: What was Mr Lennon doing just before you started to fire the shots at him?

MARK: He was approaching the door that would lead up to the security area.

EDWARDS: And what were you doing just immediately before you fired the shot?

MARK: A second before?

EDWARDS: Yes. Or a moment before. In other words, as you were standing. Did you stand and wait for him?

MARK: Yes, your Honour, as he did. As he passed me I stepped off the curb and walked a few steps over, turned, withdrew my pistol and aimed at him in his direction and fired off five shots in quick succession.

EDWARDS: Did you say anything at or about that time?

MARK: No, your Honour.

EDWARDS: Do you recall if the victim said anything that you heard?

MARK: No, your Honour.

EDWARDS: And as I understand you say that you were there with the intent to cause the death of John Winston Ono Lennon and that you fired the five shots from your pistol with the intent to cause the death of John Winston Ono Lennon?

MARK: Yes, your Honour.

The judge then asked the District Attorney if he had any questions. Allen Sullivan was a clever enough courtroom lawyer to know that, when the judge is so obviously with you, you keep yourself out of it as much as possible. He had only two questions, both absolutely on the point of whether or not Mark knew what he was doing when he shot Lennon.

'What kind of bullets did you use?' he asked tersely.

'They were .38 calibre hollow points,' replied Mark.

'What was the reason for using the hollow points?'

'To ensure John Lennon's death.'

If he had been primed to give the most damning replies, Mark could not have done better. He was convicting himself with bulls-eye effect.

The judge had heard enough. 'All right!' he said. 'Now I wish to explain to you the procedure that we will follow once the taking of your plea has been completed.' From then on, any question of further examination as to Mark's mental state seems to have been dismissed from the judge's mind. Jonathan Marks' formal motion requesting a re-opening by psychiatrists of his client's fitness to plead was technically still before the court, but Edwards simply seems to have ignored it. He went on to explain to Mark that he was not committing himself in any way but he was, for the moment, minded to impose a sentence of no greater than 'twenty years to life', giving him an allowance of five years for having agreed to plead guilty, or even 'the possibility of a smaller sentence'. But he emphasized that the final result would depend upon the probation report that would have to be filed and upon any other evidence that might be forthcoming when Mark came back to court for sentence.

He also explained to Mark that if, when he then heard all the evidence as to his background and the circumstances of his crime, he was minded to give him a greater sentence than a minimum of twenty years, he would allow him to withdraw his guilty plea and go back to his 'not guilty' stance.

It all seemed rather like cattle-trading but no one could fault Justice Edwards on his desire to be fair. Quite clearly, however, by this stage, he was taking it completely for granted that Mark was fit to plead and, therefore, fit to change his plea.

He now asked Mark if, for his part, he had any questions to ask of *him*. 'Could I consult with my attorney?' asked the defendant. 'Sure,' said the judge. After a whispered consultation with Jonathan Marks, all this time standing beside him, Mark gave this courageous reply:

> Your Honour, I appreciate the court's offer in a case where you rule 'twenty-five years to life' after reviewing the material, that I would be allowed the option to return to the 'not guilty' plea. I would like to tell you that I made the decision to plead guilty regardless of any such circumstances. So, if we did return to that position, I would still plead guilty.

There was just one more loose end to tie up. The judge allowed Allen Sullivan to ask Mark why he had decided to change his plea in the first place. Mark replied: 'It is my decision and God's decision.' Then followed this exchange:

> SULLIVAN: When you say it is God's decision, and I ask this advisedly since certain representations have been made to me by Mr Marks, did you hear any voices actually in your ears?
> MARK: Any audible voices?
> SULLIVAN: Any audible voices?
> MARK: No, sir.
> SULLIVAN: Before you made this decision did you indulge in any prayer?
> MARK: Yes, there were a number of prayers.
> SULLIVAN: After you prayed did you come to the realization which you understand to come from God that you should plead guilty?
> MARK: Yes, that is his directive, command.
> SULLIVAN: Is that a realization you came to within yourself inspired perhaps by God?
> MARK: No, I felt that it was God telling me to plead guilty and then probing with my own decision whether to do what God wanted me to do, whether to do what I wanted to do and I decided to follow God's directive.
> SULLIVAN: So would you say at this time that this plea is a result of your own free will?
> MARK: Yes.

At this point, Justice Edwards resumed the questioning: 'All right! Have any threats been made to force you to plead guilty?'

'No, your Honour.'

'Have any promises been made to compel you or induce you to plead guilty?'

'Not in such words. But I have been assured by God that wherever I will go, he will take care of me.'

'A good Christian ethic,' commented the judge. 'I presume we all feel that God will assist us in times of need and emergency.'

And that was that! One could argue that the judge was being remarkable naive in his placid reaction to all Mark's solemn talk about God but, after a few more questions to satisfy himself that, in the jargon of the New York courts, Mark had 'voluntarily, knowingly and intelligently' decided to withdraw his not guilty plea, he allowed the clerk of the court to ask Mark formally: 'Do you wish to withdraw your previously entered plea of not guilty and now plead guilty to the crime of murder in the second degree?'

Mark said: 'Yes' – and his legal fate was sealed. The judge said that 24 August would be the date when everyone should return to court for what he called 'an investigation and sentence'.

Only then were the doors of the court thrown open and the scores of people outside, wondering what on earth was going on, were allowed to file in.

When they had settled in their seats or stood attentively at the back of the court, Edwards made a brief statement: 'The defendant Mark David Chapman has exercised his right to withdraw his not guilty plea and to plead guilty to the charge of murder in the second degree,' he said. He told them the case would be adjourned to 24 August 1981 'for investigation and sentence' and thanked both counsel for 'the high degree of professionalism that they have displayed and conducted themselves and represented their respective clients'. He then invited both Sullivan and Marks to make any such statement as they desired in open court.

Sullivan merely took the opportunity to bang the nails precisely into the lid of Mark's legal coffin, emphasizing that the defendant had, indeed, made 'a knowing, intelligent and voluntary waiver of his right to trial.'

As might be expected, Jonathan Marks was more passionate and more individualistic. He also, to his great credit, stuck doggedly to his guns:

'*First*, I think there is a serious question based on my discussions with Mr Chapman as to whether he is sufficiently stable to enable him to withstand the stresses of what would have been a long trial without suffering a serious breakdown . . .

'*Second*, Mr Chapman's decision to plead guilty was his own decision. He made it against my advice and he made it principally on the ground that he believes that . . . God told him to plead guilty. Because of that belief, it has really not been possible for me to have meaningful discussions with Mr Chapman on this issue. . . . When God told Mr Chapman to plead guilty, as he believes he did, the decision was essentially made and at that point I was removed from the decision-making process.'

The whole open proceedings took only ten minutes.

Mark's day in court had been like the police investigation into his complicity in the crime: trite and lacking in depth. The legal proprieties had been satisfied but a consistently deaf ear had been turned to the realities of the situation. Apart from Jonathan Marks' fire and determination, banality had prevailed.

Justice Edwards had treated Mark Chapman's change of plea to one of the most horrendous crimes that New York had known for a long time as if the defendant were an accused shoplifter, burglar or other minor criminal following the familiar pattern of opting for a guilty plea so that he could get a shorter sentence. The two minds, that of judge and accused, had not been on the same wave-length from the beginning to the end of the whole proceedings. There had been by the judge or district attorney no real investigation into why Mark had changed his plea, just as earlier there had been no real investigation by the police as to whether or not Mark had acted on his own.

The sausage-machine-like process of the over-burdened criminal courts system of New York had not shown itself worthy of the task that this extraordinary case had presented. Honest men, under great pressure, had grappled with major issues and failed, however honourable their intentions.

Five years later, Justice Edwards justified his actions to me in these terms:

'If I had had any doubt at all in my mind that Chapman was sane, I would not have accepted his plea. I couldn't have done. I wouldn't have done.

'But by the cool, calm, collected way in which he answered my questions, I was absolutely satisfied that he was, as the law requires, "voluntarily, knowingly and intelligently" admitting his guilt. In fact, to my surprise it was one of the clearest, most articulate admissions of guilt that I have heard. He did not hesitate in any manner. I was fully satisfied he knew what he was doing. As he was speaking to me and answering my questions, I had the feeling that he was unburdening himself. He now felt that he could live with himself.'

But how could the man possibly be sane if he was to be believed when he said that his reason for pleading guilty was that 'God had spoken to him in his cell'? The answer is interesting: 'Keep in mind that we all have our right to prayer. He did not suggest that God told him to plead guilty but he wasn't guilty. All he was really saying, in substance, as it seemed to me, was that, as any good Christian might, he had prayed to the Lord and been told, "Do the right thing. If you killed him, then admit that you have killed him and plead guilty." There was no more to it than that.

'It did not mean he was insane or nuts. No way. He expressed himself very articulately. If my average defendant pleaded guilty as clearly as that I would be elated.

'He never once said: "I am not guilty. I never killed him – I didn't ever intend killing him." He didn't say a blackbird just passed the window, so because of that he decided to plead guilty. Then I'd have said: "What? Hey, wait a minute!"'

What do you think of that explanation? Whatever your views, Mark now had eleven more weeks for his day of judgement on 24 August.

20

Judgement Day

Something seems to have happened to Mark in the sequel to the events of 22 June. It was as if he had suddenly realized the horror of what he had done: inevitably committed himself to probably at least twenty years in gaol. Whether sane or insane, mentally unbalanced or in full command of his senses, the realization must have been painful – even more so, if in some way, through all his confusion and mental turbulence, someone had relentlessly compelled him to take such a course. If he had been dragooned or directed into it, despite his own natural instincts for survival, the reality of what he had done would have hit even harder.

He went into bitter seclusion. He would not even see Gloria, who had flown from Hawaii to be with him during the trial. Then exactly one week after Justice Edwards had accepted his plea of guilty, he telephoned Jonathan Marks to say that he was tearing his hair out. Sure enough, when Marks arrived at Rikers Island the next day, he found his client with his whole head shaved. He now shared his hospital wing with another prisoner under suicide watch whom he had asked to finish off the job with clippers and scissors. His name, by macabre coincidence, was Craig Crimmins, convicted three weeks earlier of the Metropolitan Opera House murder of the previous summer, in the backwash of which the twentieth precinct's investigation of Mark's own crime had been so dull and uninspired.

Five days before, Jonathan Marks had received a letter from Dr Dorothy Lewis, reporting belatedly on a visit to Mark after the 8 June incident when 'God had spoken to him in his cell.' She stated:

Mr Chapman had been experiencing auditory hallucinations while at the hospital unit at Rikers Island and these experiences clearly influenced his decision to plead guilty. . . . I question whether he was competent subsequently to plead guilty [since] it seemed to me that his fluctuating mental status made it impossible for him to understand the ramifications of such a decision or to assist his attorney in his own defence.

Marks could not let the matter rest. He had to do more, even at this late hour, to try and convince Justice Edwards that his client was insane and could not be allowed to determine his own fate. On 10 July, he filed a motion for Mark's plea of guilty to be vacated and he asked – yet again – for Mark's 'competency' to be assessed afresh by psychiatrists appointed by the court. He conceded that the defendant had 'sounded calm and lucid' during the taking of his plea but maintained he was 'delusional nevertheless inasmuch as he believed God had told him to plead guilty'.

Two days later, Allen Sullivan filed an affirmation in reply, opposing both applications. 'Defendant's clear-cut command of himself and his faculties at the time he entered his plea mandate its acceptance,' he wrote. As for the 'whacko' quality of Mark's belief that God spoke to him in his cell, Sullivan astutely observed: 'Defendant stated that he believed that this [i.e., the change of plea] was God's will and he made it clear that it was ". . . *my own* decision whether to do what God wanted me to do or whether to do what I wanted to do and I *decided* to follow God's directive."' (Sullivan's italics)

Marks, with apparent confidence, told three *New York Post* reporters that he was planning to turn his client's sentencing on 24 August into a 'mini-trial' in one last attempt to have him sent to hospital instead of prison. 'I hope to persuade the court that this was the act of a very delusional young man,' he said. 'It's going to be a trial on the only issue in the case – his mental state.'

Those were brave words but Marks was an experienced enough lawyer to know, deep in his heart, that, with a seasoned judge such as Dennis Edwards, his prospects of getting away with a 'mini-trial' or effectively re-opening the question of his client's mental condition at that very late stage were pretty low. It was a pipe-dream.

Yet there was just a chance, a slight glimmer of hope. And

that lay in the fact that the probation report that Edwards had ordered to assist him in sentencing on 24 August would include, in itself, a psychiatric evaluation of the defendant. The judge had specifically requested that the probation office supply him with 'a full and comprehensible medical and psychological evaluation' of the prisoner. Mind you, that was on the basis of his being a sane person who had pleaded guilty, in full command of his senses, to a major crime. But it was at least a chink of hope. If the probation officer or his psychiatric aide could be made to believe that Mark was insane, then they could perhaps have added their powerful voices to that of Jonathan Marks on the sentencing hearing and – who knows? – Edwards might have been persuaded to vacate the guilty plea. There was just that possibility, however slight.

So what did Mark do? He went and blew it! What no one else has disclosed is that three times the probation officer asked Mark to submit to this new psychiatric evaluation and each time the response was the same: 'No.' Why not? What, if anything, was he hiding? Why this refusal to cooperate when his own attorney was battling so hard to have his mental capacity inquired into afresh?

It could be, of course, that the man genuinely was 'nuts' (although, as we have seen, Justice Edwards thought that he was not) and that he said 'No' to these further tests because his mental processes had ceased to operate rationally. But it could also be that, like Hamlet, he was merely playing at being mad and that he did not want to take the risk of facing further psychiatric examination in case it ended up, as with the three prosecution experts earlier, in the conclusion that he was sane. Incidentally, a second EEG carried out on 31 July had registered normal – not conclusive by any means, but not without some significance.

Perhaps this is the explanation for a bizarre incident that occurred at Rikers Island in mid-August. It was totally out of character and totally unlike anything that Mark had ever done before. He suddenly went berserk. He destroyed a television set, he threw a radio across the room and began screaming at Craig Crimmins that he would be tortured in hell for his vicious crime. Guards grabbed him and slung him in his cell but he tore of all his clothing and began jumping up and down, screeching like a monkey. He tore up his Bible and stopped up his toilet with the tattered pages. Then, as his cell began to flood, he splashed water at the guards and screamed at them. Finally, six men managed to subdue him and bundle him into a van bound for Bellevue Hospital. There he quietened down but he spoke to the doctors in two different voices, completely unlike his own. He claimed they were his two personal demons: Lila and Dobar, sent by Satan to torment him.

If that did not get him adjudged mad, what on earth would? But it is difficult to assess how genuine all this was. Anyone can throw a fit and rant and rage. But was it a performance? Was he trying to get into mental hospital – and possible release as 'cured' in, say, ten years time – the easy way without having to go through months of complicated new tests which might, in the end, reveal he was really in his right mind anyway? Was it all a bluff? One can never be sure of anything in this case. But the timing of this outburst certainly does seem suspicious to my cynical mind – and, for what it is worth, I pass on this further piece of information: Walter Bowart, in his book *Operation Mind Control*, relates how Dr Bernard Diamond, Sirhan Sirhan's and Mark's defence psychiatrist, 'had Sirhan climb the bars of his cell like a monkey' in a hypnotic trance. That is exactly what Mark did as part of his wild tantrum. I am not saying for one moment that Dr Diamond had anything to do with Mark's antics but it is interesting to see what you can be made to do under hypnosis and supplies another bizarre link between the assassinations of Robert Kennedy and John Lennon.

Meanwhile, at about this time, curled up on a white sofa chair in her office at The Dakota and chain-smoking throughout, Yoko Ono was giving her first full interview since her husband's assassination. 'I have strong emotions of sorrow and hate and resentment, but where do you put them?' she asked Ray Coleman. She told him she was philosophical about the way in which Lennon's death had transferred her in many people's minds from Dragon Lady to Noble Widow. 'Do you know how that feels? For ten years I was the Devil. Now suddenly I'm an angel. Did the world have to lose John for people to change their opinions of me? It's unreal. If it brought John back, I'd rather remain hated.'

But nothing about this lady is simple. Her new album *Season of Glass*, consisting for the first time only of her own songs, had just come out. When she had gone back to the Hit Factory to record it, many of the same musicians had also worked on *Double Fantasy*.

She said she had had to force herself to carry on. 'Making the record was definitely a therapy, the only way I could survive. I felt John was with me all the time in the studio.'

One song had the crack of four gunshots on the sound track and in another an ambulance siren wailed. At one point, she actually shouted over the music: 'You *bastards*. We had everything!' But perhaps the most controversial fact about the album was the front photograph on its sleeve: it showed Lennon's blood-stained spectacles, retrieved on the night of the murder, alongside a half-filled tumbler of water on a table by an open window in their apartment at The Dakota looking out over Central Park. Was that not rather tasteless?

Yoko did not agree. 'John would have approved,' she told Coleman, 'and I will explain why. I wanted the whole world to be reminded of what happened. People are offended by the glasses and the blood? The glasses are a tiny part of what happened. If people can't stomach the glasses, I'm sorry. There was a dead body. There was blood. His whole body was bloody. There was a load of blood all over the floor. That's the reality. I want people to face up to what happened. He did not commit suicide. He was *killed*. People are offended by the glasses and the blood? John had to stomach a lot more.'

On Monday, 24 August 1981, Mark David Chapman, his hair close-cropped from the incident when, with Craig Crimmins' help, he had totally shaved his head, walked into Justice Edwards' court under his usual heavy armed guard. He carried with him a copy of *The Catcher in the Rye*. He wore dark slacks and a light-blue T-shirt with no jacket. One could clearly see the bullet-proof vest beneath.

The courtroom was full, the atmosphere tense. Some spectators openly wore T-shirts bearing John Lennon's face or buttons proclaiming his name. They looked at Mark with hatred in their eyes. He did not look once in their direction.

Gamely, Jonathan Marks presented his formal motion that Edwards should vacate his client's guilty plea and order a new competency examination. But for all his proud words to reporters before, it was a forlorn gesture. The judge ruled tersely against him. This was to be solely a normal sentencing procedure on a sane defendant who had pleaded guilty to the charge. The only concession that he was prepared to make was that the defence attorney could call such psychiatric evidence as he wished 'for the limited purpose of assisting the court in imposing sentence'.

There was certainly going to be no 'mini-trial'.

In fact, Marks called two witnesses: Dr Daniel Schwartz and Dr Dorothy Lewis.

Sitting on the stand, to the judge's right-hand, the dark-haired, heavily-jowled Dr Schwartz, with his notes in front of him to which he occasionally referred through large-lensed spectacles, looked like everyone's idea of a typical, earnest psychiatrist. He told the court of Mark's fantasies about 'the little people' and about how he had come to be obsessed with 'the phoniness and the corruption of the world'. His replies to Jonathan Marks' simple, almost terse questions were long and complex. The judge did not interrupt.

Here is the essential part of his testimony to the defence attorney:

MARKS: Is there any psychiatric significance to his mental condition that's attributable to religious beliefs?
SCHWARTZ: I cannot call them, in and of themselves, delusional, since they are not unique to him.

His concept of religion, of God, is an extremely fundamentalistic one. As he himself says, he doesn't just believe in Satan, he knows that Satan is here on earth. Moral questions, therefore, are not issues over which he so much struggles within himself. And I would comment that's consistent with this – at least, in my mind, that his government had no judiciary, no court would decide right or wrong. Right or wrong to a great extent is decided in his life by a struggle between God or God's angels, and Satan, or Satan's demons, who struggle for possession of his will.

He tells me that he can feel the presence of Satan's demons around him . . . 'I can feel their thoughts. I hear their thoughts. I can hear them talking, but not from the outside, from the inside.'

His faith in God has fluctuated over the years, but his basic orientation to this kind of primitive fundamentalistic religion . . . has never wavered. He tells me that it was Satan's demons that gave him the strength and the opportunity for the present offence.

He struggled over the idea, knowing that he would be killing somebody, and mindful that the Bible states, 'Thou shalt not kill.' He told me that he prayed to God for strength to resist.

Even up to the last minute, he continued to operate under this primitive kind of thinking, in which he believed or believes that forces outside of him, supernatural or otherwise, determined his behaviour.

You will recall that there were two other fans standing outside The Dakota with him – a woman and a man. She left first, and finally the man, the photographer, but he pleaded with each of them to remain with him outside The Dakota, feeling that if someone were there with him, he would not go through with the shooting.

MARKS: As a result of your examination and your review of all the material relating to Mark Chapman, have you reached a diagnosis?

SCHWARTZ: I think that he is a chronic paranoid schizophrenic, that he also has a narcissistic personality disorder.

MARKS: Can you explain the killing of John Lennon in light of your diagnosis and in light of your examination of the defendant?

SCHWARTZ: I am not addressing myself at all to the question of criminal responsibility. I am just trying to explain why a man who had never done anything violent like this before in his life would at this point in his life do it. I think that he has to be understood, or is best understood, as a schizophrenic who is subject to major depressive episodes.

By the fall of 1980 . . . he believed that he could retire. His wife's income was adequate for both of them at that time, and she enjoyed her work, and he then tried to model himself after John Lennon, who you recall, like himself, was married to a Japanese woman who was the working member of the family.

However, in a way peculiar to schizophrenics, the closest he came to achieving this goal of identifying with Mr Lennon, the more he came to believe he was John Lennon.

You and I try to model ourselves after somebody, we can try to identify with that person, but we will not run the risk of believing that we are that person. We will always know who we are and who that person is. But I believe that he became perilously close to losing his own identity, and actually, on the day that he retired, 23 October, he signed himself out from work as John Lennon.

Now, this identification with Mr Lennon, after a while, became quite threatening. He was in his mind, then, really losing his own identity, and he didn't want to do that completely. So he tried to reintroduce some organization into his life . . . but it was not sufficient.

He then saw his only chance to survive, psychiatrically, psychologically, as being able to make an abrupt break from Lennon. Whereas he had idolized and adored this man, now he suddenly switched to the opposite direction and began to hate him, and he had no real reason, no justifiable reason for the intensity of his feelings against Lennon. He thought of him as a phoney.

Actually, what he was doing, psychiatrically, was distracting his mind from himself. He knew that deep within, he wasn't entirely the way he wanted to be. There were things about himself that he believed were phoney, and he had now projected all the phoniness from himself to Mr Lennon. He now viewed himself as pure and honest, and Lennon was the evil person who had to be destroyed.

I think, too, that he found his role in life at this point as too threatening for him. He had retired; his wife was now working. She had adopted the role that's usually taken by the man in most married couples.

In fact, this is what the Lennons had done. I think he found this intolerable, too threatening to himself, to his own concept of himself, and this was another motive for him to experience anger at the man who was living that lifestyle.

Finally, I think that his obsession with his preoccupation of killing Mr Lennon was serving now as a defence against his own unconscious suicidal wishes. . . . Indeed, he has always been rather inarticulate about explaining the killing itself. At first, in his statement to the police, he could not really give any explanation. Usually, he would say that the explanation is to be found in Mr Salinger's book. He has insisted he is the 'Catcher in the Rye' for our generation.

For a long time he was concerned primarily with promoting the book and was fascinated by the similarities. He would talk to me at length about the similarities that he saw between himself, the last three days up to the killing, and Holden Caulfield's last three days in New York City in the book.

MARKS: When Mark Chapman says that he is "The Catcher in the Rye" does he mean that metaphorically?

SCHWARTZ: I cannot be sure. I think he means it more literally than you and I do. He has the belief that by promoting the book he would help save countless lives.

But I am trying to point out that he was, at the time of the killing, struggling with severe depressive feelings and even suicidal wishes. . . .

I think that what finally happened was this: killing Mr Lennon was, in his kind of schizophrenic reasoning, a compromise, a way of handling these suicidal wishes, but in a sense, staying alive himself. He killed the person who, to him, now represented evil and hypocrisy. He killed him physically, and he killed himself psychologically. . . . Mark Chapman would no longer exist.

Well what do you make of all that? I must confess that for myself I regard it as so much psychiatric hogwash.

For a start, there is a fundamental error of fact that, at least for me, vitiates in itself most of the tortured theorizing about Mark's alleged identification with Lennon.

For look back at what Dr Schwartz said: 'By the fall of 1980 . . . he [Mark] believed that he could retire . . . he then tried to model himself after John Lennon, who . . . like himself, was married to a Japanese woman who was the working member of the family.' Then a few moments later: '. . . on the day he retired, 23 October, he signed himself out from work as John Lennon. Now, this identification with Mr Lennon, *after a while* (my italics), became quite threatening. He was in his mind, then, really losing his own identity. . . . He *then* (my italics) saw his only chance to survive as being' to kill Lennon.

The clear implication of those two statements is that quite some time, weeks perhaps even months, passed between Mark's 'retirement' and the process of identification with Lennon having become so great that he was forced into deciding to kill Lennon. 'After a while' is the exact term used.

But this is, with respect to Dr Schwartz, viewing the facts in the light of his theory, a common failing among historians, psychiatrists, journalists and (I do not deny it) lawyers. For remember the

273

dates: Mark left work on the afternoon of Thursday, 23 October 1980 and had already made up his mind to kill Lennon by, at the most, four days later, Monday, 27 October 1980, when he bought his gun and booked his flight to New York. There was no gradual process of finding himself turning into Lennon. There simply was not the time. Indeed, he had almost certainly made up his mind to kill Lennon on the Thursday, for Dr Schwartz totally ignores the significance of the fact that Mark did not merely 'sign himself out from work as John Lennon', as he said on the witness stand: Mark then put two vicious lines scratched through Lennon's name. He was already saying, 'I am going to kill this man.' He did not have to think about it any more. The decision had already been made. Dr Schwartz was misreading the available evidence.

But then his testimony, as a whole, amounts to no more than surmise based upon conjecture presented for the most part as solid fact.

Another flaw in Schwartz's reasoning is that he seems to have made no allowance for the fact that the information on which he based his theorizing came from a highly suspect source: Mark himself. That too is a common failing among psychiatrists: they tend to have regard only for what their patient tells them. The only other person Dr Schwartz seems to have spoken to is Gloria Chapman, and then not until very late in the day. Like most psychiatrists, he based his views essentially on his interviews with his patient: there was little outside corroboration.

Dr Schwartz was, in effect, presenting as factual reality what was really only his professional opinion.

And if you counter: what about my own theorizing about the possibility of Mark having been a programmed assassin? Am I not doing the same thing? I say: not at all. I do not foist my views upon you as if they were holy gospel. I seek to give all the relevant facts, as I see them, so that you can make up your own mind. And that is something very different.

When he rose to cross-examine, Allen Sullivan must have realized that, with the down-to-earth kind of judge he had in front of him, he would not have to work too hard to attack the credibility of the witness. I take my text again from the hitherto unpublished official transcript.

After a courteous 'Dr Schwartz, good morning,' Sullivan homed in at once on the fact that all the doctor's theoretical house of cards came from one source: the defendant.

SULLIVAN: Dr Schwartz, with respect to the material, the information, that you have just given the court, I think that you told Mr Marks that the conversations with the defendant were the primary source of your information; is that correct?
SCHWARTZ: Yes, sir.
SULLIVAN: With respect to the first – what you described as a depressive episode in 1973, and 1974, did you receive any information from any source other than the defendant?
SCHWARTZ: I am sure that I did. I cannot tell you exactly what.
SULLIVAN: Did he receive any medical treatment at that time or psychiatric treatment at the time to your knowledge?
SCHWARTZ: I don't think so.
SULLIVAN: With respect to the 'little people' that you described, going back to the age of nine or ten or thereabouts, did you get that from – did you get that information from any other source of – or any other conversations with the defendant?
SCHWARTZ: Well, he had described it to other people with whom I spoke.
SULLIVAN: Do you know of him having described that to any other people prior to 8 December 1980, people with whom you spoke?
SCHWARTZ: I cannot be sure. He has spoken of other delusions to his wife prior to the present offence.
SULLIVAN: Did you discuss those delusions with his wife?
SCHWARTZ: The ones about the government.
SULLIVAN: The one about Freedom from Debt [referring to a campaign to cut heavy credit card debts by rigid economizing in the early summer of 1980]?
SCHWARTZ: Yes.
SULLIVAN: Other than what you described as his delusions, during Operation Freedom from Debt, did you discuss any of his other delusions with his wife?
(Witness perusing document.)
SCHWARTZ: Not that I know of.
SULLIVAN: Incidentally, when did you have these discussions with the defendant's wife?

SCHWARTZ: On 22 June.
SULLIVAN: And I think you told Mr Marks that you had approximately eight interviews with the defendant?
SCHWARTZ: Yes, sir.
SULLIVAN: What did they consist of?
SCHWARTZ: 3 February, 17 March, 19 March, 14 April, 21 April, 19 May, 2 June, and 17 June.
SULLIVAN: And were those interviews conducted in connection with the preparation of the defendant's 305 defence under the Penal Law? [i.e., the insanity defence]
SCHWARTZ: With the possibility of it, yes.

He then went on to elicit the fact that, after some early interviews with the patient, Schwartz had been, as Sullivan brusquely put it, 'fired' – only later, and with no explanation given in court, to be re-engaged. He banged home the fact that Mark had been, in no true sense, a Lennon fan and had not taken 'any particular interest in him during a ten-year period between age fourteen and age twenty-four' and that his 'favourite musician' was, in fact, Todd Rundgren. Schwartz surprisingly confirmed the prosecution's key point that it was Mark's 'belief or at least one of his beliefs that killing John Lennon would make him famous'. Then embarrassingly he was forced to give the one-word answer 'Yes' to a whole series of questions (some of which I have quoted earlier in this book) in which Sullivan put to him, in most specific detail, some of the intricate stages of Mark's preparation for the crime, including the expressed desire for hollow-point bullets. (But, of course, omitting his three missing days in Chicago in the first week of December en route from Honolulu to New York.)

The district attorney certainly knew what he was doing. It was a good cross-examination. He even hinted at the possibility that Mark had faked his suicide attempt in Hawaii in 1977 because he did not like the manual work he was doing and it was a way, so Sullivan suggested, of getting on public assistance for two months after his discharge from the Castle Memorial Hospital. (His fees there had been reimbursed by public assistance.)

Yet, more important, he banged away at the fact that far from freeing himself by killing Lennon, with whom he was alleged to have so totally identified, Mark had hardly thought about him at all *as a person*. He ended his cross-examination in this way:

SULLIVAN: I think, Doctor, you described the defendant as having left his most cherished possessions behind him in the Sheraton Hotel, arranged some sort of a display?
SCHWARTZ: Yes.
SULLIVAN: Doctor, to your knowledge, did any of those cherished possessions relate in any way to the victim?
SCHWARTZ: No.
SULLIVAN: Are you aware of any cherished possessions that the defendant owned, after the age of fourteen, that related in any way to John Lennon?
SCHWARTZ: Unless you mean the records, no.
SULLIVAN: Those were records that his wife owned prior to their marriage; is that correct?
SCHWARTZ: Yes.

Even the few Lennon or Beatle records that Mark had in his family collection were not his own but had been bought by Gloria before their marriage. It was a well-chosen moment to sit down. The theory that Mark-was-Lennon-was-Mark had been exposed for the nonsense that it was.

Dr Dorothy Lewis was on the stand for a much shorter time. She said nothing about Mark's 'little people' or *The Catcher in the Rye* or fanciful theories about killing Lennon so that Mark could survive as himself. Split-personality psychosis did not seem to be her concern. She was more interested in telling Jonathan Marks about her theory that Mark had had some kind of a convulsion. She believed it was 'extremely likely' that a seizure disorder had caused his psychotic delusions and hallucinations, although she conceded that another psychiatrist might consider those to be symptoms of schizophrenia.

Sullivan did not cross-examine her at any length. He knew that by then he did not need to. And anyway Justice Edwards was hardly likely to have been impressed by her testimony: if she were right, he had been 100 per cent wrong in rejecting Jonathan Marks' motion to vacate Mark's guilty plea at the beginning of the morning's hearing.

There was no medical evidence for the prosecution – but this was entirely in character. Throughout Mark's half-dozen appearances in court from the day of the murder to his conviction on 22

June 1981, not one person – policeman, detective, psychiatrist or witness – had been called to the stand by the district attorney. There had not been one piece of evidence against him presented on behalf of 'the People of the State of New York'. It had not been necessary. Mark had been convicted entirely out of his own mouth and on his own version of what had happened. And, when it came to sentence, it was the same: not one prosecution witness was heard or cross-examined, on his behalf, by the defence. It was an easy ride for the New York police.

Even so, Sullivan was unrelenting. He now told the judge that he should pass more than the minimum sentence of 'fifteen years to life'. He did not ask for the maximum sentence of 'twenty-five years to life' because he knew, of course, that the judge had already indicated he was unlikely to follow such a course. He argued, however, that Mark deserved more than fifteen years in gaol because he was a man who 'has never exhibited any true remorse' and who 'remains only interested in himself, his own well-being, what affects him, what's important to him at this particular moment'. His 'primary motive', he claimed, was 'personal aggrandizement, to draw attention to himself, to massage his own ego'.

If the district attorney's speech, though powerful, was entirely predictable, so was the defence attorney's. He conceded that his client was 'a very dangerous man' but he pleaded for leniency for a defendant who, he maintained, did not understand what was going on. He still said that his client was not of sound mind.

What about Mark himself? He had spent several hours listening to other people talking about him. What did he have to say in his own defence? Asked if he had anything to say to the court before sentence was pronounced, Mark opened his copy of *The Catcher in the Rye* and read an extract to the hushed 'Part 49'.

He had worked it out carefully. If you want to check it for yourself, it is to be found on page 173 of the Bantam paperback (the same edition that Mark had in court).

Holden Caulfield is talking to his young sister Phoebe, the only person in the world whom he really loves, about what he wants to be when he grows up. She suggests a lawyer like their father, but Holden dismisses lawyers as 'phoneys'. What he wants to be is a 'catcher in the rye', and he explains what he means in this passage cited by Mark David Chapman on his day of judgement:

Anyway, I keep picturing all these little kids playing some game in this big field of rye and all, thousands of little kids, and nobody is around, nobody big, I mean, except me. And I am standing on the edge of some craggy cliff. What I have to do, I have to catch everybody if they start to go over the cliff. I mean they are running and they don't look where they are going, I have to come out from somewhere and catch them. That's all I'd do, all day, I'd just be the catcher in the rye.

Do you think anyone in court understood what he was saying – least of all, the judge? I doubt it. Nothing was going to be permitted to raise these proceedings from the level of the humdrum. Justice Edwards had said, back on 22 June, that, if he received a good probation report, he would adopt what was really the easy way out of his sentencing dilemma and halve the difference between the submissions of the prosecution and the defence: i.e., choose twenty years as the minimum period to be served instead of fifteen or twenty-five.

All eyes turned to him as he now delivered judgement:

I disagree with the defence attorney's suggestion that it is an insane crime. An act of a person who is insane. It may well not be a crime committed for the classic motives, revenge or for money; but it was, as the district attorney carefully pointed out, an intentional crime. It was a crime contemplated, planned and executed by an individual fully aware of the situation and the consequences of his conduct.

There is no question in this court's judgement that the defendant may benefit from psychiatric attention, although equally beyond any possible challenge, there is no doubt in the court's judgement that he is to be held accountable and responsible for his knowing, voluntary and intelligent act.

Five years later he told me, 'Chapman had received a good probation report and I felt able to honour my promise,' to give him a middle-of-the-road sentence. In court, however, he merely said: 'I do not think it would serve any purpose to detail' the probation report's contents. He then pronounced the formal sentence of the court: 'Mark David Chapman is sentenced to State Correctional Facility for a minimum gaol sentence of twenty years and a maximum gaol sentence of life.'

What was the probation report that so impressed the judge? Its contents have, in accordance with his wishes, never been revealed but I can disclose that its kernel, its very essence, that which most moved this devoutly Christian judge, was this verbatim extract that it cited from the probation officer's interview with the defendant:

I know I am guilty under God's law. I found my faith in Christ again while in gaol and I know Christ wants me to plead guilty. By pleading, I am acknowledging my guilt and no longer trying to manipulate events, such as a trial with a lot of notoriety, but am placing myself in God's hands for him to do his will with. I am not absolutely sure of my guilt under New York State Law. I cannot say exactly how much I was in control of myself. Certainly, I have been mentally ill to one extent or another for at least five years. To what extent on that day I cannot say. I have allowed my faith to lapse. Sometime in October or November, I heard God say to me, 'thou shalt not kill.' So I had the choice religiously and rejected God's call. Therefore, to God I am guilty and to myself I am morally guilty. I even invoked the 'forces of darkness'. I don't mean a demon with a tail and horns, but as a religious person I believe there are spiritual powers in the world and an evil side of the spirit. The point is I did the invoking, so the responsibility is mine.

Basically, Mark David Chapman was a decent individual and the judge responded to that innate decency. But there are others who will say that, in this complex modern world, decency is not enough. There have also to be other, more sophisticated standards with which to assess, and deal with, human behaviour.

Be that as it may, Jonathan Marks stood up and shook his client's hand, Mark was taken off for the last time in his windowless van to Rikers Island and the 'Trial of the Decade' had ended, like T. S. Eliot's world, 'not with a bang but a whimper'.

21

A Hard Day's Night

Mark had played his role in court with conscious dignity. The reading from *Catcher* had been poignant, his quiet calmness at the moment of sentencing impressive, his handshake with Jonathan Marks a fitting culmination to a well-scripted scene.

But the chill reality was that he now faced at least the next twenty years of his life in gaol before he could even be considered for parole, and 57 per cent of all first applicants were refused. There were even those who muttered (and still do) that Lennon's killer should never be released.

As against that, if only he had stuck to his original not guilty plea, he knew that his attorney thought he stood a good chance of victory with a nice comfortable hospital and not prison as his reward. Why had he changed his plea? He would not have been human if, back at Rikers Island that night, and once again on 'suicide watch', he had not played over in his mind's eye the scenario of the last turbulent weeks and tormented himself with thoughts of his fate.

It is impossible to tell to whom he was speaking over the telephone at this time – or, indeed, at any time since his arrest – or what visitors he had received or would receive in the future (in *People* in March 1987 Jim Gaines was to name one more hitherto unknown Southern pastor as seeing Mark in the summer of 1983). But if he was indeed controlled, his controller had certainly let him down badly. Mark had to be shut up at all costs. There could be no trial, that was for sure. So cynically he had been thrown to the wolves.

'Change your plea to guilty, say that God told you to do so, throw a really wild tantrum – and I guarantee you the judge will say you're nuts, the "shrinks" will have to have another look at you and you'll end up at Marcy, the state mental hospital, and not at Attica, and you'll charm your way out of there in no time as you did at the Castle back in Hawaii,' could have been the 'advice' a friendly voice had told him. And just look where it had got him! He had got the people behind him off the hook, but at what cost to himself?

Mark was in turmoil. Outside Justice Edwards' court, Jonathan Marks had said that his client had taken a 'vow of silence'. That extract from *Catcher* would be the last words he would ever speak so long as he lived.

The so-called 'vow' lasted exactly two days. After one last night at Rikers Island when he communicated with the guards only in writing, he was moved to Fishkill Prison in downstate New York – where he almost immediately found his tongue again and cooperated fully with prison psychiatric and psychological evaluations to select the gaol to which he would be sent to serve his sentence. Of course, he cooperated. So long as he was seen to be helpful, there was just the chance that he might not be posted upstate to New York's toughest and most dreaded prison, Attica, where in September 1971, thirty-seven men had been killed in a four-day riot.

Yet despite all his newly found friendliness with the authorities, Attica is where he was ordered to be confined.

Mark had nothing to lose. He accepted the indefatigable Jonathan Marks' advice to appeal and not take Justice Edwards' decision lying down. Not many people know it (and Jim Gaines in all his three articles for *People* in February/March 1987 does not mention it) but, within three weeks, Mark appealed against Edwards' ruling that he had been mentally competent to change his plea. This was a complete turn-round from his original point of view. First, he had said that God 'spoke to him' in his cell on 8 June and told him to plead guilty and, despite all his attorney's efforts to talk him out of it and persuade the judge not to allow it, he had insisted on doing exactly that – but, now that he was in gaol for 'twenty-to-life', he was permitting his attorney to argue that, after all, he *was* 'nuts' and his change of plea should not have been accepted. Jonathan Marks could not possibly have appealed without his client's permission. How contrary – or desperate – can you get?

But then Mark was just like anyone else: when reality sinks

in, few people like the thought of spending at least the next two decades in gaol even if it does mean flouting the wishes of God.

On 10 September 1981 Jonathan Marks lodged formal notice of appeal in the appellate division of New York's State Supreme Court. He was not asking for a trial. That was the opposite of what he needed. He wanted Mark's guilty plea to be vacated and a new psychiatric examination ordered of his fitness to stand trial in the hope that, even at this later stage, the court's psychiatrists would say that Mark *was* unfit and he would, after all, have to be transferred to Marcy.

It was Marks' swan song. Weary of the battle and not anxious to undertake the long hassle of the appeal procedure, he handed over the case to his friend, William E. Hallerstein. On 17 November 1981, the appellate division formally named Hallerstein as Mark's new legal aid attorney.

Allen Sullivan also now withdrew from the fray. Norman Barclay, another assistant district attorney specializing in appeals, took over. In a somewhat world-weary reply to the notice of appeal, Barclay wrote in the prosecution's brief prepared for the appellate judges: 'By the time the defendant was sentenced, he was undoubtedly among the most thoroughly examined psychiatric subjects in the United States. Over an eight-month period, he has been examined by at least seven psychiatrists and five psychologists and been the subject of a CAT scan, a glucose tolerance test and two EEGs, which in turn were monitored by still more medical personnel. In spite of all these examinations, and the approximately ninety pages of reports they generated, defendant now argues that the inquiry into his mental capacity to plead guilty was inadequate.'

Over three years dragged by until finally, on 1 May 1984, a five-member panel of the appellate division, under presiding Justice Theodore R. Kupferman, ruled that Mark had not been denied due process of law when Justice Edwards accepted his guilty plea. In June 1988, I asked Gerald McKelvey, the New York district attorney's special assistant, if I could have a copy of the court's judgement, but he could not find one and, in the end, said he thought there had been no detailed judgement spelling out why the appeal was dismissed but merely a brief formal order saying that the lower court's order still stood. That is a time-saving device often adopted by the United States' hard-pressed appeal judges.

The result is that the American courts have by now well washed their hands of Mark David Chapman. And the country's penal system has not been too bothered about trying to comprehend his crime either. Back in August 1984, Harold J. Smith, then super-intendent at Attica Prison, wrote to me: 'I could see little value in your sitting down and talking with me about Mr Chapman. So far he has been a rather model inmate, causing no problems. . . . I have no idea about what his motivations were for his crime and I do not feel any of my staff could give you any useful information in this regard either.' One might have thought they would at least have tried to find out for their own enlightenment – or for better understanding of how to treat him in custody.

So, against this background, how has life been for Mark since 24 August 1981? How has he adjusted to existence behind bars?

Whether because he genuinely for the first time felt remorse or because he had been stung by Allen Sullivan's dismissal of him as a man who 'remains only interested in himself' and who 'has never exhibited any true remorse', or because he was cynically trying to put himself in best odour with his new prison guardians or because it was a calculated commercial decision (with Mark you always have to give yourself as many options as possible), he wrote to Yoko in September 1981 at The Dakota 'profusely apologizing for what I had done'. Those were his own words in an interview with the *Buffalo Evening News* (Buffalo is the nearest large city to Attica) in February 1984. He described his letter as 'sincere and sympathetic'.

In the same letter, he also saw fit to mention that he was involved in a book that might be coming out and noted that New York State law prohibits criminals from profiting from their crimes.

So: 'I wrote asking Yoko Ono to assign my portion of the profits that I might earn from a book about myself to a children's charity.' He told her that the offer was an attempt 'to do some good from the position I'm in.'

Perhaps not surprisingly Yoko did not reply and, in fact, the book proposal lapsed after Mark refused to sign a contract. Later he did sign another contract for a book with Jim Gaines and Jonathan Marks was also involved; but to date the book has not seen the light of day.

Anyway, shortly after the first letter, as Mark told his *Buffalo*

Evening News interviewer, 'I thought I had made a mistake. I should not have put my apology in the same letter as the idea about assigning my portion of the book profits to a charity.' So he wrote again, giving a 'really sincere' apology and offering to decline any book project 'if you don't want to see a book'. Once again there was no reply.

Part of the text of this second letter, written in November 1981 (when Mark had already arrived at Attica), appeared in an article in *Playboy* in January 1984 by David and Victoria Sheff (subsequently reprinted in the *Sunday Times Magazine* in London in August of that year). The article was an exposé of the betrayals and exploitation to which Yoko had been subjected by former friends and employees of Lennon in the early years after the murder, and the Sheffs included the letter as a typically unsavoury episode. It was indeed a very strange letter for a killer to write to the widow of his victim:

Dear Yoko,
. . . My new attorney, Marshall Beil, may have contacted you concerning a possible agreement that would consist of seeking to use any funds – earned by the release of certain materials – toward charitable [child relief organizations] purposes . . .
    Yoko, if you feel that what I might enter into (even though all funds would be given to charity) is against your wishes, I would honour this completely . . .
Sincerely,
Mark David Chapman

Mark, who had begun by reminding Yoko that he had earlier written to her to 'apologize' for murdering her husband, ended by saying that if she did not want him to proceed with the release of his story, she could be assured of his 'cooperation in this delicate matter'.

The authors of the *Playboy* article commented: 'The implication is immediately clear to Ono: her husband's assassin is proposing that she assent to his participation in a book. He assures her that all funds would go to charity. Sick, Ono heads for her bedroom.'

For some reason, this really hit home with Mark. The reading of *Playboy* was not one of life's delights denied to him at Attica and the Sheffs' article really got up his nose. He contacted the

Buffalo Evening News and requested the interview (although every month since his conviction he regularly turns away requests for interviews from all over the world). 'I am tired of writers' lies,' he told the reporter who was amazed to find himself talking to John Lennon's assassin. 'I have read so much garbage about me. I never spoke up before. But that article was the last straw. Now I can speak up.'

What really angered him was the Sheffs' conclusion that he had proposed – over two years previously, let it be noted – that Yoko 'assent to his participation in a book'. 'That's the exact opposite of what I was doing,' Mark told the local journalist. 'I wasn't asking for her help. I was asking that she assign some portion of the profits to charity.' He said that he would abandon another book project he had begun (presumably the one with Jim Gaines) if Yoko asked him to. He claimed that he dreamt about talking to her. 'I asked Yoko if she wanted to meet with me so that I could apologize,' he said. 'I want her to accept that I'm sincere. I have a theory that some of the pain for both parties goes away if they meet and talk.'

One thing is clear: he *was*, and, I believe, still is, in pain. 'As far as I am concerned, he is just one of my 2100 inmates here,' Walter R. Kelly, the superintendent, told me in October 1985; but the reality is that, save for one hour a day for exercise, he has since his arrival at the prison been locked up by himself in cell BS10 for his own protection. 'APC (administrative protective custody)' is the technical term. The reason is that, as a prison guard has told Philip Finn, New York correspondent of the *Daily Express*, 'If he got loose for one minute, someone would have him in a flash. Guys back there [inmates] would love the glory of killing him. Most of them are in there for murder anyway. They hate him because he struck down John Lennon, someone everyone loved.'

So he spends twenty-three out of every twenty-four hours in a cell measuring ten feet by seven feet and painted pastel blue – the size (and colour) of an average bathroom. It is on the first floor (second floor in American numerology) of the prison in a drab gallery nicknamed the Box. At least seven heavily built guards, among the most experienced men in the prison service, watch him night and day.

He has contact with only four other convicts who live in cells along the same gallery. But it is very limited contact. Like him, they are there for their own protection from Attica's other inmates – but they can walk out into the corridor and eat their meals or watch television in the gallery's small private lounge. He is not permitted to do that. His food is served to him in his tiny cell and he is not allowed to watch television with the others.

I have been in an identical cell and I have seen for myself that his only view of the world, through the bars of his window, is a small patch of lawn and the massive thirty-six-feet high, three-feet deep grey stone wall of Attica Prison.

It is a Kafka-like existence and the pain by now must have reached the level of a numbed ache that is almost unbearable. But, even if you believe that he was sane before, it has not yet driven him mad – at least according to the US prison authorities. In the United States, as in Britain, a sane prisoner can be removed to a mental institution if the authorities decide that he has become insane while in custody. This happened in Britain in March 1984 to Peter Sutcliffe, the notorious Yorkshire Ripper convicted at the Old Bailey as sane nearly three years previously of murdering thirteen women, twelve of them prostitutes, in Leeds and Bradford. Explained the Home Secretary, Leon Brittan: 'I have received recent reports from which I am satisfied that Sutcliffe's mental condition has seriously deteriorated. He is now suffering from a grave form of mental illness.'

This has not happened to Mark, but he has twice on brief occasions – from 9 February to 8 March 1982 and again from 5 to 10 August 1983 – been transferred from Attica to the state mental hospital at Marcy, despite ex-superintendent Harold J. Smith's claim that he was throughout this period 'a rather model inmate, causing no problems'. William R. McAnulty, the deputy superintendent, explained to me in October 1985: 'It's sort of like taking a car in for repairs.'

Apart from those two brief visits to the 'repair shop', Mark is adjudged by the New York State prison authorities, backed up by their vast resources for psychiatric examination, as being a sane individual. In May 1988, superintendent Walter R. Kelly wrote to me: 'The status of Mr Chapman has remained constant during the past few years.'

He has his good days and his bad days. Jim Gaines, who has frankly written that he thinks Mark is mad, has described incidents when

Mark's demons speak to him and Satan takes over, when his mood changes and he embraces God and when he again thinks he is Holden Caulfield and '"The Catcher in the Rye" of this generation'. All this, of course, is out of Mark's own mouth in gaol. Yet, for all his APC, he is not isolated from the outside world. 'His visitors are never quite sure which Mark Chapman they will be meeting,' Gaines has written – but we have no idea who those visitors may be, or what poison they still may be pouring in his ears.

Soon after he was sentenced, he asked his wife to think about a divorce because, as he said, he did not want to hurt her any more. Her family said she should do as he suggested. But she prayed for an answer, and refused. 'I would sometimes even search [the Bible] for an answer that would have me able to say "yes" but I never found one,' she later told the *Honolulu Sun*'s Beverly Creamer.

In June 1982, she moved to upstate New York to be close to Mark. She took a job as a night-time sales clerk in a clothing shop so that she could visit him every other day for several hours at a time. Sitting opposite one another across a large formica-topped table, they studied the Bible together and refound the earlier days of their close Christian fellowship. They even applied for a conjugal visit so that they could enjoy marital sex together, as some US states permit their long-term prisoners; but it was denied. 'We had a lot of good quality time together,' Gloria told Beverly Creamer. 'I felt very fortunate compared to a lot of couples. They see each other maybe a few minutes in the morning and then after they come home. Maybe an hour they get to talk, if that.'

But this bizarre second honeymoon, like most honeymoons, did not last. Mark's high pitch of new religious devotion passed, his moods became erratic, the strange marriage-without-a-bed did not work out. After eight months, in February 1983, Gloria returned to Hawaii by mutual consent and picked up something of her old life: she moved back in with her parents and returned to the Castle Memorial Hospital as a part-time admitting clerk.

Yet this loyal Japanese-oriented wife could not cut her husband out of her life. Soon she and Mark were writing to each other again, and now every year she takes a whole month off work and goes to the 'Attica Hotel' for inmates' visitors and every other morning takes the courtesy bus service to visit Mark. 'She loves him very much and without question,' says her friend Ruth Brilhante. 'And that is all there is to it!'

His moods fluctuate. When Gloria was living nearby, the two of them wrote and published a Christian newsletter for his fellow inmates called *New Block*. That ended with Gloria's return to Hawaii but he still has times when he feels again the call of Jesus Christ. At other times he jettisons the Bible for *The Catcher in the Rye* but never since he arrived at Attica has he ever again claimed that he actually is Holden Caulfield. At one stage, he thoroughly researched all the works of *Catcher*'s author, J. D. Salinger. At another, he started to compile a chronological record of every book he had ever read. He has studied Zen Buddhism and Judaism. His cell is literally stacked with hundreds of books at any one time. Todd Rundgren is still his favourite musician and he often plays his tapes – but never the music of John Lennon.

He can never escape the reality of what he has done. One of the four APC inmates on his gallery once mentioned in a loud voice outside his cell that sightseeing buses now pass the entrance to The Dakota for tourists to stare at the spot where Lennon was gunned down. 'Get off my case,' Mark shouted out. 'Don't ever mention that again!'

June Blankinship, the mother of his one-time girlfriend Jessica, says that as the anniversary of Lennon's death approaches each year he gets depressed and particularly low. Back in 1982, out of the blue, Steve Spiro, the cop who arrested him and whom he felt he could trust, received a letter from Mark asking him to correspond with him. For several months he did. But Spiro could not resist trying to get out of him why he really committed his crime – and the correspondence abruptly ended with a one-line letter in May 1983: 'Read *The Catcher in the Rye*.' (If this book was, indeed, his controller's trigger for the crime, Mark was perhaps saying more than he knew.)

He broke off with the Rev. Charles McGowan in early 1981 after the Alabama pastor had made public their two meetings in gaol soon after the assassination and McGowan had tried to launch a fund to help pay his legal costs (unnecessary as it turned out because of New York's legal aid provisions). But Jim Gaines, as part of his research, later contacted McGowan for his impressions of Mark and McGowan used the occasion to make contact again with the ex-member of his flock. He was going to be vacationing in New England in the spring of 1984 so it was agreed that he should make a detour and visit Attica to see Mark. But by the time he got there, Mark had changed his mind. 'I couldn't believe it,' says McGowan. 'I sent the guard back to tell him to make sure he knew who I was and the guard came back and said: "He said he doesn't want to see you" – and he added, "Frankly, I think if you were the president of the United States he wouldn't see you. He's in a bad mood!"'

But he still keeps in contact with most of his old close friends: Gene Scott, David C. Moore, the Blankinships. In March 1988, he wrote to Moore: 'My memory is fully intact, as you might have gathered. And so is my sanity, but that is debatable in some circles.'

As for John Lennon, the years since his death have only served to prove how great was his fame and how universal the love in which he was held by those to whom his music and his message were dear. If he was killed to silence his live voice, the honour and adulation done him since his death – always excepting the views of Albert Goldman – have confirmed how potent a threat he would have been to the newly flourishing forces of arch-conservatism, if he had been allowed to live into the Reagan era and even beyond.

The tributes to the man who once said 'What is the point of all the fame, if I cannot do something useful with it?' have ranged from the personal to the universal. From his photograph, still displayed in the window of the West Side Pharmacy on Columbus Avenue near West 72nd Street beneath the sign: 'Let us not forget our beloved JOHN LENNON. His message of Peace and Love will last Forever,' to the $2000 annual scholarship set up in his name by Britain's Performing Rights Society for students to learn new recording techniques. From the Lennon Peace Tribute Committee that assembled 1000 people to sing his songs and demonstrate for peace and gun control at the Washington Memorial on the nearest Sunday to the first anniversary of his death to Mikhail Gorbachev thanking Yoko for Lennon's and her efforts for peace in the Lenin Palace at Moscow at an International Forum for a Nuclear-Free World in the winter of 1987. From the individual visitors to New York who every day of the year make a pilgrimage to The Dakota to the spot where he was gunned down to the hundreds of thousands of people, some only children when he died, who still buy his records and the millions more who still live and dream to his music.

Even Yoko Ono has given up the battle to fight against his fame. In November 1982, she told Steve Morse of the *Boston Globe*: 'I don't want to be "Mrs Lennon" living on a pension for the rest of my life. I wouldn't respect myself and I wouldn't expect Sean to respect me. I want to keep my independent career going, and for that it's important for me to be professionally accepted and to make a viable product.' But two years later *Rolling Stone* commented: 'Whatever her wishes, her identity has switched irrevocably from Yoko Ono, Avant-Garde Artist, to Mrs Lennon, Keeper of the Flame.' Finally, in October 1988, with only three moderately successful solo albums of her own in the past eight years, she admitted to *Newsweek*'s Cathleen McGuigan that her independent musical career was on hold: 'It's silly to bring out something where there's no demand,' she said with a wry smile.

Instead, she has thrown herself heart and soul into her dedication to Lennon's memory. 'Work is her best weapon,' Barbara Graustark has said. 'She behaves as if she is the keeper of the flame. As if it's almost a sacred task. You may not swallow it, but I think it's sincere.'

As sole executor of an estate estimated in 1980 at $150 million, she has seen herself included in *Forbes Magazine*'s annual list of the 400 Richest People in the United States – but only for one year (1984). In the following year, *Forbes* down-graded her because of 'no signs of substantial business activity and much charity'. Even so, from what seems like an inexhaustible supply of largely unpublished Lennon material, she has released two books (*John Lennon Summer of 1980* and *Skywriting by Word of Mouth*), three albums (*Milk and Honey* – the other 'half' of *Double Fantasy* – *Menlove Avenue* and *John Lennon Live in New York City*), a video, hundreds of signed lithographs and 300 hours of *Lost Lennon Tapes* (cassettes of music and interviews widely played over the air-waves and hopefully to be later marketed in records and CDs) – plus mugs, T-shirts, sweat-shirts, kites, rugs and posters bearing Lennon's drawings. She has sold the estate's world-wide licensing rights for $20 million – but she and Paul McCartney were unwilling to pay the price of retaining the rights to the Lennon-McCartney catalogue of songs and it went to Michael Jackson for $40 million.

Perhaps her most ambitious project to date has been the film *Imagine: John Lennon*, a 103-minute-long biography that was released by Warner Brothers on 7 October 1988, two days before what would have been his forty-eighth birthday. She conceived the idea for the $7 million movie in 1986 and it was a tour-de-force by producer David Wolper and director Andrew Solt, who contrived to have it narrated by the dead Lennon himself from material culled from 100 hours of tape. It begins with Lennon's voice saying: 'I was always a rebel . . . but on the other hand I wanted to be loved and accepted,' and ends with Yoko saying direct to camera: 'He was my husband, he was my lover, he was my friend, he was my partner. And he was a soldier who fought with me.'

It is possible to have two views about this film: adulatory – people in the Los Angeles cinema where I saw it applauded spontaneously at the end – or less than enthusiastic. 'This version of the legend still leaves you vaguely dissatisfied,' wrote Mike Clark in *USA Today*. It is a 'flattering but uncomprehending documentary portrait that aspires to a presentation of the man, but settles instead on one of the masks – and the least interesting one at that,' wrote Hal Hinson in the *Washington Post*.

But there can be no reservations about Yoko's most meaningful tribute to her husband.

In 1984, she donated $1 million to turning an uncultivated area of two and a half acres of Central Park, just across from The Dakota where she and Lennon used to stroll, as an 'international garden of peace' under the name 'Strawberry Fields'. That was taken from the name of the Salvation Army children's home in Liverpool in whose grounds the child Lennon had played and which spawned the title of one of his most haunting melodies, 'Strawberry Fields Forever'. 'I didn't want a funeral for John because I felt that his spirit lives,' she told a reporter. 'Instead, this garden – it's a living memorial.'

Before work began, open meadows on either side of a path, surrounded by trees and outcrops of rock, sloped unadornedly up towards the view of a lake. When the site was formally reopened on 9 October 1985, the day that would have been Lennon's forty-fifth birthday, it had been planted with hundreds of trees and thousands of plants and shrubs, including 25,000 strawberry bushes, donated by over a hundred different countries. Today a plaque set into a rock commemorates its name as Strawberry Fields and cites Lennon's perhaps most famous line: 'Imagine all the people living in peace.' And that one evocative word IMAGINE is set into a mosaic pattern on the ground. It has become one of the standard tourist sights of New York, more positive and uplifting than the stretch of drear paving stones outside The Dakota where a man was assassinated.

But the true legacy of John Lennon goes far beyond New York's 'international garden of peace' or the several streets that now bear his name in countries around the world or his star embedded in September 1988 in the sidewalk of the Hollywood Walk of Fame in front of the Capitol Records Building in Los Angeles. They are just symbols. His true inheritance is to be found in the minds of millions of people for whom popular modern music today is now no longer merely a form of entertainment but a political force in its own right. Without Lennon and 'Give Peace a Chance' there could have been no Band Aid. Rock music came of age as a world power in 1985 with the recording on 28 January of 'We Are the World', under Quincy Jones' production, in Los Angeles and with Bob Geldof's brilliantly conceived simultaneous Live Aid concerts in London and Philadelphia on 13 July, which together brought in a staggering $98 million to feed the starving in Ethiopia; but it was born in Ann Arbor with the 'Free John Sinclair Rally' in 1971. John Lennon, despite five years of silence in his 'house-husband' era, somehow contrived right up to the day of his death to keep his place in people's minds as a unique spokesman for peace and reform. Hence, perhaps, the reason for his assassination.

As Michael Poole has written in *The Listener*, the BBC's weekly review: 'Sport Aid [another Geldof creation], with its royal patronage and its celebrity trappings, may be a long way removed from the radicalism of sixties' counter-culture, but its version of a different way of getting things done is still recognizably an "alternative" one . . . capable of mobilizing what is now a growing spectrum of opinion that finds no expression in conventional party politics.' It could not have happened without the historical role played by Lennon.

'Your way of life,' Lennon once said, 'is a political statement.' So may have been his death.

PART FIVE

EPILOGUE

Attica

At 7 o'clock in the morning – every morning – a uniformed guard bangs on the door of cell BS10 at Attica Prison and prisoner 81A2860 hauls himself wearily from his iron-framed bed.

He relieves himself into his private toilet in the corner, then washes and dresses in prison-issue blue denim trousers and shirt. His breakfast, like all his meals, is brought to him.

At 9.30 a.m., his cell door swings open and, flanked by guards, he is led through a maze of passages and stairways to the exercise yard in the prison's grounds. He stands, looks up at the sky, then around at the grey stone walls, every crack and imperfection in the surface of which he has come to know like an old friend as he now trudges round in solitary gyration. For other prisoners, this is a time of movement and vitality, of ball games and 'pumping iron'. For him it is at least an escape from the torture of his cell – to which, after an hour, he is led back by the same circuitous route.

At 11.30 a.m., his cell door again opens and it is time for lunch. He munches through it, drinks his cup of weak prison coffee then settles down to his main work of the day: reading the books that spill out from his desk into neatly stacked piles on the floor. Or typing replies to the large deliveries of mail that still come in from all over the world or writing long personal letters to his wife and small band of friends. He has no radio but he is allowed newspapers and magazines which he underscores heavily with a felt pen if any particular passage strikes his attention.

At 4.30 p.m. it is time for dinner, again served alone in his cell. From then until his small barred home is plunged automatically into darkness at 10.00 p.m., he is left entirely to his own devices. To listen to music on his tape recorder, to read or just to think.

He has to endure this mind-numbing routine, without even the prospect of asking for parole, for 365 days a year (and one extra day in a leap year) until at least December 2000. If he was not mad when he went into Attica, the wonder is that he has not become so today.

On 2 June 1988 I wrote to him: 'I consider that, although you did not know it, you were not acting alone in the murder of John Lennon. You were under the influence of someone else to commit the crime. You were programmed to commit it at just the very time that Lennon had decided to become active again on the left-wing of American politics. You struggled and you were in torment but in the end you gave way to the command which someone else had planted in your mind. . . . I believe that, even as late as 28 November 1980, when you bought a return ticket to Chicago, you still had not finally made up your mind to kill John Lennon. . . . You alone are paying for a crime for which you are not alone responsible.'

I invited his response to those statements. I have heard nothing. The sad thing is that, even if I am right, he could long ago have been programmed into complete memory-loss.

'Ladies and gentlemen of the jury,' as we say in court, 'the verdict is yours.' Do you believe there was – or might have been – a conspiracy to murder John Lennon? Should other people be in gaol as well as – or instead of – Mark David Chapman? Is he truly an innocent?

Or are you satisfied that he was, after all, just one more lone nut?

To help with your deliberations, I leave the last word to Mrs June Blankinship who knew him so well all those years ago: 'Christians can be beset by a demon and Mark was beset by a demon. Whether it was a human, two-legged demon, I do not know.'

Footnote: After this book had been delivered to the publishers and over five months after I wrote to him, Mark replied to my letter of 2 June denying that he had been part of a conspiracy. 'The reasons for Mr Lennon's death are very complex,' he wrote, 'and I am still trying to sort them out emotionally myself.' He claimed that he had now given his life to Christ who 'brightened it and gave it purpose'. There was no mention of *The Catcher in the Rye*.

Bibliography

John Lennon by Ray Coleman (Futura Publications, London, 1985).

The Playboy Interviews with John Lennon & Yoko Ono by David Sheff (Berkley Books, New York, 1982).

The Last Lennon Tapes by John Lennon, Yoko Ono and Andy Peebles (Dell Publishing Co., Inc., New York, 1983).

J. D. Salinger by Warren French (Twayne Publishers, Boston, 1963).

Come Together by Jon Wiener (Random House, New York, 1984).

The Lives of John Lennon by Albert Goldman (William Morrow and Company, Inc., New York, 1988).

The Struggle Over Lebanon by Tabitha Petran (Monthly Review Press, New York, 1987).

The Insanity Defense and the Trial of John W. Hinckley, Jr. by Lincoln Caplan (Dell Publishing Co., Inc., New York, 1987).

John Lennon One Day at a Time by Anthony Fawcett (Grove Press, Inc., New York, 1976).

The Agency: The Rise & Decline of the CIA by John Ranelagh (Sceptre [Hodder and Stoughton Limited], London, 1988).

VEIL by Bob Woodward (Simon & Schuster, Inc., New York, 1987).

American Assassins by James W. Clarke (Princeton University Press, Princeton, 1982).

The Control of Candy Jones by Donald Bain (Playbody Press, Chicago, 1976).

Operation Mind Control by Walter Bowart (Fontana [William Collins Sons & Co. Ltd.], Glasgow, 1978).

The Search for the 'Manchurian Candidate' by John Marks (McGraw-Hill Book Co., New York, 1980).

Shout! The True Story of the Beatles by Philip Norman (Corgi Books [Transworld Publishers Ltd.], London, 1982).

Secrecy and Democracy by Stansfield Turner (Perennial Library [Harper & Row, Publishers], New York, 1986).

Strawberry Fields Forever: John Lennon Remembered by Vic Garbarini and Brian Cullman with Barbara Graustark (Bantam Books, Inc., New York, 1980).

Contract on America: The Mafia Murder of President John F. Kennedy by David E. Scheim (Shapolsky Publishers, Inc., New York, 1988).

The Book of Lennon by Bill Harry (Delilah Communications, Ltd., New York, 1984).

The Troubled Mind by Solomon H. Snyder, M.D. (McGraw-Hill Book Company, New York, 1976).

Under Cover: Thirty-Five Years of CIA Deception by Darrell Garwood (Grove Press, Inc., New York, 1985).

The CIA and the Cult of Intelligence by Victor Marchetti and John D. Marks (Dell Publishing Co., Inc., New York, 1975).

The Lawless State by Morton H. Halperin, Jerry J. Berman, Robert L. Borosage, and Christine M. Marwick (Penguin Books Ltd., England, 1976).

Inside the Company CIA Diary by Philip Agee (Penguin Books Ltd., England, 1975).

The Pursuit of the Presidency 1980 by David Broder, Lou Cannon, Haynes Johnson, Martin Schram, Richard Harwood and the staff of *The Washington Post* (A Washington Post/Berkley Book [Berkley Books], New York, 1980).

The Election of 1980 by Gerald Pomper with colleagues (Chatham House Publishers, Inc., Chatham, 1981).

The Lennon Companion ed. by Elizabeth Thomson and David Gutman (Macmillan Press Ltd., London, 1987).

John Lennon Summer of 1980 by Yoko Ono with Eight Photographers (Perigee Books, Putnam Publishing Group, New York, 1983).

The Catcher in the Rye by J. D. Salinger (Bantam Books, 1964).

Rock of Ages: The Rolling Stone History of Rock & Roll by Ed Ward, Geoffrey Stokes and Ken Tucker (Summit Books, New York, 1986).

Index

Urwand, Vincent, 122, 189
US Army Chemical Corps, 38,
   39–40
USA Today, 292
Uviller, Judge Rena K., 230

Vietnam War, 57, 62–3, 66, 80,
   82, 108–9, 187, 212, 214
Village Voice, 142
Visscher, Paul, 159

Waikiki Mental Health Clinic,
   128, 169, 170, 171–2
Walker, Judge Herbert, 48
Wallace, Mike, 89, 151
Walls and Bridges, 113–14
Walters, Barbara, 221
Warmflash, David, 219
Warner Brothers, 292
Washington Post, 26, 39, 154–5,
   292
Watson, Peter, 41
Weatherby, W. J., 253

Weidner, Robert P., 75
Wender, Dr Paul H., 34, 244
Wenner, Jann, 67
White Album, 70, 84–5
Wicner, Jon, 7, 8, 63, 64, 71, 72,
   79, 81, 83, 119, 121
Wildes, Leon, 81, 112
Williams, Judy, 159
Wilson, Sir Harold, 214–15
The Wizard of Oz, 193–4
Wolf, Janice, 170–1, 172–3
Wolper, David, 292
Women's Own, 97, 100, 159
Woodward, Bob, 103–4
Wright, Walter, 131–2, 171, 172,
   181

Young Men's Christian
   Association (YMCA), 28–31,
   46, 87, 100–10, 124, 134–5,
   158–9, 189–90, 192